in their shoes

Doing It Right
Bronwen Pardes

The Social Climber's Guide to High School
Robyn Schneider

 # in their shoes

extraordinary women describe their amazing careers

Deborah Reber

SIMON PULSE

New York   London   Toronto   Sydney

SIMON PULSE
An imprint of Simon & Schuster Children's Publishing Division
1230 Avenue of the Americas, New York, NY 10020

Copyright © 2007 by Deborah Reber

Designed by Joel Avirom and Jason Snyder

The text of this book was set in Caecilla.

Manufactured in the United States of America

First Simon Pulse edition April 2007

10 9 8 7 6 5 4 3 2 1

Library of Congress Control Number 2006928451

ISBN-13: 978-1-4169-2578-1
ISBN-10: 1-4169-2578-3

PHOTO CREDITS:
Photo of Missy Park copyright © by www.traceyprever.com
Photo of Danielle Aust copyright © by Deborah Reber
Photo of Chiyo Ishikawa copyright © by Kevin P. Casey
Photo of Severn Cullis-Suzuki copyright © by Jeff Topham
Photo of Joyce Roché copyright © by C. Craddock
Photo of June Ambrose copyright © by Matteo Trisolini
Photo of Melissa Block copyright © by Meghan Gallery
Photo of Lauren Faust copyright © by Deborah Reber
Photo of Amanda Koster copyright © by Maggie Soloday
Photo of Kay Lakey copyright © by Deborah Reber
Photo of Sara Lynch copyright © by Deborah Reber
Photo of Maura Tierney copyright © by Isabel Snyder
Photo of Roxanne Coady copyright © by Tricia Bohan

*To Derin, my workmate,
playmate, and partner for life*

* *

acknowledgments

writing this book didn't actually feel like work at all. I mean, bringing together an incredible group of women to inspire and inform teens? How lucky am I? For their help, guidance, and support in writing *In Their Shoes*, I am filled with gratitude to:

My husband, Derin (aka my rock): Thank you for believing in this idea and encouraging me to make it happen from the very beginning. You are my constant source of support, insight, and love, and your faith in me makes me feel like I can do anything!

My son, Asher: Though you're too young to read this now, the gifts you give me every day help me grow in ways I never knew possible.

My mom and dad, Dale and MaryLou: You have always believed in my ability to do and be anything. Thank you!

My sister, Michele: Thank you for reading countless outlines, notes, and drafts and giving me invaluable feedback at every stage of this book. Your positive reinforcement is a huge force in my life.

My in-laws, Barbara and David Basden: Thank you for your encouragement and interest in my writing ventures.

My "support team" of Alice Wilder, AnneMarie Kane, Ed Adams, and Renée Adams: I know I can come to you at any time with anything and you're there to share your honest insight, valued opinions, and most of all, your belief in me. I couldn't do what I do without you!

My dog, Baxter: For keeping me company by lying under my desk day after day.

My intern, Anna Minard: Thank you for sharing your great research skills with me, but even better, sharing your enthusiasm for this project and being an excellent sounding board at every step of the way.

Bridget Perry: Thank you for "getting" what I was trying to do and helping me brainstorm the ideas that shaped this into the book it is!

My friends who allowed me to babble on endlessly about my process: Tip Blish, Alison Bower, Mardi Douglass, Peter Koorey, Stephanie Lucash, Darcey Pickard, and Marty Silano.

Ed Adams, Renée Adams, Crai Bower, Britta Couris, Lee Davis, Loch Phillipps, Dave Rosencranz, Lee Skaife, Lisa Viscardi, and Chad Willett, as well as Avon, CARE, the Massachusetts State Police Crime Lab, Scripps Oceanography Institute, and Seattle WriterGrrls: thank you for introducing me to some of the incredible women inside this book.

My agent, Susan Schulman: Your belief in me and my vision for bringing important media to teen girls is truly valued and appreciated.

Jen Bergstrom: Thank you for bringing this seed of an idea to life and realizing its potential.

Michelle Nagler: You know how I feel about working with you. You are a dream editor! Thank you for trusting in me to do what I do best, and for sharing your incredible creative and business skills with me.

Cara Bedick: Your perspective and enthusiasm throughout this project has been invaluable. Thank you for taking a special interest!

The extraordinary women in *In Their Shoes*: This book would be nothing without your stories, inspiration, and advice to bring it to life. Thank you for opening up and letting us inside your work and personal lives. Each one of you is making a powerful mark on the career women of tomorrow!

Russell Gordon, Ann Zeak, Mike Rosamilia, Lisa Fyfe, Joel Avirom, Jason Snyder, and Meghan Day Healey, the incredible designers who brought the content of this book to life: You took a lot of material and packaged it beautifully to make it readable and accessible. Thank you for doing such an amazing job!

My power team at Simon & Schuster, who put their all into making this book a success: Bethany Buck, Paul Crichton, Katherine Devendorf, Jaime Feldman, Lucille Rettino, and Orly Sigal.

And last but not least, to all the teen girls who gave me feedback and provided questions to ask each woman in the book: Thank you for sharing your dreams, goals, and point of view. This book is for you!

contents

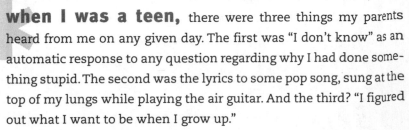**when I was a teen,** there were three things my parents heard from me on any given day. The first was "I don't know" as an automatic response to any question regarding why I had done something stupid. The second was the lyrics to some pop song, sung at the top of my lungs while playing the air guitar. And the third? "I figured out what I want to be when I grow up."

This last one always raised eyebrows and drew laughter from my family. After making my announcement at the dinner table (for example, "I'm going to be an animal conservationist and save the giant panda from extinction"), my parents would ask to have it in writing. Apparently they wanted to get it on the record, so the next time I flip-flopped they could wave it in front of my face, as if to say, "Uh-huh, Deb. *Sure* you're going to join the Peace Corps."

Maybe they had a point. I did change my mind about careers a lot. There was the time I wanted to be a teacher. Then a veterinarian. A rescue worker. Come to think of it, the animal conservationist phase did last a couple of years. Oh yeah, and let's not forget my personal favorite, a "farmer's wife." (I'm not joking. My only defense is too many years of watching *Little House on the Prairie* as a kid!)

Then everything changed. I saw *Broadcast News*, this movie where Holly Hunter plays a high-stakes network news producer. Her character, Jane, was smart. She was sassy. She was even neurotic. *She was me!* From that matinee on, I wanted to *be* Jane in the worst way. I wanted her job, her cool Georgetown apartment, her simple bob hairdo, and her invites to press dinners at the White House.

So I went to college and studied journalism and television production, and even put together a few of my own "news pieces" for classes along the way. (I specifically recall producing a hard-hitting segment about the different steps involved in feeding my dog, Ari. Clearly I was well on my way to big-shot newsmaker.)

I researched everything I could about the news industry and interned at the local NBC affiliate in my small college town. It was all falling into place. I'd be Debbie Reber, VINP (Very Important News Producer). I'd waltz through the revolving door at Rockefeller Plaza wearing Prada, my hair in an up-do that looked sensible, smart, and sexily disheveled all at the same time, and hurry off to meet a pressing deadline.

I landed a summer internship at NBC News the summer before my senior year, where I sat less than a hundred feet away from Tom Brokaw's anchor desk. Al, Matt, and Katie at the *Today* show were right down the hall. There I was. Just like I'd imagined. Except it was anything but.

In my internship I saw the real side of news. The windowless work spaces, the layers of foundation worn by on-air personalities, the rigid divide between godlike anchors and lowly production assistants. The drama. The backstabbing. The politics.

Once I graduated, I quickly learned that the kind of job I wanted was nearly impossible to score. I mean, I knew there'd be competition, but I had no clue that I'd be up against recent grads with family connections and no student loans to worry about while they earned next to nothing fetching coffee for the teleprompter guy. I also learned that most news professionals got their start in smaller television markets like Dayton or Little Rock and worked their way up. Of course I assumed my brilliance and savvy would enable me to go straight to playing with the big boys and girls.

So I gave it a whirl. I used my internship connections to con Tom Brokaw's assistant into letting me interview him under the guise of

"postgraduate work" and got meetings with the executive producers of some prime-time news shows who promised to put my résumé "at the top of the pile," but I just couldn't land a job.

Over time, I let go of the dream of becoming "Jane" and began navigating my way through different jobs and careers. Over the past fourteen years I've done everything from producing a campaign for children's rights for UNICEF to developing original animation for Cartoon Network. Going from the *Nightly News* to *The Powerpuff Girls*? It wasn't exactly what I'd had in mind. But how was I supposed to know? How was I supposed to understand what my career of choice was all about when I was using a Hollywood movie as a training manual?

And now, here I am. In my thirties and already on my third career—a writer. This one's going to stick, though, because I finally figured out what I want to do when I grow up . . . and I'm doing it. Even though it took me a while, I wouldn't be sitting here today if I hadn't gone through all those different jobs. Still, maybe my journey would have been more direct if I'd had straightforward information about what to expect when I got into the real work world. That's where this book comes in.

I've come to realize that *information* is the most valuable commodity any of us can hope for. And this book is chock-full of it. This book tells it like it is. The real scoop. The dirt. The DL.

I've reached out to women across the country who are not only great at their jobs but love them to boot, and I've asked each one of them to share what it's really like to be in their shoes. You'll learn not only about the realities of different careers, but even better, what successful women behind these careers actually look like, from *Grey's Anatomy* creator Shonda Rhimes to surgical veterinarian Anke Langenbach.

I approached the interviews for *In Their Shoes* by asking myself what you—on the verge of making your own career choices—would want to know. So I asked the women to describe the moment they realized what they wanted to do with their lives, what a typical day looks like, what the highs and lows of their job are, how they juggle it all, and what career advice they have for today's girls.

I learned more than I could have imagined. I learned that for most women, there is no such thing as a "typical day." I learned that while almost all the women I interviewed work long hours and consider their job extremely stressful, they wouldn't trade it for anything in the world. I've learned that when it comes to following your career dreams, you can't make a "bad choice"—everything we do along the way somehow fits in with where we end up. Lastly, I've learned that *you really can have it all.*

I absolutely loved meeting the women in this book. In fact, I have to admit that after each and every interview, I had a moment of pause where I thought about making another career shift. (*Is it too late for me to be a forensic scientist? Hmmm . . . what's the cutoff age for joining the Coast Guard?*)

Read on for "a day in the life" of some pretty impressive women, and then ask yourself, *which one feels most like me?*

there are all kinds of words and abbreviations that are used when talking about college degrees, positions within a company, and other job stuff. Here are some of the more common words and abbreviations you'll find throughout *In Their Shoes:*

AA Associate of Arts, a two-year college degree

AS Associate of Science, a two-year college degree

BA Bachelor of Arts, a four-year college degree

BFA Bachelor of Fine Arts, a four-year college degree

BS Bachelor of Science, a four-year college degree

BUSINESS CASUAL A work wardrobe that's somewhere between jeans and T-shirts and suits—slacks and a top, a skirt and a sweater, etc.

BUSINESS DRESS A work wardrobe that is dressy and professional, like business suits

CEO Chief Executive Officer, a title in business (usually the number one at a company)

CFO Chief Financial Officer, a title in business (usually the number one finance person at a company)

COO Chief Operating Officer, a title in business (usually the number one or number two at a company)

DOCTORATE Another way of referring to the graduate school degrees EdD, PhD, or MD

EDD Doctor of Education, a graduate school degree

EVP Executive Vice President, title in business

EXPENSE ACCOUNT The reimbursement of work-related expenses by a company—anything from taxi fare to a lavish entertainment account

GRADUATE SCHOOL Education that takes place after undergraduate school, usually to earn an advanced degree such as an MA or a PhD

MA Master of Arts, a graduate school degree

MBA Master of Business Administration, a graduate school degree

MD Doctor of Medicine, a graduate school degree

MFA Master of Fine Arts, a graduate school degree

OFFICE POLITICS The term used for difficult work situations or relationships within the workplace

PER DIEM A daily monetary allotment provided for people when they're traveling for work, to cover expenses while out of the office

PHD Doctor of Philosophy, a graduate school degree

PR A common abbreviation for public relations

SVP Senior Vice President, a title in business

UNDERGRADUATE Another way of referring to two- or four-year college degrees

VP Vice President, a title in business

![in their shoes]

in their shoes

Shonda Rhimes

TV show creator

the facts

Shonda Rhimes, Creator & Executive Producer, Grey's Anatomy

▶ **what?** Television show creators dream up TV show ideas—from sitcoms to dramas to reality shows—and convince a network to buy, produce, and broadcast their show.

▶ **where?** Most TV show creators work out of L.A. or New York City, since these are television industry hot spots, although they can write and develop their ideas anywhere.

▶ **how?** TV show creators need to be amazing writers and have supersmart ideas that fit in with the current television climate. On top of that, they need an agent to set up meetings with television executives so they can pitch their idea. If the execs love the pitch, then the real fun begins in production.

▶ **$$$:** Ranges dramatically depending on the show and the network . . .

▶ **dress code?** Creative and cool . . . or whatever you like

▶ **stress factor:** On a scale of 1 to 10, an 8

she's one of the hottest show creators in Hollywood, and I was thrilled to finagle an interview with Shonda Rhimes, the woman behind *Grey's Anatomy*, for this book. I spoke with Shonda about how she got her start, what it's like to create a hit TV show, and how she gets it all done. Here's our conversation:

ME: What did you want to do when you were a teenage girl?

SHONDA: I actually thought that I would be a novelist. I read a lot and I also watched a lot of television and old movies. But I really somehow thought that I would be a novelist. I thought that real writing was sitting in a garret somewhere, cold, starving, and pounding out the "great American novel." I loved literature and I majored in English lit in college, but really, when it came down to it, I'm more of a pop culture girl. That's what excites me and the stuff that I sit down to write.

ME: So how did you decide that you'd rather be writing screenplays instead of novels?

"Most of my time is spent hunched over a computer trying to come up with more ideas for the show, which if you're at all a writer, you find to be extremely fun and liberating."

SHONDA: When I got out of school, I was working as an assistant at an ad agency. In my spare time I sat down to put pen to paper, and what came out felt much more like a screenplay than a novel. It was mostly dialogue, and that was the stuff that was really exciting to me, so I went to USC film school.

ME: And look at you now . . . you not only created *Grey's Anatomy*, but you're also an executive producer of the series. What do you do as a creator and executive producer?

SHONDA: Well, I came up with the idea for the television series, and thus created the series. I wrote the script, I helped pick the director, and we shot the pilot, which is the first episode of a show. When your show is chosen by a network to become one of their shows, you become an executive producer, which means that I oversee the writing on all the scripts, the hiring of all the cast members, and all the editing and post-production. In an interesting way, it's like running a small country. . . . *Grey's Anatomy* is a small country and I have to run it.

ME: That's a good analogy. It sounds like an amazing job. Is it?

SHONDA: There are parts that are glamorous. I spend a certain amount of time doing interviews and walking down the red carpet and having hair and makeup done for those events. And you know, you do get to hang out with actors and be part of that really great creative process. But the reality of the situation is that most of my time is spent hunched over a computer trying to come up with more ideas for the show, which if you're at all a writer, you find to be extremely fun and liberating.

ME: Is *Grey's Anatomy* the first television show you've created?

SHONDA: It's the second television show I pitched and sold, and it's the first television show that was picked up and made.

ME: Wow, that's amazing. I'm sure you know that teens are really into your show.

SHONDA: Yes . . . and it's really exciting because for me, a little bit of what I love about *Grey's Anatomy* is that it's "high school in a hospital."

you asked . . .

"What do you tell yourself that helps you be successful?" Alex, age 14

shonda answered . . .

"My father always said to me, 'The only limit to your life is your own imagination. The only thing that's going to stop you from doing whatever it is you want to do is your ability to envision doing it.' When I was a teenager and he'd say that I always felt like, 'Oh, come on.' But now it makes so much sense to me. If I come up with the idea, I'm pretty sure I can make it happen."

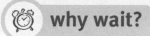

why wait?

▸ Read articles about television show creators and find out how they did it.

▸ Come up with your own characters and write, write, write about them.

▸ Follow the trends in TV and watch the highest-rated shows so you can see what makes a hit.

ME: Yeah, totally . . . that's why I'm hooked! So, what are the hours like? What's a typical day like for you?

SHONDA: I try to get in between eight o'clock and eight thirty a.m., because it's so quiet around here. I do a little writing, answer e-mails, and do phone calls. Everybody else sort of bustles in at about nine and the days are spent doing whatever's necessary at the time. You know, I'll spend a couple hours writing, I'll spend a couple of hours in editing, and I spend a lot of time sitting in a room with the rest of the writing staff coming up with more ideas. Sometimes we'll sit down with the cast and read the script out loud, and that gives me more ideas, and we'll have more notes to go back and keep writing. Now that the show's more popular, it feels like I spend an hour a day doing interviews. I grab lunch if I remember, I try to get home between seven and eight every night, which is not always possible, but I try really hard. And then I spend time with my family, write for a while longer after my family has gone to bed, and then go to bed and get up the next day and it starts all over again.

ME: That's a packed day. Do you have a life on the weekends?

SHONDA: On the days that I take off, absolutely . . . no question. I definitely always take off Sundays. That's my constant. I do not work Sundays mostly because I want at least one full day that I can spend with my family, giving them my full time, my full attention. Sometimes I'll work a little bit in the morning on Saturdays, sometimes I'll work a little in the afternoon. But sometimes I don't do any work at all.

ME: So tell me, is working in Hollywood as cutthroat as some movies and shows portray it?

SHONDA: At *Grey's Anatomy*, we're not very cutthroat. I mean, I think we're fairly relaxed. I think the fact that everybody here really loves their jobs and we're really focused on what we do keeps us from being cutthroat, because there's a lot of work to be done and we don't have time to worry about other people on other shows.

ME: Do you feel like a pioneer in television?

SHONDA: I don't feel like a pioneer. It was a surprising statistic when it was quoted to me that I was probably the first black woman to have her own show on one of the big four networks. But I don't feel like a pioneer so much as I feel like I'm busy still learning and I'm having a really good time while doing it. I'm trying to keep my head down and do a good job.

ME: After reading your blog on the *Grey's Anatomy* website, it came through loud and clear that you love your job.

SHONDA: I spend my days with the doctors of Seattle Grace Hospital, and that is not a bad thing by any stretch of the imagination. You know, whether they're in my head or I'm going to the stage to talk to the actors, it's a very pleasant way to pass the time. And when you have a job like that, that's the thing you're meant to do because it doesn't feel like work.

ME: What's the most difficult part of your job?

SHONDA: The pace. The pace in television is lightning fast. Which means that every eight days we need a new script to shoot, every eight

 then to now

1991: Graduated from Dartmouth College with a BA in English literature

1994: Received MFA from USC School of Cinema-Television

1995: Worked as research director for Tollin-Robbins/Mundy Lane Productions

days I need to have a new script edited, and every eight days I need to have something ready to go on the air. So the pace is really, really exhausting and you have to keep up. I think it was David Mamet who said that writing a movie is like running a marathon, and writing in television is running a marathon until you die.

ME: That's a great quote.

SHONDA: Yeah. And that's what it feels like. It's a constant never-ending pace. That's the hardest part. That and not getting to spend as much time at home as I like.

ME: What's it been like watching your show not only survive on the schedule, but become a breakout hit?

SHONDA: It's been pretty shocking. It feels really surprising to me that the stuff I come up with in my head at home while wearing my pajamas is stuff that people want to watch. The stuff that the ten writers and I sit around and brainstorm is stuff that people are really interested in. It's always amazing when you feel like people out there can look at something you've created and say, "I see myself in that." They look at one of the characters and they think, *That person's a little like me.* That's an amazing feeling.

ME: Are there any misconceptions out there about being a TV show creator? Anything we'd be surprised to know about?

SHONDA: Many people think creating shows is a thing that men do, but more and more women are creating shows. Any time you let

1999: Wrote HBO original movie, *Introducing Dorothy Dandridge*

2002: Wrote screenplay for *Crossroads*, starring Britney Spears

2004: Wrote the screenplay for *Princess Diaries 2: A Royal Engagement*

2004: *Grey's Anatomy* premiered on ABC

someone tell you it's a closed door and you believe them, you're setting yourself up for defeat.

ME: Do you have any advice for girls looking to do what you do?

SHONDA: Go to college. Honestly. And not just go to college, but the best thing you can do to strengthen your writing is to read as much as possible . . . to have a huge knowledge base of literature in all of its forms. I spent my entire childhood living in books, and I feel like that was the one thing that really helped me.

ME: Is there anything else you want to add?

SHONDA: The women around you can be the people who uplift you. The other girls you meet, the other women you meet who are your peers, can be the people who support you and help push you forward as opposed to being your competition. That to me is the most important thing. Some of the great people who helped me in this town have been other women.

in the field
Five More Careers Working on a TV Series

production assistant (entry-level position) Production assistants, or PAs, support the work of a producer, director, or other production executive. They do their fair share of fetching coffee and running errands, but they also have an opportunity to prove their commitment while learning on the job.

tv script writer TV script writers work together to develop a series arc and story episode ideas, and then work solo or paired with another writer to write individual episodes. They must have a solid understanding of the show's sensibility, as well as the characters in the series, in order to write scripts that will work on the air.

casting director Casting directors work with talent agents to identify potential actors to play the roles in a show, screening a ton of reels and reviewing headshots. After holding auditions, casting directors make their recommendations about who they think should be cast for each role.

location manager Location managers handle logistics that arise when shooting at a specific location. For example, if a scene from a TV show needs to be filmed at a baseball stadium, the location manager will work with the stadium personnel to work out any logistical details so the TV show can shoot as needed.

prop master Many TV series hire prop masters to figure out what props are needed for each episode and then buy, find, or build them. Prop masters have to be creative and resourceful in figuring out ways to get the necessary props, especially when they're working under tight budgetary constraints or the item isn't readily available.

 you need to know about

Scenarios USA is a nonprofit organization that gives young people ages twelve to twenty-two the chance to write scripts for short films addressing important social issues like peer pressure, HIV/AIDS, self-esteem, and body image. Winners of the "What's the REAL DEAL?" writing contest work with professional filmmakers to turn their scripts into short films. Find out more at www.scenariosusa.org.

For more on writing in Hollywood, check out the screenwriter profile on page 240 and the movie studio executive profile on page 60.

Joanne B. Sgueglia

forensic scientist

the facts

Joanne B. Sgueglia, Technical Manager of Forensic Biology, Massachusetts State Police Crime Lab

▶ **what?** Forensic scientists study samples and evidence collected at a crime scene to provide proof for police and attorneys as they solve their case and take it to trial.

▶ **where?** Forensic scientists usually work anywhere within the local, state, or federal law enforcement arena to support the work of detectives, police, and district attorneys. Others might work in independent crime labs, hospitals, or universities.

▶ **how?** To get in the door, forensic scientists need a bachelor's degree in a natural science, like chemistry or biology, although many get graduate degrees in their area of specialization, such as chemistry, botany, or entomology.

▶ **$$$:** An average salary of $40,000 to $85,000, depending on level of experience and work environment

▶ **dress code?** Business casual to casual

▶ **stress factor:** On a scale of 1 to 10, an 8

the popularity of shows like *CSI: Crime Scene Investigation* has spawned a surge in wannabe forensic scientists, but how realistically do those shows portray the career? I caught up with Joanne B. Sgueglia, the technical manager of forensics biology at the Massachusetts State Police Crime Lab, to find out.

ME: From the outside, your job sounds so cool, and you've been doing it for more than seventeen years, so you must like it. Was it what you expected when you first got started?

JOANNE: To get in and be trained to do DNA profiling was very much utilizing the skills that I gained in college, but I think the part that was more of a surprise was testifying in court. When you're taking chemistry and biology in college, you don't anticipate that. A lot of very good scientists don't necessarily make very good witnesses, so it takes a certain personality type to be a forensic scientist. So that was the surprise with a twist—it was a different set of skills that I learned on the job. I was testifying after only six months on the job. In those days you were sort of just thrown to the wolves.

> *"The biggest fallacy on CSI is the amount of time it takes to do things, along with the fact that one character on the show does what is actually the job of about twelve different people."*

ME: Can you tell us what you do at the crime lab?

JOANNE: I oversee four main units. There's the crime scene response unit, which is the unit that goes out into crime scenes and recognizes, collects, preserves, and transports evidence to the crime lab. I oversee a criminalistics unit, which is the unit that triages* all of the items that come in from a crime scene and do things like biological fluid identification, identify a particular garment, a rape kit . . . things like that. Then we have our DNA unit, which is my field of expertise, whereby

* **THE LINGO:** In forensic science, the term **triage** is another word for classifying or sorting evidence.

joanne answered . . .

"I was a biology major in college and a lot of my professors wanted me to go pre-med, but I found that whole environment very competitive, and I wanted to do something that could incorporate street knowledge along with formal education. So I went into a career guidance office and found out about forensics. I always loved shows like Quincy *and* Columbo, *but I didn't realize that the career existed in the same way. I thought it would be fascinating to integrate my love of science with wanting to be part of crime fighting."*

we do DNA profiling on those items that are amenable for DNA testing. And then we have the CODIS or Combined DNA Index System Unit, which is a database of DNA profiles from crime scene samples that gets searched against convicted offender profiles so we can get what we call "cold hits." Within the DNA unit, I make sure that all interpretations of DNA are done correctly and complete a whole host of duties that are overseen by the FBI.

ME: So then how do you actually spend your day?

JOANNE: Earlier in my career, the day would be spent getting items of evidence and bringing them into the laboratory, cutting stains off items, going through different methodologies in our laboratory to get DNA off the fabric, extract DNA, find out if we had enough DNA to continue with the test, and then do some sort of detection method to see if the DNA from the crime scene sample matched the DNA from a particular victim or suspect. That type of day would be working in the lab and looking at the final data to see if little bar codes match up or not. I've come a long way from that. That would be what the staff is doing now. I might spend my day looking into funding for new laboratory instruments, things like that. One of the frustrations and challenges in DNA testing is it's so progressive that as you're using

the technology, there's new technology on the way, so you are constantly in a state of transition.

ME: I've read a lot about how DNA testing has gotten so much better in the last twenty years, and that jurors expect a ton of DNA tests for cases now.

JOANNE: A lot of people in the legal field are calling that the "CSI effect." Those types of shows have raised a new awareness of DNA testing, and now jurors have more questions and more knowledge. They want DNA on everything, and it's actually overburdened the system both for the attorneys and for the scientists, because you have to test more stains on more items that may not necessarily need to be tested, but the jurors are expecting it. Today you have investigators wanting more and more samples tested for comprehensiveness, because it looks better to the jury to say that you tried it.

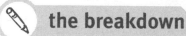

the breakdown

IN MEETINGS: 0–2 hours per day for entry level, 5+ for senior level

SITTING: Most of the day

PUBLIC SPEAKING: Occasionally

READING: Depends on level

WORKING SOLO: At least half the day

ME: What are your hours like?

JOANNE: At this level, I work pretty set hours, eight thirty a.m. through five o'clock p.m., Monday through Friday. At different times in my career, though, I've worked really long hours. I was part of the team that identified human remains from the crash of TWA Flight 800 that occurred on Long Island in 1995. We worked for about a year and a half on that project. So if you're working on a disaster or if you're on a rush case, you'll work extra hours.

ME: What kinds of things happen for you to have a good day?

JOANNE: A good day could be if you have a rush case and you get some information so you can solve the case and help the victims' families.

That's a good day. When you finally have some sort of DNA match to something in a case that has been unsolved, that can be very rewarding. Or if you have an old unsolved case, called a "cold case," and you get a DNA hit and can finally have an answer, that's a really good day.

ME: Would you say that's one of the best parts of your job?

JOANNE: It's difficult to say. It's complicated, because we do the analysis and we may get a result, but we can't make that result be the answer to a case. So sometimes it's frustrating, especially if it's a highly publicized case. Let's say we get a good DNA profile from a crime scene sample but we can't find the perpetrator. That's out of our hands. But when a rape victim tells you how they feel like they can breathe again because the rapist was caught following a DNA match you made, that's gratifying.

why wait?

▸ Take biology, chemistry, and physics classes in high school.

▸ Request an informational interview from a forensic scientist at a crime lab.

ME: When do things get tense?

JOANNE: Things are very stressful in a forensic crime laboratory. There's constant pressure to get more done with less. It's also a very stringent field as far as quality assurance goes, so bad days might be when you have audits, inspections, or one of your employees fails a proficiency test.

ME: If readers want to become forensic scientists because they think it will be like the show *CSI*, do they have a realistic idea of what they're in for?

then to now

| 1982: Graduated from State University of New York, Purchase, NY, with BA in biology | 1983–1984: Took graduate courses at John Jay College of Criminal Justice | 1988–1991: Worked at Lifecodes Corporation as a senior forensic scientist | 1991–1999: Worked as forensic scientist II at Suffolk County Crime Lab |

JOANNE: The biggest fallacy on *CSI* is the amount of time it takes to do things, along with the fact that one character on the show does what is actually the job of about twelve different people. Forensic science is a field of specialists. For example, our crime lab has a forensic biology department and a forensic chemistry department. There's someone to do the work on the databases; there are different people to go out to do crime scenes; there's a drug unit, which deals with controlled substances; you have bomb arson and fire debris; you have toxicology to see if any date rape drugs are involved; you have a trace department that does hair and fibers and paint and things like that. There is a specialty for any type of substance you're going to analyze. On *CSI*, only a few people do all of that, plus they also go out and do the detective's job. That is very unrealistic.

ME: So one person's job alone might be just collecting trace evidence.

JOANNE: Yes. In trace, for example, they do hair work, fiber work, and paint. So let's say a car hit a bicyclist and paint from the car got onto the bicycle in the accident. Trace will take the paint that came off the car and do some testing. They can look at all the different colors and layers in the paint and try and identify what type of vehicle hit the victim.

ME: How many cases might your DNA group be working on at once?

what it takes

▶ Attention to detail

▶ A compulsiveness to be organized

▶ A perceptive personality

▶ Being comfortable speaking (and testifying) in public

1993: Completed training at the FBI National Academy/ University of Virginia

1997: Awarded the American Academy of Forensic Sciences Regional Award

1999: Became technical manager of forensic biology at the Massachusetts State Police Crime Lab

2003: Certified by the American Board of Criminalistics

JOANNE: Each DNA analyst handles approximately forty cases a year. They get their own batch of assignments, about five cases or so at a time. The crime lab itself takes in hundreds of cases a year, and we're backlogged by over a thousand.

ME: Is there anything else you'd like to add?

JOANNE: The one thing I would say is that as much as forensic science can be exciting, every day's not an exciting day. You have to be the type of person who likes putting puzzles together, and in this job, you might be dealing with different puzzles every day.

INTERESTED IN DNA FORENSICS? HERE'S JOANNE'S ADVICE

▶ *Take coursework in molecular biology, genetics, biochemistry, and forensic statistics.*

▶ *Be sure that you're emotionally able to handle the graphic nature of a crime scene.*

▶ *There's nothing sacred when you're in a lab . . . we have to talk about things that may make some people uncomfortable, so you can't be shy.*

in the field

Five More Careers in Forensic Science

forensic pathologist Pathologists specialize in examining blood work and determining the cause of an illness or death. Shows like *Law & Order* and *CSI* feature forensic pathologists—you usually see them working in a dark room, wearing gloves and performing autopsies.

forensic entomologist Because there are insects that literally feast on dead bodies, bugs can be helpful in providing clues as to time of death. Through examining the life stage of insects like

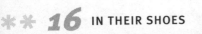

blowflies on a dead body, forensic entomologists can pinpoint the exact time of death, a clue that can be very important in murder investigations.

forensic psychologist Forensic psychologists are experts in the criminal justice system. Some work closely with lawyers, helping them figure out what a criminal's state of mind was during a crime, or testifying in court about the psychology behind a crime. Others might consult with lawyers on jury selection.

ballistics expert The work of ballistics experts usually focuses on ballistic evidence at crime scenes, which is anything relating to guns. Ballistics experts might look for bullets or slugs, help identify what kind of gun was used, and testify about the ballistic evidence in trials.

fingerprint classifier Making a fingerprint match can be a tedious process, and while technology has facilitated it, the actual matching is still a very exact science. Fingerprint classifiers examine fingerprints from crime scenes and use their skills to find a positive match in the hopes of identifying the perpetrator.

 ## you need to know about

The American Academy of Forensic Sciences (AAFS), which you can find online at www.aafs.org, has information on everything concerning forensics and even hosts the Young Forensic Scientists Forum, where you can learn more about schools with forensic science programs and learn how to break into the field.

For more science careers, check out the marine biologist profile on page 95.

Leah Faresh Karp

real estate agent

the facts

*Leah Faresh Karp,
Real Estate Agent*

▶ **what?** Real estate agents buy or sell real estate—anything from houses or lots of land to office buildings. Real estate agents handle every aspect of a deal, including negotiating offers, coordinating a ton of paperwork, meeting with inspectors, and making sure everything goes smoothly.

▶ **where?** Everywhere

▶ **how?** There are no college requirements for real estate agents, but a high school diploma is required, as well as being at least eighteen years old, taking thirty to ninety hours of training, and passing a written test to get a real estate license.

▶ **$$$:** Real estate agents get a percentage of the price a home or apartment sells for, so one who brokers a deal for a celeb could potentially make a million dollars in one shot. Agents working in more typical markets have an average annual salary of $30,000 to $50,000.

▶ **DRESS CODE?** Depends on the market

▶ **STRESS FACTOR:** On a scale of 1 to 10, between a 7 and an 8

from the outside, being a real estate agent seems like a pretty great gig. They get to drive around in deluxe cars, help people find the home of their dreams, sign a few pieces of paper, and sit back and collect their big fee. A closer look shows that it's not as easy as it looks. In fact, a real estate transaction is kind of like a complicated ballet, and the agent is the choreographer.

To get inside the life of a real estate agent, I met with Leah Faresh Karp, an agent in the San Francisco Bay area's hot Marin County market, where a simple three-bedroom home can easily go for more than a million bucks. Leah has been working in the biz for more than fifteen years, and she's figured out the secrets of success in her competitive field. I asked Leah what was at the heart of real estate, and she gave me a one-word answer: *marketing.*

> *"I love matching buyers and sellers together—that's probably why I set my friends up all the time too."*

"For me, marketing means always trying to create and tweak new ideas for either showing a property or advertising it differently. I'm always trying to highlight unique aspects of a property and figure out what needs to be said in order to draw the buyers to it. The great thing is that by

you asked . . .

"How has your career changed your life?" Carrie, age 15

leah answered . . .

"I've been doing it from such a young age that I learned about the importance of not just working to get a paycheck, but that it's what you do with the money you earn that determines how you succeed financially. If all I did was work because I wanted to get a paycheck, I would never get ahead. So now I work, get that paycheck, and turn around and invest it in what I do . . . that's given me a vehicle to be financially successful."

attracting buyers to my website or by advertising the listing, I'm also marketing myself, which helps me find new buyers to work with," Leah explains. "So I do the creative marketing work, and then I have someone who I employ full-time who does my online marketing."

Because real estate agents work with two different kinds of people—those who have property they want to sell and those who are in the market to buy—and they're sometimes working on a bunch of deals all at once, they are often swamped. In busy markets, they can literally work around the clock.

"The agents that I meet who are at the top of their game work *a lot* of hours. They probably couldn't even tell you how many hours they work because it's sort of like *all the time*," says Leah. "You really can sell real estate twenty-four hours a day."

Leah used to be one of those agents, but having a baby last year has changed everything.

"Being a new mom is forcing me to face one of the biggest challenges of the job, which is finding balance in your life and being okay with saying, 'These are the hours that I can meet you,' and if it doesn't work and I can't get someone else in my team to cover for me, accepting the fact that maybe this isn't a client I can work with. Before I had a baby, it was never an issue. I would find a way to make anything happen. Now it's all about making choices and working only with the clients who fit my lifestyle."

the breakdown

IN MEETINGS: 2–3 hours a day

ON THE PHONE: 4–5 hours a day

ONLINE: 1–2 hours a day

STAYING UP-TO-DATE ON INVENTORY/ HOUSE SEARCHING: 1 hour a day

DRIVING IN CAR: Half the day

then to now

1986–1990:
Sales associate, Nordstrom

1990–1994:
Took classes at American River College, Sacramento, CA

1990–1992:
Bank teller, Wells Fargo Bank

1992–1994:
Office manager, State Farm Insurance

That's not to say that Leah is slacking off these days. Hardly. In fact, she still pulls in at least thirty hours of work a week (she worked fifty plus pre-baby), balancing the million different pieces that make up her job. Here's what Leah's day looks like:

 ## LEAH'S (UN)USUAL DAY

6:00–7:00 a.m.: I like to get up before anyone else is awake at my house, because that's when I'm able to fit my exercise in and spend a few minutes actually thinking out my day. I make a list of "to do's" and think about what the day is going to look like and what I need to accomplish. The exercise and quiet time is my favorite time.

8:30 a.m.: I head off to work, and the first thing I always do is return e-mails and phone calls that are a priority. I try to do the things I like to do the least first, because that's when I'm the most alert and ready. I spend a lot of time prospecting—finding new buyers, finding new sellers, and working on the marketing. The smaller portion of my day is looking at homes or showing real estate.

12:30 p.m.: I usually don't take lunch—I eat at my desk or in the car. And I always bring my lunch with me, because I don't want to take the time during the day to sit down or go out to lunch, unless I'm meeting a client or having a staff meeting with people who work for me.

1:00–5:00 p.m.: The afternoon is spent focusing on people who are currently in the process of buying a house, whether it means meeting inspectors, reviewing documents or negotiating and working on contracts, dealing with mortgage brokers and title companies, or returning phone calls. I need to keep all of the pieces moving forward.

1994: Started working as real estate assistant for father's business

1996: Became business partner for father's business

1998: Went out on her own

⏰ why wait?

▶ Scour the real estate listings in your weekend paper and visit properties to learn about how they were marketed.

▶ Get experience working in retail or sales to strengthen your communication and business skills.

You're probably getting the sense that real estate agents have to be skilled at many things, and you're right. Leah says she always has to think one step ahead, not only when it comes to what's happening with her deals and marketing, but in how she works with people as well.

"I have to be personable, so that clients feel comfortable talking with me and feel that I understand what their needs are. Part of that is what I consider to be the basics of my job—it's getting dressed and looking presentable, having a clean car with a full tank of gas and just being prepared to go to work. I make sure my cell phone is charged, and I always keep bottled water and snacks in my trunk to make sure my clients are comfortable and happy," says Leah. "You have to wear a lot of different hats for this one job if you're going to do it successfully."

Challenges

Leah says the biggest challenge of her job is keeping her pipeline full. That means that while she's working with Client A, who is just starting to look at properties, she's also got to make sure she has Client B in the middle of escrow (the financial process regarding the transfer of funds in a sale), and Client C just about ready to finish a deal. Because real estate agents get paid only when all the loose ends of a sale are wrapped up, without this steady stream of clients in different stages of the process, it could be months between paychecks.

To make matters more challenging, there are a lot of aspects of the job that are out of the agent's control, and that can be frustrating and stressful. There are multiple people in the process, all of whom have to do their jobs right in order for a deal to go through—and of course, the buyer and seller need to cooperate too.

paying your dues

Don't expect to get your real estate license and dive right into selling multimillion-dollar homes. Beginning real estate agents typically start with less desirable properties and work as associate agents under a more experienced agent to gain experience.

Rewards

So if real estate is so challenging, why are so many people drawn to the field? Leah summed it up again in one word: *matchmaking*.

"I love matching buyers and sellers together—that's probably why I set my friends up all the time too. When I understand my client's needs and I know what they're looking for and I find *the* house, I can walk in and say, 'Oh my God, this is the one.' Watching my clients recognize that this is exactly what they were looking for . . . it's just so great. When they have their house-warming party and they call and tell you that they're so happy in the house and the kids love the neigh-bors' kids—when they really love where they live—that is probably the most rewarding moment.

what it takes

▸ Being a "people person"

▸ Having a good memory

▸ Being honest, trustworthy, and professional

▸ Attention to detail

LEAH'S CAREER ADVICE

▸ *Make a commitment to what you're going to do and do it for a set period of time before you walk away.*

▸ *Be passionate about your work—if you don't have a passion for it, you're not going to have what it takes to get through the negative aspects of a job.*

in the field

Five More Careers in Real Estate

mortgage broker Unless the person buying a home or office building can pay in cash, they'll be working with a mortgage broker. Mortgage brokers help buyers find a loan to buy the property and handle all the necessary paperwork between the lender and the borrower.

real estate appraiser For just about every real estate transaction, appraisers need to get involved. Appraisers check out the house or property that is being bought or sold and determine how much it is worth in the current market.

property manager Every apartment building or rented business space has a property manager who handles everything from making sure rent is paid on time to dealing with plumbing and heating problems. Many property managers say they love their jobs because they never know what to expect from one day to the next.

developer Some people make small (or large) fortunes as real estate developers. Developers are the people who look for opportunities to build new properties—townhouses, shopping malls, apartment buildings, high-rises—oversee their planning and construction, and then hope to make a profit by selling the building or renting it out.

insurance sales agent Before any bank will lend someone money to buy a home or a commercial space, they need to see proof of insurance, and that's where insurance sales agents come in. These agents sell policies to the person buying the space so if the property is damaged by a fire, flood, or other disaster, the lender's investment is safe.

Missy Park

entrepreneur

the facts

Missy Park, Founder & CEO, Title 9 Sports

▶ **what?** An entrepreneur is someone who starts his or her own business—basically creating something out of nothing. Entrepreneurs must have innovative ideas and find creative ways to get their business up and running.

▶ **where?** Absolutely anywhere!

▶ **how?** Depending on the kind of business they want to create, some entrepreneurs might start small and fund their venture by themselves, while others might write a detailed business plan and apply for a business loan.

▶ **$$$:** $0 to millions . . . it all depends on how good the idea is, how committed the entrepreneur is to it, and how successful the idea is on the market.

▶ **dress code?** Whatever you want!

▶ **stress factor:** On a scale of 1 to 10, between 5 and 10 (Missy says it changes on a daily basis)

there's something impressive about people who take an idea that they're passionate about and bring it to life, with no one telling them how to do it, writing them a paycheck, or giving them health insurance . . . no one guaranteeing them that their idea will be successful. How do entrepreneurs know what to do? Where do they get their confidence?

There are thousands of women entrepreneurs in the United States, but I chose to interview Missy Park, founder of Title 9 Sports, a hub for

"I'm pretty good at failing, and for me that seems to be the best way to learn."

women's athletic apparel that started as a tiny catalog business in 1989 out of Missy's garage and is now a national name in women's sportswear. Last year alone they mailed out more than twenty-five million catalogs and opened their seventh store. Missy had a strong vision when she started her company, and I couldn't wait to sit down and find out how she did it. Here's our conversation:

ME: What were your career dreams when you were younger?

MISSY: My mother and father both said that it was important that I know how to "think." My dad's big thing was, it really doesn't matter what your major is, but you need to learn to write, you need to learn to think critically, and you need to understand how statistics work, because they're important no matter what you do. But I don't believe that you need to know what you want to do at the age of eighteen. I majored in history, mostly because Yale is known for its history department.

ME: I read that you and your college friends talked about trying to create the women's version of Nike when you first got out of school. Is that true?

MISSY: I think that anyone who has played team sports at the collegiate and even the high school level spends the rest of their life trying to re-create the unanimity of purpose that you have when you're part of a team. Women's basketball had been a varsity sport at Yale for about five years when I got there, and it was very clear that we were second-class citizens. And there was a very tight group of us who had an idea about how to change that in the marketplace once we had graduated.

ME: So how did you get Title 9 up and running?

MISSY: I coached for a couple of years after college and then moved out to the West Coast because my brother lived here and it was free room and board. I got a job working for the North Face when it was quite small, and Fisher Mountain Bikes, companies whose founders were very much still there and there was a real passion for the product. My father had his own business when I was growing up, so I think the idea of that was very familiar to me . . . it seemed like a good life. I think it was in my genes to start my own thing, and at a certain point I was like, "Wow, I want to have my own business." I had a total of maybe two and a half years of industry experience. And then I decided to do it and proceeded to learn the business by trial and error. I'm pretty good at failing, and for me that seems to be the best way to learn.

you asked . . .

"What do you like most about remembering the old days and your journey to where you are now?" MaryBeth, age 12

missy answered . . .

"You know how we don't always notice when someone we're around all the time changes because it happens so gradually? That's almost the way it is with our company. Sometimes I'll look back on our old catalogs and think, Wow, we've really come a long way. *I mean, we started in my house and the inventory was in the garage, and now I walk over to our warehouse and it's twenty-five thousand square feet. It's like,* Wow, we've accomplished a lot. *So I certainly have a sense of pride and progress."*

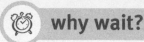

why wait?

▸ You know those little kids selling lemonade on the sidewalk? They're entrepreneurs! It's never too early to try starting your own business.

▸ Read about famous entrepreneurs like Oprah, Anita Roddick (The Body Shop), and Martha Stewart to find out how they got started.

▸ Take on leadership roles in activities and clubs to get experience in management.

ME: Do you think that not being afraid to fail is an important quality for someone who wants to be an entrepreneur?

MISSY: I do, actually. A buddy of mine once said, "You know, I've seen all kinds of entrepreneurs—some of them are really extroverted, some are really introverted, some are supersmart and some aren't that smart at all, some are really good with people, some aren't. The only thing I can say that they all have in common is that none of them really care about what other people think." Yeah, it's hard to fail and I don't like it, but I'm never thinking, *Oh, I've failed, and what do other people think?* I'm like, *Damn, I wish I hadn't screwed that up,* you know?

ME: Without having someone show you the ropes of starting a company, how did you know that you could make Title 9 work?

MISSY: I didn't. For the first three or four years, I'd resolve that we were going to quit at least once every six months. You know that saying, "Courage is not the absence of fear, but the mastery of it"? The absence of fear is really stupidity. You show me somebody that's never

then to now

1984: Graduated from Yale with BA in history	1984–1988: Worked various jobs in retail	1989: Started Title 9 Sports at the age of 26	1990: Title 9 hired first employee (now she's the president!)

been afraid and I'll show you someone that's either superstupid or living in a box. There were times when I was really nervous and I had a ton of doubts, and that still continues now. But I think that mastering your fear can fuel you to focus on the right things. I think that a lot of girls hate making mistakes, and it just kills me. They're so worried about making mistakes, it's like, "Wow, if you don't make mistakes, how are you going to learn?"

ME: What does your day-to-day work actually involve?

MISSY: I have a lot of interest in the creative side of the business, so I spend a lot of time on that—like looking at products, deciding what's going to go in the catalog, reviewing how we talk to our customers on the phone—that's probably 50 percent of my time. Then I spend 25 percent of my time figuring out what's next . . . some people would call that "new business development." I think that's a pretty fancy name for what I do, which is trying to develop other opportunities for us and learning new businesses. I spend the other 25 percent of my time working on employee development stuff—thinking about what the next opportunities are for the people who work here.

 what it takes

▶ A great idea (or several)

▶ Confidence (and, as Missy says, a healthy dose of fear)

▶ A willingness to fail and assume a financial risk

▶ The ability to think outside the box

▶ Being extremely self-motivated

ME: Wow . . . it sounds like you wear many different hats.

MISSY: Yes, which is good for me . . . I have a very short attention span.

1994: First year Title 9 made a profit

1997: Opened first Title 9 store in Berkeley, CA

2000: Title 9 got first photocopier

2002: Held first "Title 9 Olympics"

2006: Opened eighth retail store

ME: So, what do you do when things get tense at work?

MISSY: Well, often I'm the one who is causing the tension. . . . I feel like that's my role. I actually think it's a good thing. I need to be able to do it in a way so that we all still love one another at the end of the day, but it's how we get better. One of the things that we talk a lot about is this idea that when we hire people here, you need to feel comfortable both being challenged and challenging others rather than just sort of doing what you're told, because we're growing and things are always changing. You need to be able to think on your feet and say, "Well, this doesn't work anymore."

ME: If you're having a great day, what is it that makes it great?

MISSY: It used to be that a great day at work for me was having the phones ring like crazy, trying to process credit cards, packing up orders while talking on the phone, chasing after the UPS truck, throwing orders at the truck, and then running back and cleaning everything up. That was really fun for me. Now I think a great day for me is when I'm working with a small group of people, all of whom are sort of at the top of their game, and together we come up with a product or an idea that none of us could have come up with on our own. I find that incredibly gratifying.

ME: That's such an interesting perspective, because when I think of an entrepreneur, I think of this sole person running a company. Is it possible to have a balance between work life and personal life when you run your own company?

MISSY: I think work/life balance is probably a lot like finding the job you love—it's an ongoing process. When I was first starting the business, I slept here. I worked all the time, I traveled on the weekends to play rugby or to do photo shoots and I was really happy doing that. I mean, there might be people who say that wasn't a good work/life balance, but for me it worked great. Then my business became more mature, I grew up, and now I have two kids. When our first child was born, my partner and I were both working in fairly high-level jobs that required a fair amount of travel, and that was a time where we didn't have it right. And it was like, "Okay, now there's a kid in this equation that we really want to spend time with." But about four years ago, Dana left her job and is at home full-time, and we have very clear roles now. And I focus entirely on the business and I have the freedom to do that. Having said that, people always ask me, "Oh, it must be hard juggling a family and a baby and work," and I'm like, "No, it's not hard at all. Family always wins." I've made some compromises. . . . I think I'd rather have more than two kids, but I would have had to start a lot sooner and I wasn't ready then. I don't see work and life as two separate things. I like both a lot, so I don't need to wall them off.

ME: What's it like being able to do what you want with your company?

MISSY: It couldn't be any other way for me. And there are strengths and weaknesses to that. I am someone who needs complete autonomy to do what I think is right—that's why I have my own business.

MISSY'S ADVICE

Take more risks. That's it . . . just take more risks.

in the field
Five More Careers Where You Can Be Your Own Boss

small business owner More than ten million women own small businesses in the United States. While it can be risky, being your own boss is great if you've got the passion. Small business owners may handle product development, marketing, advertising, accounting . . . even pounding the pavement in search of new business.

independent contractor or consultant This is one career that's difficult to embark on until you've had solid work experience. Independent contractors can be found in any field—the thing they all have in common is an expertise that someone needs. For example, a marketing executive might leave her firm to consult for companies who don't have their own marketing department.

freelance writer Freelance writers usually work from home, and they might write anything from magazine articles to marketing materials. Like most self-employed people, freelance writers are always looking for their next job, even as they're working on a dozen projects at once.

dog walker In big cities, you can spot dog walkers a mile away because they look like a moving ball of fur. Dog walkers might have up to twenty clients, whose dogs they typically walk while the pet owners are at work. They charge up to twenty-five dollars a day per dog—this can be a pretty good gig!

stay-at-home parent This might not seem like a "career" in the traditional sense, but stay-at-home parents have more than a full-time job. Never off duty, they work around the clock—feeding, dressing, entertaining, and educating their children, as well as possibly cooking, cleaning, and doing laundry. The pay's not great (as in . . . there is none!) but the benefits can be.

 you need to know about

Junior Achievement, or JA (www.ja.org), is a national organization for children and teens with high school programs that help students foster skills that will be useful in the business world. A number of their programs, like JA Company, JA Titan, and GLOBE, are geared toward educating future business owners and entrepreneurs.

Kamala Harris
district attorney

the facts

▶ **what?** If you've seen *Law & Order*, then you've seen Hollywood's take on the role of a district attorney. Elected or appointed into their position, district attorneys, or DAs, are the chief legal officer in their jurisdiction, and they prosecute crimes that occur in their counties or cities on behalf of the people.

▶ **where?** Most cities and counties have a district attorney, as well as a number of assistant district attorneys (ADAs).

Kamala Harris, District Attorney, San Francisco

▶ **how?** District attorneys need a bachelor's degree and a law degree. They must also pass the bar exam in their state.

▶ **$$$:** An average of $40,000 to $50,000 a year for attorneys starting out in the district attorney's office, and an earning potential of more than $100,000 a year, depending on the city they work in.

▶ **dress code?** Business dress, especially in court

▶ **stress factor:** On a scale of 1 to 10, an 8

kamala harris, the district attorney of San Francisco, made national news in 2005 when she was featured alongside Oprah and eighteen other incredible women in a *Newsweek* special report called "How Women Lead: 20 of America's Most Powerful Women on Their Lives—and the Lessons They've Learned."

Kamala is the first woman to ever be elected district attorney for San Francisco, and the first African-American woman to hold the office in the entire state of California. Since being elected in 2003, Kamala has been busy—trying murder cases in San Francisco, creating a new specialist team to deal with gun violence, and calling for legislative changes to better protect women and children. On top of this, she oversees a whole team of attorneys and the multiple cases they are prosecuting. Kamala squeezed in some time to give us an inside glimpse of her career.

"It is not only about what I can do in the office during business hours. It's also about what I can do out in the community."

ME: What were your career dreams when you were younger?

KAMALA: I have always been drawn to issues of justice, public service, and equal rights. Both my parents were involved in the civil rights movement, and some of my earliest childhood memories are of the marching, the passion, the debate, and the emotion about this concept called "justice." My earliest role models and examples of public service were those who were more concerned with work that benefited others, rather than work that made money. My heroes were the architects of the civil rights movement, individuals who were agents for change. Conversations that I heard while growing up were always about the responsibilities of government and the fair distribution of public resources so that those in need are protected and supported. Early on, it was very evident to me that if you were going to have some impact in making sure that justice occurred, becoming a lawyer was a good place to start.

ME: What kind of tasks might you do on any given day?

KAMALA: First of all, it would be erroneous to call this wonderful work "work" in the traditional sense. It is not a nine-to-five job, and no day is like another. It is not only about what I can do in the office during business hours. It's also about what I can do out in the community, whether it is speaking at community events or before fellow lawyers at bar association events. It is continually talking about the need for a criminal justice system that sees and thinks about all the people it is supposed to protect, including immigrants, children, seniors, and others who may not feel empowered. It's the work of brainstorming and thinking about the most creative and efficient ways to solve some of these problems.

ME: What's the first thing you do when you get to work in the morning?

KAMALA: I meet with my executive assistant to identify the most urgent and time-sensitive matters of the day so we can address them first thing in the morning.

you asked . . .

"How did you manage to keep a positive attitude and allow the benefits of your dream to outweigh your fear and doubts?" Brooke, age 16

kamala answered . . .

"I think that all of us, no matter who we are or what we aspire to do, can sometimes feel overwhelmed with fear and doubt. My mother was a great influence and motivator in my life. She is a very smart woman who is fierce in her honesty and her opinions about what is fair, just, and right. My mother raised my sister and me with a standard that it was never acceptable to do anything other than your best. She never had any doubts about what I could accomplish and always inspired me to overcome any obstacle. In fact, one of the most important pieces of advice she gave me was, 'You may be the first to do many things, but make sure you are not the last.'"

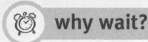

why wait?

> ▶ Good public speaking skills are important for most lawyers, so join the debate team at school and brush up on your skills.
>
> ▶ Find out about public hearings in your community. If you feel passionate about the debate, you can even argue your side of the issue in the hearing, no matter your age.
>
> ▶ Some law firms offer internships for high school students, where they can perform administrative tasks like filing and answering phones.

ME: What is the last thing you do before you go home?

KAMALA: Before heading out to any of the one to two community events that are usually scheduled each evening, I debrief with my chief assistant district attorney and executive assistant about the day's events. We also look ahead and prepare ourselves for the next day.

ME: Your job appears so cool from the outside, especially for fans of TV shows like *Law & Order*. What's the reality?

KAMALA: The reality is that a prosecutor's job is not glamorous in the least. Shows such as *Law & Order* do not really depict how closely prosecutors work with victims and witnesses of crime, as well as their families. Our interaction with these victims, with their raw pain and struggle and grief, always drives home the seriousness and grittiness of the work that we do. So in that regard, TV shows are sanitized versions. And there is no neat conclusion to the day like there is at the end of an episode. After the conclusion of one case, we can't

then to now

| Graduated from Howard University | 1990: Graduated from Hastings College of Law | 1990–1998: Deputy district attorney in Alameda County |

paying your dues

Attorneys fresh out of law school usually start out as junior associates, or if they're at the top of their class, as law clerks for a judge. In these positions they'll do a lot of research for the attorneys or judges they work for, putting in long hours and using their salary to start chipping away at law school debt.

afford to rest on our laurels and watch the credits roll. We have to prepare ourselves for the other twenty cases on our desks. But there are "*Matlock* moments," such as when we really connect with a jury at trial, or when we make the perfect argument. Knowing that we have done the work necessary to hold a perpetrator accountable for causing harm or injury to another can be immensely gratifying.

ME: What's the best part of your job?

KAMALA: The best part is achieving my goal of creating a world-class district attorney's office. We are focused on the work of keeping San Francisco and its residents safe, and doing that work in a way that is smart. I'm proud that we have significantly increased the conviction rate at trial for felonies. There was a significant backlog of cases in this office, and we have reduced it by more than 60 percent. We have created a priority around the prosecution of gun cases. For the first time in the history of this office, we created

what it takes

▶ Attention to detail and a love of research

▶ A strong sense of justice and integrity

▶ Being a great communicator, both written and verbal

▶ Long, hard hours

a child assault unit, an environmental unit that prosecutes environmental offenses, and a public integrity unit to go after corruption. We have been reaching out to traditionally underserved communities and taking our show on the road to different neighborhoods instead of waiting for them to come to us.

ME: And the most challenging aspect?

KAMALA: Frankly, how much there remains to be repaired and fixed.

KAMALA'S CAREER ADVICE

The advice I would give to young women, whether they aspire to a law career or otherwise, is to own your power. Know your value and your potential. Don't be afraid of it, don't be intimidated by it, and certainly don't deny it.

in the field

Five More Careers in the Law

judge Judges are the authority in the courtroom, and they conduct trials and ensure that trials are fair. In trials where there's a jury, a judge explains to the jury how to come to a decision and sentences people who are found guilty. In trials with no jury, they decide the verdict. Most judges are elected into their positions after practicing law for a number of years.

paralegal Also known as legal assistants, paralegals do much of the same work as lawyers, including tons of researching, writing legal briefs, and helping to prepare arguments for trials. Unlike lawyers, paralegals typically don't have law degrees, so they can't give legal advice or present cases in court.

mediator Mediation can save legal fees and provide parties with a quicker and potentially "nicer" way to resolve disputes by helping two parties at odds with each other resolve the issue by employing an unbiased middle person. Some mediators are on staff at courthouses, while others work for organizations that offer mediation services.

corporate attorney While most legal TV shows involve dramatic trials, many attorneys never see the inside of a courtroom as part of their job. Corporate attorneys handle legal business for companies. They are required for just about every business transaction, and they must have an intimate knowledge of the business laws on both the state and local levels.

court reporter Court reporters transcribe every trial as it happens to ensure that there is an accurate legal record of the procedure. Most court reporters use keyboards called stenotype machines, which let them type every word as fast as it's said—good court reporters can type two hundred words per minute.

For more careers in law enforcement, check out the sheriff profile on page 298.

lunch break

have big plans for your future? Setting goals can be an incredibly powerful tool to keep you plugging ahead. Here are some ideas to keep in mind when setting goals. See which ones work for you!

Try Writing a Mission Statement

A mission statement is basically a sentence or two explaining what the ultimate goal of an organization (or person) is. For example, the mission statement for Girls Inc. is "to inspire all girls to be strong, smart and bold."

You don't need to know exactly what you want to be to write a mission statement, and you can also constantly revise it. For example, my mission statement for the past five years has been to "work on creative projects that inspire and empower girls and women." When you have a mission statement that's clear, it's so much easier to make smart choices.

So how about you? Want to give it a try? Here are a few lines to write your own mission statement. Write down something very broad and focus on the things that make you feel excited and inspired:

_____

_____

_____

Set Some Goals

There's something about putting our dreams and goals down on paper that makes it more likely that we'll accomplish them. Even if no one else ever sees your goals, the act of thinking about what you want to achieve and writing it down forces you to think about the smaller steps that go into reaching the bigger dreams. Try breaking the big goals down into smaller steps. It makes them feel attainable . . . because they are!

Here's an example: Say you want to be a successful screenwriter. You might map out your goals like this:

MAIN GOAL:

▸ To be a successful screenwriter by the time I'm twenty-five

SUPPORTING GOALS:

▸ Read William Goldman's book *Adventures in the Screen Trade* this year.

▸ Watch all the movies that are nominated for best screenplay each year.

▸ Read one screenplay each month.

▸ Write in my journal for five minutes every night.

▸ Look into taking a screenwriting class.

Why don't you give it a shot?

MAIN GOAL(S):

_____

_____

_____

SUPPORTING GOALS:

_____

_____

_____

_____

_____

_____

Keep Your Goals Visible

Writing down goals works the best when we put them somewhere we can see them, preferably every day—on your bedroom wall, tacked above your desk, or tucked inside your journal. Goals are almost like "to do" lists . . . and there's nothing more rewarding than checking off a goal once you've accomplished it.

Be Flexible

Goals change . . . and that's totally fine and completely normal. It doesn't mean that you failed—it just means that you're open to all different kinds of possibilities for your future. There's no better way to be fulfilled in your career and your life than by recognizing when things really connect for you. If you follow your passion, you can't make a wrong turn, because you'll always be happy doing what you're doing, and it will lead you to other amazing opportunities.

Jessica Weiner

actionist

the facts

Jessica Weiner, Actionist

▶ **what?** When Jessica Weiner couldn't find a career title that encompassed everything that she did, she made one up. The result? *Actionist*. According to Jessica, an actionist is someone who takes action in her everyday life. For Jessica, that job entails everything from speaking and motivating to writing and performing, all in a quest to make peoples' lives better.

▶ **where?** Actionists do their thing anywhere, anytime.

▶ **how?** Don't expect a course called How to Be an Actionist 101 to pop up in colleges anytime soon. Actionists take action by feeding their interests and following their passion to inspire change.

▶ **$$$:** The sky's the limit.

▶ **dress code?** Pajamas to dress pants—depends on where that day's adventures take you

▶ **stress factor:** On a scale of 1 to 10, a 9

when I first heard about what Jessica Weiner was doing with her life, I thought, *How cool is that?* Here's a woman who created a career by following her passion and working on projects that connected with her *purpose.* Like any trailblazer, Jess is a risk taker with a clear vision, and following her gut has certainly paid off. Not only is she a successful author, writing books like the recent *Life Doesn't Begin 5 Pounds from Now,* but she juggles a column for Mary-Kate and Ashley's website (www.mary-kateandashley.com), travels around the country speaking to teens and young adults about body image and self-esteem, and even makes appearances on shows like *Oprah* and the *Today* show. Her message? To inspire people to take *action* in their everyday lives to make the world a better place.

"I didn't have anyone showing me how to do exactly what I wanted to do."

I caught up with Jessica while she was on a book tour and spent an afternoon hanging out with her in her "author's suite" at a hotel downtown. Here's our conversation. . . .

ME: Can you tell me how you started going down this path of being an actionist in the first place?

JESSICA: From the time I was a little girl, I always wanted to be an actress. I loved to perform, loved to create, loved to make up stories. And so as a little girl of eight or nine, I wrote a story that my teacher found to be very wonderful. I read it to my class and they were laughing and that was it—I was hooked. And I was like, "Wait a minute. I can make something up in my mind and then share it with people and they'll get enjoyment out of it? I want to do that!" So I decided I wanted to be an actor and performer. Then when I was in my teens, I struggled with eating disorders, and as I dealt with figuring out who I wanted to be in the world, I was afraid of going further into acting because I thought people were going to tell me all the time to lose weight or straighten my hair or change my nose or look different.

When I was eighteen, I came to the conclusion that I didn't want to put myself out there in a way that would damage my self-esteem any further.

ME: That was pretty insightful at eighteen years old.

JESSICA: I just knew I didn't want to make a career out of having people comment on what I looked like. At the same time, as part of my recovery from my eating disorder, I was sitting in groups with women and talking about body image and our addictions, plus I still was in love with storytelling. So I started writing stories about the girls in my treatment program and performing them as one-woman shows on campus. That's kind of where it all began, and over the years, I've refined it into being the career that I have today. I didn't have anyone showing me how to do exactly what I wanted to do.

ME: I love that, the whole idea that there are many different ways to go about reaching the same destination.

JESSICA: Yeah, me too. But when I was in college, it was challenging to be a twenty-one-year-old senior trying to figure out how to make money at it. All my friends were going out to get their "jobs,"

you asked . . .

"If you could do it all over again, would you?" Crystal, age 12

jessica answered . . .

"Absolutely. I would even take all of the bad stuff that happened to me as a teenager and all of the things that wrapped themselves around into making this a career for me. All the hard work, frustration, pain, and discouragement gets wiped away when you do what you love and you see that you've affected someone else. That kind of happiness is irreplaceable."

the breakdown

IN MEETINGS: 10 to 20 meetings a week

ON THE PHONE: Constantly

ONLINE: Constantly

SITTING: Not very often!

PUBLIC SPEAKING: All the time!

WORKING SOLO: A lot

WRITING, DAYDREAMING, AND IMAGINING: A lot

and there I was with no idea how to make a living at what I was doing. I just knew that I loved it so much I was going to have to break the rules and make something up.

ME: So how did you get started?

JESSICA: I took a grant-writing class at a community college because I thought that maybe I wanted to start my own business. My final exam was to write a grant and submit it, so I did that. My grant application was accepted and I got five thousand dollars from the Eli Lilly Foundation, and at the age of twenty-one I started a social issues theater company in Indianapolis without a clue as to what I was actually going to do. So I wrote plays and got actors together to perform for anybody who would have us—high schools, middle schools, colleges. We'd put on these plays and get people to talk about things. And my career just slowly started taking off after that.

ME: Let's shift to the present. My gut is that you don't have an "average day," but could you tell me what a typical day might look like if, say, we were peeking through your window?

then to now

1995: BA in theater arts, Pennsylvania State University

1995: Created the ACT Out Ensemble in Indianapolis

2000: Founded Parallax Entertainment, Beverly Hills, CA

2003: First book, *A Very Hungry Girl*, is published

JESS'S (UN)USUAL DAY

I usually get up between six thirty and seven in the morning. Then I go for a walk, usually for about a half hour, just so I can start to clear my head. Then I come back and I write in my journal. I write in my journal every day, even when I don't feel like it, because it's the one place I can get out all the crazy thoughts in my head. My whole morning routine takes about an hour, and it starts my workday.

Next I go into my office and begin answering e-mails. A lot of girls write in to my advice column, so I start answering those questions, or if I'm preparing to speak or do a seminar, I'll do some of my research or gather my materials and make sure that everything's in place. I have someone that helps me with my bookings, so when she comes to work, we'll talk about what schools have called or what my speaking tour looks like, what projects have come in for me to work on.

I live in Los Angeles, so everyone does a "lunch meeting." I usually have one of those where I'm networking. So I go and meet with people and talk about what projects are going on.

I usually write in the afternoon. Maybe I'm writing an essay for CosmoGIRL! or writing an entry for my blog on my website, or a blog for someone else's site. Sometimes I'll read. I actually have the luxury of being able to read magazines and books and new things that are out just so I understand what my audience is reading. And then I try to connect with friends in the evening. As best I can, I try to carve out time that's just for my friends when I'm actually in town.

When I'm on tour, like I am right now, I'll come into a city and I'll usually have some kind of press interview—radio, TV, newspaper—and then I'll go back to my hotel room. And if I haven't journaled yet, I'll journal. Then I'll prepare to go and speak. I just get really quiet, write my thoughts out, and think about if I was in my audience, what I would want to hear that night.

2003: Appeared on *Oprah*

2004: Founded No. 11 Media

2005: Second book, *Life Doesn't Begin 5 Pounds from Now,* is published

2006: Became advice columnist for Mary-Kate & Ashley's website

▸ Discover where your passion lies.

▸ Volunteer with organizations whose cause feels close to your heart.

▸ Offer to be an intern for a person you admire (Jess offers internships through her website, www.jessicaweiner.com).

JESSICA: As you can see, I have a really unstructured day. The trick for me and my job is to not overwork. The tendency is for me to push myself because there's no one over my shoulder telling me I only have fifteen minutes here and fifteen minutes there. The challenge is to strike a balance, because my life is my work, and my message is my life. And so if I'm not taking care of myself, I have nothing to give my audience.

ME: Traveling, speaking, press appearances . . . it all sounds very glamorous. But how does it really feel in the moment?

JESSICA: I've been doing it for so long that I sometimes forget what a cool job I actually have. Because the other part of this job is that there is nobody who does it with me. And even though I have people who support me in my office at home and I have tons of friends and family, I don't get to create with other people until I go out and speak. So there's a little bit of loneliness. And sometimes I feel like the lone crusader out there. But when I'm in front of an audience, all of that melts away, and I feel the most in tune with my purpose. And that's when I know that I've got the right job.

ME: Did you have an "aha" moment where it all just clicked for you and you knew what you were supposed to be doing with your life?

JESSICA: I wrote a play about eating disorders when I was in college, and when the show was over, I went onstage with my actors, took a bow, and realized that nobody was moving out of the theater.

Everyone was just kind of sitting there. And I thought it was because we had really sucked. And then a woman in the back raised her hand and said, "My mom and my sister have thrown up after everything they eat, and I never knew it was called bulimia." Another girl who was sitting not far from her turned around and said, "My roommate throws up all the time. How could you not know that that was an eating disorder?" And suddenly this spontaneous conversation broke out. When I saw that what I had created had sparked that kind of debate in an audience, I was hooked. I knew I needed to figure out how to make a career out of doing it.

ME: What's the most frustrating thing about what you do?

JESSICA: For every one of my performances in front of fifteen hundred people, there are thirty tabloid magazines, ten television shows, and forty other media properties that send out the message that all girls need to look a certain way in order to be loved. And while I'm trying to make having self-esteem cool, I continuously come face-to-face with my detractors, which in many ways is the very world we live in. And that's a big obstacle. My work also has the same frustrations as other jobs . . . things just don't go right, or somebody mispronounces my name or people in the crowd heckle me, or a microphone doesn't work and I have to speak loudly for an hour and a half in front of an audience. And then there are just days when I don't feel like putting myself out there. And when I've been paid to come stand in front of the room and inspire somebody and I'm not feeling particularly inspirational that day, I have to dig deep and push myself to be "on." And that can be a lot of pressure.

 what it takes

- ▶ Being self-motivated and a self-starter

- ▶ Passion, passion, passion!

- ▶ Confidence in yourself and your message

- ▶ Being a good communicator

ME: And how about the opposite? When are you happiest doing your job?

JESSICA: When I finish giving a talk, there's usually a group of people waiting to tell me something afterward. But it's the ones who wait because they just really want to hug me and say "thank you"— that single moment makes my entire job worth doing.

JESS'S CAREER ADVICE

▸ *Make it up—all of the great career niches out there have been created by someone!*

▸ *Surround yourself with friends and family who say yes to your dreams and validate your vision.*

▸ *If you see somebody doing what you want to do, don't be afraid to grill them. Offer to take them to lunch. E-mail them! Ask them to be interviewed. Find out what their lives have really been like.*

in the field
Five More Careers Where You Can Inspire the World

motivational speaker To be a good motivational speaker you need: (1) a strong message that inspires other people, (2) a healthy dose of charisma, and (3) a love of being in front of an audience. Motivational speakers might work for themselves or for an organization that wants to promote a cause or message.

life coach This is a fairly new career, but its future looks pretty hot. Most life coaches work for themselves, and they're hired by people who want to get their life on track—everything from creating a plan for landing their dream job to helping them keep their life in balance.

youth program director Have you ever joined a youth organization like the Girl Scouts, or maybe a religious youth group? Every one of these organizations has directors who figure out what programs their organization's members might be interested in, like writing workshops or group volunteer activities, and then make them happen.

activist Activists are passionate about a cause or idea, and their work is all about creating change. Activists are the people behind all the big "movements," like the civil rights movement or the women's lib movement, and they usually work for organizations that are trying to change government policy.

volunteer coordinator Most of us have volunteer experience, and it's a good thing, too—the work of volunteers is what helps keep even multinational organizations running. Volunteer coordinators help find new volunteers, train them, and make sure their work has a positive impact.

 you need to know about

Action Without Borders, otherwise known as Idealist.org (www.idealist.org), is the online hub for people from more than 165 countries who want to take action and change their world. You'll find links to thousands of nonprofits, opportunities to volunteer, and a section with info and resources just for teens and kids, including tips for starting your own movement.

Jocelyn Warner
social worker

the facts

▶ **what?** Social workers offer support to people facing hardships or experiencing difficult situations in their lives. Social workers find services for their clients, as well as offer emotional and informational support through counseling.

▶ **where?** Social workers might work for government agencies in welfare or foster care, health agencies and clinics, schools, or—like Jocelyn—in a hospital setting.

Jocelyn Warner, Social Worker, Department of Gynecologic Oncology, Mount Sinai Hospital

▶ **how?** Most social workers have a four-year degree in social work (called a BSW) or psychology, but many choose to get a master's (MSW) on top of that—which is required for many clinical and health-related jobs—or get further certified by getting their license (licensed master social worker, or LMSW).

▶ **$$$:** An average of $30,000 to $47,000 a year, depending on the kind of social work

▶ **dress code?** Casual to business casual

▶ **stress factor:** On a scale of 1 to 10, a 7

jocelyn is a social worker in the gynecologic oncology department at Mount Sinai Hospital in New York City, which means that she works with women who have cancer. As a social worker, her job is all about supporting the patients in the department. Usually her interaction with them starts when they're first diagnosed, and she'll introduce herself to them in case they want to use her services right away, or just so they know she's there for them when and if they need her down the road.

"A lot of my early meetings with patients are me talking with them and their partners about the shock of a new cancer diagnosis," Jocelyn explains.

She ran through the kinds of things she might do as part of her job; the list is long, the tasks many. Here are some examples of what her work entails:

"Although a lot of social workers deal with depressing situations, I don't think our role is depressing at all . . . we're the people families can turn to."

▸ Meeting with newly diagnosed cancer patients

▸ Coming up with a discharge plan for patients going home or to a health-care facility, including arranging for transportation and home IV medication and handling other logistical details

▸ Helping people get resources, like applying for disability or Medicaid

▸ Counseling patients and their families about their diagnosis or their needs

▸ Arranging for end-of-life care when necessary

"As a social worker, our role is one of supporting and empowering people. And although a lot of social workers deal with depressing

jocelyn answered . . .

"I've always wanted to work with kids. My first job out of college was teaching preschool at a Head Start program, which are government-sponsored programs for low-income families to send their kids to preschool. While I liked the work itself, it was a lot of classroom management. We had a social worker on staff who'd come in and work with kids in the class who were dealing with some kind of psychosocial issue. I talked with her about her work, and that's what got me interested in the general field of social work."

situations, I don't think our role is depressing at all, because we're being a support . . . we're the people families can turn to," says Jocelyn.

I asked Jocelyn to paint a picture of what her typical day might look like. Here's what she had to say.

JOCELYN'S (UN)USUAL DAY

For the most part the hours are pretty good, basically nine a.m. to five p.m. Sometimes things take longer and you get wrapped up in someone's discharge from the hospital at the end of the day, but in general, you work pretty decent hours.

When I first get to work, I print out my list of who's in the hospital. I usually deal with my "inpatient" stuff first. Usually I will page the resident or intern who's on duty and we'll go through all the patients, and I find out who's going home, if they need anything, who's newly diagnosed, or who I should introduce myself to. A lot of work involving patients in the hospital is about planning for them to go home and figuring out what their needs are. You know, if a person needs a walker, or this person needs a list of rehabilitation centers, this person is interested in getting counseling, etc.

Next I'll try to touch base with the clinic to find out if there are any outstanding issues with patients who aren't currently in the hospital that I need to know about. For example, if I'm helping a patient with an application for government assistance, I'll follow up on that when I have time, or sometimes I'm writing letters for people to show their employers that they missed work because they were in the hospital.

I usually attend to patients leaving the hospital first. If someone's being discharged, I'll talk with them about what they need, or call the medical equipment company for them, call the pharmacy to make sure they can have their medication delivered to their home. That's kind of my busywork for the day, and it's dispersed between seeing patients and running around.

Next I'll go to see some of the people who are newly diagnosed, unless someone calls me and says, "We have this patient who's hysterical in our lounge, she can't stop crying and you need to see her now." But if it's just a new diagnosis and I'm just going to introduce myself and let them know about my services, I'll usually wait until my other work slows down so that I can be more relaxed when I see the new patients.

I have about two or three meetings a week. Sometimes home care facilities hold lunches for us so they can tell us about their services, or we'll have meetings where we talk about issues affecting the staff. A lot of times I have family meetings too, which usually happen when we need to have an end-of-life discussion as to how the family wants to proceed or when a decision needs to be made about a patient's treatment.

 the breakdown

IN MEETINGS: 1–2 hours a day

ON THE PHONE: 1–2 hours a day

ONLINE: Not very often

PATIENT CARE: 4 hours a day

CHART DOCUMENTATION: 1 hour a day

RUNNING AROUND: Most of the day

On days when it's slower, I'll sit down with a patient who comes in for a four-hour chemotherapy drip or the like, and talk with them, ask them how they're doing. I'll also try to follow up with a patient who's been discharged just to make sure everything is in place and they're not running into any bumps on the road.

Usually I try to spend the last hour of my day sitting in my office so I can type up all my notes, maybe do some personal e-mails. That's the one thing about my job . . . I definitely do not sit around and stare at my computer, and when I do have the time it's such a treat to sit and relax for a few minutes. No two days are ever the same—and the day usually goes by pretty quickly.

paying your dues

After getting your master's in social work (MSW), you're likely to spend two to three years working in an entry-level social work position, where you'll have to do all of the "busywork"—faxing referrals, copying forms, and managing paperwork—by yourself.

One of the things that Jocelyn loves about her work is that it's always interesting and different, especially since social workers are interacting with people, all of whom are unique and have their own personalities.

But what about the challenges? How does Jocelyn handle the stress of working in an environment among people who are seriously ill? She shared a story that gives some insight into not only how she deals, but also what it takes to be able to succeed at this career.

"My cousin died of cancer when he was eight years old—that's actually how I got interested in working with cancer patients. My aunt and uncle both loved their social worker; they said that she was the most supportive woman ever. Flash forward years later, and I ended up getting an internship at Sloan-Kettering in pediatrics. I had been doing it for about month when a girl with a very big family came in to have a tumor removed. We were pretty sure it was cancerous, and the case took a lot of my time in the week leading up to the surgery.

"On the day of the surgery, the whole family was in the waiting area, and I think the family must have reminded me a little bit of my own. I went down to see the family and while I was there, the surgeon

then to now

2000: Graduated from Washington University in St. Louis with a BA in educational studies and dramatic literature

2000–2001: Worked as teacher at Early Head Start Montessori preschool, Denver, CO

2001–2002: Worked as a child welfare specialist at Seguin Services, Inc., Chicago, IL

2002–2004: Attended New York University for master's in social work

came out and said that they took out the tumor, and it was benign, which means it wasn't cancerous. The entire family was ecstatic and everyone was crying with tears of happiness. . . . It was a wonderful moment.

"At the end of the day, I got on the subway to go home and suddenly I just lost it. I started crying hysterically on the subway. I was a mess. I came home, ended up getting a good cry out, and then I was fine. So I talked to my supervisor the next day and told her the whole story, and she said, 'You know, that's totally fine, it happens to everybody once. You just need to figure out if it's going to happen to you often. Some situations spark an emotional attachment and you have to recognize it and let yourself be sad about it, but this is why it's an internship. See how much it affects you on a regular basis. If it does, it doesn't mean you're a bad social worker, it just means this particular area of social work might not be a fit.'

"And now that I'm doing this work, somehow I'm able to separate myself. I try to take a few minutes before I leave at the end of the day to shift gears. I also have a nice forty-five-minute commute where I can sit on the subway and clear my head—I read the paper or my book, put on my iPod, and chill out. Then I get off the subway and I have my evening."

2002–2003: Interned in social work at Woodhull Hospital, Brooklyn, NY

2003–2004: Interned at Memorial Sloan-Kettering Cancer Center, New York, NY

2004: Passed social work licensing exam to become an LMSW

2004: Started working at Mount Sinai Hospital as a social worker in the Department of Gynecologic Oncology

▶ Look for volunteer opportunities as a social work assistant at a hospital or with a foster care case manager.

▶ Volunteer with community agencies like a local branch of the Boys and Girls Club of America.

▶ Schedule an informational meeting with a social worker at your school.

Many Possibilities

"Social work really is five hundred careers in one, and one of the things I love about this field is that if I ever feel like I'm bored with hospitals, I have so many other avenues I can pursue, whether it be working in a school or a community agency, opening a private practice, or doing advocacy work—you find social workers in so many settings. But right now I'm really happy with what I do. I think there's something very unique about working with cancer patients. They are some of the strongest people I've ever met, and it can be very humbling to work with them," says Jocelyn.

INTERESTED IN SOCIAL WORK? HERE'S JOCELYN'S ADVICE

▶ *It's important to be understanding of what your patient is going through in every interaction and really try to be fair.*

▶ *Learn patience—it's the most useful skill you can have, especially in the hospital setting.*

in the field
Five More Careers in the Field of Social Work

family social worker Also known as a family services social worker, these people specialize in family dynamics and provide support for issues ranging from parenting problems and difficult relationships to children with special needs. Family social workers usually work for government agencies or family services agencies.

foster care case worker The foster care system finds temporary homes for more than a half million kids in the United States who have been abused, neglected, or abandoned, and case workers act as advocates for these kids—matching them with foster parents, recommending programs, and helping to determine when and if a foster child should be reunited with his or her parents.

substance abuse counselor Substance abuse counselors work with people who have drinking or drug problems, and help them address their abuse and come up with strategies for recovering from their addiction. Substance abuse counselors might work at rehab centers, for hotlines, or in hospitals.

social policy maker These social workers help shape government laws and policies that affect populations who might not have a lot of support, such as the homeless, child abuse victims, and drug abusers. Social policy makers work with the government to develop ideas, programs, and policies to create positive change.

clinical social worker Clinical social workers specialize in counseling people or providing what's known as "psychotherapy," or therapy that deals with mental and emotional disorders. Some work in mental hospitals or in psychiatric wards at hospitals, while others might start their own private practice to see clients independently.

Alli Shearmur

movie studio executive

the facts

Alli Shearmur,
Movie Studio Executive

▶ **what?** Movie studio executives wield much power when it comes to what movies get made, who stars in and directs them, and how they get produced.

▶ **where?** Most movie studio execs work on the big movie studio lots like Universal, Paramount, and Sony, which are primarily located in Los Angeles, although a number of movie studio execs work out of New York City.

▶ **how?** These jobs are super-competitive—a background in film, being in the right place at the right time, and a willingness to pay lots of dues are all key.

▶ **$$$:** Between $100,000 and $500,000 a year, plus bonuses, depending on level

▶ **dress code?** Business to business casual, with creative flair

▶ **stress factor:** On a scale of 1 to 10, an 8 for stress (and "a 10 for enjoyment!" says Alli)

alli shearmur has been a part of the movie studio power structure in Hollywood for a number of years. As an executive at Walt Disney Pictures, Universal Pictures, and Paramount Studios, she has overseen the day-to-day development of big studio features such as *Erin Brockovich*, *The Bourne Identity*, the *American Pie* trilogy, and *Charlotte's Web*.

I caught up with Alli in Los Angeles and swung by her office on a studio lot full of old Hollywood charm and bustling with activity. While I waited outside her door, I caught up with her assistant, who was doing ten other tasks at the same time, bolstering the stereotype that the movie industry is extremely fast paced. Once inside her office, Alli and I got comfortable on plush couches, and she shared with me the ins and outs of the job of a movie studio executive.

"The reality is, this job is like being in a class where you have tons of reading and way more homework than anybody else."

ME: What were your career dreams when you were younger?

ALLI: The first memory I have of even thinking about what I wanted to be was when I was in first grade. My teacher asked us, "What do you want to be when you grow up?" And I remember drawing a picture of the answer, not writing it out. I literally drew a princess with a crown and wand. That changed, because by the time I got to junior high, I had already become deeply obsessed and fallen in love with the movies, and I knew with all my heart that I wanted to work in the movie business. I didn't know that a job as a studio executive even existed until seventh or eighth grade, when I read a magazine article about a prominent studio executive. And I remember thinking that maybe someday, that could be me. From then on, anytime I had any exposure to film or a conversation about film, I knew that it was a world I wanted to work in.

ME: It's amazing that you had such a clear vision of what you wanted at such a young age.

you asked . . .

"Did you have any struggles along the way?" Tiffany, age 19

alli answered . . .

"I'd say the biggest struggle I had was self-doubt. But I stayed connected to my passion and my dream and stuck it out long enough to find people who mentored me and showed me the way."

ALLI: It's a really strange thing, I admit. But it was really luck that I stumbled upon that article back when I was a teenager and got to read about the movie executives of the day and track their careers. It was also really lucky that there were so many amazing women in Hollywood paving the way at studios like Sony, Universal, and Paramount. It truly inspired me to believe that this career was a possibility.

ME: I have to say, in writing this book I haven't met many women who are doing exactly what they dreamed they would be doing when they were so young. What does it feel like?

ALLI: It is the luckiest thing in the world. I remember one of my best friends in high school went to California and she came back with a plaque for me that said, "I'd rather be in California." At my sweet sixteen party, I'm literally photographed with a director's clapboard. That's how much I loved it. I would stay inside and watch *Roman Holiday*, *Philadelphia Story*, every version of *Phantom of the Opera*, while my siblings were playing outside.

ME: So is it still exciting to you?

ALLI: Yes! I have not lost the love and excitement for being around screenwriters, directors, and actors. I never will, ever. But what I have learned is what unbelievably hard work making a movie is, and how much hard work all people working in all the facets of the movie industry do. It's hard work, it's long hours, and it's not always glamorous.

ME: So what does the hard work really entail? What does being a movie studio executive mean?

ALLI: As a movie studio executive, you are the godparent of a film from the moment it's an idea until it's completed. First you buy an idea that someone has verbally pitched to you, or you've read a screenplay, a book, or an article and you've decided, "Hmm, that's a good idea for a movie." So you hire a writer and, just like an editor does at a publishing house, you work with that writer to develop the best written version of that story for the screen that is emotional and unpredictable, and funny if it's a comedy, moving if it's a drama, or terrifying if it's a horror film.

You're also responsible for figuring out how much the movie would cost to make. Then you go out and you find a director. When you have the director, you actually "cast" the movie. Then you bring this entire package to your bosses and tell them that this is a movie you believe in your heart and soul will be entertaining and profitable.

Then when they say yes, your job is not over. Because then your job is to be the godparent of that project through every phase of production. In prep, when the crew is hired, in production while the film's being shot, and in postproduction while the editor is putting the film together, the composer is scoring music, and the effects people are adding effects. And at the same time, it's making all the people involved in all of those decisions feel good about their role. Depending on what level you are in your career, you may be doing this for more than one movie at a time. When you become a VP, you're responsible for one or two of these a year. As SVP or EVP, you're responsible for maybe three or four. And as a president of production, you might be responsible

 the breakdown

IN MEETINGS: Half the day

ON THE PHONE: Half the day

ONLINE: At least 4 hours while on phone, at least 1 hour at home

READING: At least 1½ hours a day, plus 3–4 hours each weekend

for a slate of between sixteen to eighteen of these a year, as well as managing all of the people in the staff who are part of the creative group, production, legal, business, and music, and who help make these movies possible.

ME: Wow! It seems like having a great assistant is critical for a movie studio executive.

ALLI: Yes, it is. And assistants to movie studio executives work extremely hard and put in long hours, but it can be a great opportunity for the right person to discover if the path of a movie studio executive is for him or her.

ME: I e-mailed your assistant at eight a.m. on a Sunday to confirm our meeting, and I got a reply back from him within minutes. I couldn't believe he was working on a Sunday morning!

ALLI: Well, I started out working as an assistant when I first got into this business. And it's a great learning experience, because you're not just answering the phone and handling schedules—you're really a part of the process, and it is just such a great glimpse into the career.

ME: So are the TV shows and movies that portray the job of a movie studio exec as being hip and glamorous unrealistic?

ALLI: The reality is, this job is like being in a class where you have tons of reading and way more homework than anybody else. Imagine doing a term paper on every script that you're reading. That's just one part of the job. Watching dailies, which is the film that's shot on a daily

 then to now

| Graduated from University of Pennsylvania | Received law degree from University of Southern California Law Center | Interned at Triad Artists in Los Angeles | Participated in Columbia Pictures Management Associate Program | Director of comedy development, Columbia Pictures Television |

basis, is also required. And watching dailies is a privilege and needs to be done with complete concentration, so phone calls and e-mails have to wait until the screenings are done. On top of that, there are a lot of people who call you because they have questions that need answers, and most of the time, the answers can't wait a day or two. On top of that, you have to read several papers a day—the *New York Times*, the *Los Angeles Times*, the *Hollywood Reporter*, *Variety*, the *Wall Street Journal*. And it's not unusual to read an entire novel or six-hundred-page manuscript in one night. So imagine you're in a class where you have more reading and more written homework than any of your friends— that's what being in my job is like.

ME: With such an incredible amount of work to do, how do you get it all done and still stay sane?

ALLI: You prioritize and focus only on those scripts that need attention by the end of the weekend. You create your own due dates and deadlines. You hire very smart people and you rely on them, let them do their jobs, and trust them.

ME: How about being a woman in your career—is it particularly difficult, especially because you're a mom, too?

1992–1994: VP of Stewart Pictures	1994–1997: VP of production, Walt Disney Pictures	1998–2004: EVP of production, Universal Pictures	2004: EVP of production, Paramount Studios	2005: Promoted to co-president of production, Paramount Studios

paying your dues

You'll need to spend one to three years being an assistant to a movie executive, where you'll earn little money, work long hours, and do a lot of phone and scheduling work. The great part is, you'll be on the inside, and after paying your dues, you'll have a greater chance of moving up to the next level.

ALLI: I don't really feel like there have been any limitations as far as being a woman in the business. I actually feel like I've had the good fortune of working among great women who make it seem very doable, and not one of them seemed to have their personal life impaired because of their job. It just happens to be that like many working women, we can't be home during the day for our children. I also work around my daughter's schedule. She's up at six thirty, so I set the alarm clock for five in the morning. That way I get an hour and a half of work in every day before she even wakes up. What I won't do is be around her and be on my BlackBerry or on a phone call or be reading a script. She is the center of my attention when we're both home.

ME: Tell me what kinds of things make a studio executive's day.

ALLI: A great day can be when an actor you're dying to do a movie with says yes, or a script comes in better than you ever imagined, or maybe a director you dreamed of directing a movie says yes. Or sometimes you'll just be sitting in a creative meeting with a writer, director, actor, or producer, and it's just an absolutely fulfilling conversation that you know is going to end with the movie being better. Any one of those things can make a great day.

ME: And what are the biggest challenges, besides having more work than you have time to do?

ALLI: There are two main challenges. There tends to be a lot of change in the entertainment business, and you have to be a personality that can remain fluid and not become shaken by a business that

is in constant transition. Another interesting challenge is that it's a very social business, so your work doesn't end when you leave for the day and go home to do your homework. There are no regular hours. And there are very few boundaries. There's nothing regular, routine, or predictable about it.

ME: Is there a particular project that you're most proud of?

ALLI: I'm proud of all of them, but two of the films about which I have the greatest pride are *The Bourne Identity* and *The Bourne Supremacy*. That franchise is something that I nurtured from the beginning. The director of the first film brought the book to me and together we developed the screenplay, and together we dreamed that Matt Damon would play Jason Bourne. I participated in many decisions relating to that movie, and the idea that the films were considered by some to be redefining the spy genre felt incredibly exciting for someone who loves film as much I do. When I watched the final cut of *The Bourne Supremacy*, I was moved when I saw that the filmmakers had named the hotel where Jason gets his memory back the Brecker Hotel, which is my maiden name. That meant a lot to me.

what it takes

▸ Being persistent and willing to pay your dues

▸ A blend of creative and business sensibility

▸ Able to handle change and instability

in the field

Five More Careers Working in the Movies

director of photography Every shot of every movie has been carefully planned out by directors of photography (DPs or cinematographers), who need to understand lighting, cameras, and different types of film stock. Those at the top of their game can leave as much of an impression on a film as the director or the actors.

script supervisor Script supervisors take detailed notes about what happens every day of a film shoot, including dialogue changes, what scenes were shot, and how many "takes" the director filmed for each shot. They also help prompt actors who forget their lines while rehearsing or filming.

film editor After a movie has been filmed, the music scored, and the sound effects created, it is handed off to an editor, who works with the director to put the pieces together, scene by scene, note by note, frame by frame. Editors dictate the pacing of a film—the tiniest tweak to a scene or shot can change the way an entire film feels.

casting director Before an actor can be cast in a new movie, they must first impress a casting director. Casting directors work with talent agents to identify potential actors to play the roles in a film, screening a ton of reels and reviewing hundreds, if not thousands, of headshots. After holding auditions, casting directors will make their recommendations about who they think should be cast for each role.

gaffer In the production of a film, the gaffer is another word for "chief lighting technician." Gaffers not only plan what lights are needed for each scene, but they also work with the crew to get the lights set up and make any necessary changes on the set as shooting progresses.

 you need to know about

The Internet Movie Database (www.imdb.com) is the go-to source for any and all info relating to movies. Here you'll find a searchable database of every movie ever made, inside scoop and trivia on the movies and their stars, and articles on moviemaking.

For more on writing in Hollywood, check out the TV show creator profile on page 2 and the screenwriter profile on page 240.

Danielle Aust
firefighter

the facts

Danielle Aust, Firefighter/ EMT, Tualatin Valley Fire and Rescue, Oregon

▶ **what?** Firefighters are trained in fighting fires, rescuing people trapped in fires, and handling other critical situations such as car accidents or medical emergencies.

▶ **where?** Most firefighters work for county or city fire departments.

▶ **how?** Firefighters don't need a college degree, but many get an AS in fire science. To get a job, firefighters need to pass a series of written and physical tests, go through a three-month "academy" which is like boot camp for firefighters, and prove themselves through a year of probation on the job.

▶ **$$$:** Between $25,000 and $50,000 a year for a full-time firefighter, depending on the city and number of years on the job

▶ **dress code?** A heavy protective uniform made of fire-resistant material, boots, gloves, and a helmet, as well as an oxygen tank and mask

▶ **stress factor:** On a scale of 1 to 10, usually a 4 (but Danielle says it varies from shift to shift)

less than 2 percent of firefighters are women, but more and more are making the choice to break into this traditionally male career. Firefighter Danielle Aust invited me to spend the day with her at her fire station in Tualatin, Oregon, for a "ride-along." Here's my journal entry about my visit:

When I rang the fire station, Danielle greeted me wearing her uniform, which consisted of dark blue pants and a short-sleeved button-down shirt made of a fire-resistant material called NOMEX, and black leather boots with a zipper down the front so she can easily switch them out for her fire boots if a call comes in. Danielle has a great energy and smile, which instantly made me feel at ease, and she led me into the main room of the station to meet the rest of the guys on her crew: Jeff, Dave, and Bob.

> "I love being able to go into what might be a terrible, chaotic, fearful situation for someone and know that we can make it better by the time we leave."

The fire station wasn't what I thought it would be (I guess I've seen too many old firehouse movies). It was one story (no pole to slide down) and looked like a relaxed office building, except instead of offices and cubicles, there was a kitchen with three refrigerators (one for each shift), a dining room and patio with a grill, and a living room area with four recliners facing a big TV.

After initial introductions were made, Danielle showed me around. In a hallway off the main living area were little dormlike rooms. Because firefighters work twenty-four-hour shifts (they're on for twenty-four hours, then off for forty-eight), they spend the night at the station, and unlike some stations where everyone bunks in the same big room, here each person gets his or her own room while they're on duty. As the only woman on her shift, Danielle also has her own bathroom to use when she's working, complete with private shower.

In the front end of the station was an office with a few computers and phones. Firefighters have to keep electronic records of every call they go on, and they use a special computer program to log information—what the call was about, who did what, whether there were injuries, what medical attention was given, how long everything took, and so on.

As we walked around the station, Danielle told me it had been a busy morning, but visitors are often plagued with "ride-along syndrome"—that's when no calls come in when someone is visiting the station.

Next Danielle showed me the "garage" where all the big vehicles were. At the front of the garage were two large fire engines, and as Danielle walked me around and opened up doors and compartments along the sides of the engine, I was blown away by all the equipment and gear on board. There were hoses of all shapes and sizes, medical equipment and supplies, huge lights, a water tank with a dozen or more water pressure gauges, and tools such as axes and saws. I suddenly started to get a picture of what a firefighter's work really involved, and it felt intense—this was some pretty serious equipment.

Even more serious was the fact that all the engine's doors are left halfway open, so that when a call comes in, there's no time wasted opening them. To speed things up even more, the firefighters strategically place their boots and firefighting pants

you asked . . .

"Did you ever feel like giving up and you almost did, but something kept pushing you not to?" Rebecca, age 12

danielle answered . . .

"I don't know if it was to the extreme that I felt like giving up, but there were definitely times that it became very challenging, because it is a male-dominated career. When I questioned myself about whether or not I should continue, the passion and the drive kept me moving forward. I just knew I had to find the strength to keep going."

⏰ why wait?

▸ Start getting in great shape now . . . being physically fit is an important requirement for firefighters.

▸ Get certified in CPR and first aid and take a class in American Sign Language—knowing sign language is a good skill for firefighters.

on the floor outside the fire engine, and their jackets and hats are hanging on the side, the idea being that they can just slip into their fire boots, pull up their trousers with suspenders, slip on their coats and hats, and head out. Their oxygen tanks and masks are hooked into their seat backs, so they can pull on their tanks and slip on their masks while they're driving to the emergency.

While we're on the subject of the firefighting gear, which I mistakenly called an "outfit" but learned is called "turnouts," I was surprised by the amount of things Danielle kept in the pockets of her coat and trousers: tools, flashlights, all kinds of little gadgets to help her get in or out of different situations. I was even more blown away when I found out how much it all weighed: seventy-six pounds! That's like carrying around a small person! I suddenly got why firefighters need to be in excellent shape.

After our tour was over, Danielle and I sat down in the front office to talk. She told me that landing a job as a firefighter is so competitive that some people say it's easier to get into an Ivy League school. It's always been an extremely tough field to break into, but since September 11, the number of people applying for jobs has skyrocketed.

As we continued talking, every now and then I would look at the clock and wonder when we'd get the call . . . when the lights in the fire station would start flashing and news of an emergency would blast over the intercom. But things were pretty quiet, so I asked Danielle some questions about her job.

ME: Was it intimidating when you first started out because there are so few women firefighters?

DANIELLE: I was exposed to it at such a young age that I was mostly excited, although when I started testing to get a job, it was scary. The academy was probably the most stressful for me. During the academy, which lasts three months, you're continuously physically and mentally tested, and you have to score very high. You can be let go at any point, so you have to do a lot of studying, and you're physically wiped out. You're drilling nonstop, so you're in your turnouts all day long, pulling hose, throwing ladders, breaking through stuff.

ME: Is there a whole group of you going through academy together?

DANIELLE: I was hired with a group of sixteen, and only fifteen of us graduated. Then two more people were let go during the nine months that we were "on the line" (active duty) and on probation. It's very rare that an entire academy makes it all the way through without losing anybody. The biggest thing that you're let go for is attitude and not getting along with other people, because that's a huge part of this job.

ME: What was it like being the low man on the totem pole and a woman at the same time?

DANIELLE: I wish I could say that women coming into the fire service would never encounter any kind of criticism from the guys, but I would be lying. It's a hundred times better than what it used to be and hopefully will only get better.

ME: How many women are there in your department?

 then to now

1992: Was exposed to the world of firefighting while in high school through a cadet program

1995: Worked as a ramp agent for an airline

1998: Graduated from Pacific Community College with a degree in fire protection technology

DANIELLE: Fourteen out of about 345.

ME: What would you say are the biggest challenges for you?

DANIELLE: The hardest thing for me has been that I continuously have to prove myself. Nobody's pointing fingers, nobody's saying anything, but if I get transferred and I start with a new crew, I've got to prove myself all over again. Some other guy that's been here five years like me, he's not going to have to prove himself. But I will. But overall the job is so worth it, I would not discourage anybody.

ME: How do you deal with the heavy, sad stuff that comes along with the job?

DANIELLE: I honestly haven't had anything callwise that's affected me so badly that it's created an issue for me. We make a lot of jokes amongst ourselves . . . that's a lot of how we cope. For incidents that are very, very traumatic and possibly very gruesome, we have what's called CISD, Critical Incident Stress Debriefing. They'll bring in another crew to cover our station, and everybody who took the call will sit together in a room and talk about it. It's a known fact that at some point in your career you will have a call that's going to get you, and some people can't finish out the rest of their shift. There are times when I'm like, "That's pretty sad," and some people may think I'm a little coldhearted, but I think it's just a different way of thinking. You truly have to disassociate yourself.

ME: Let's move on to the good stuff. What do you love the most about your job?

1999: Passed the firefighting written and physical exams

2001: Started working as a firefighter at Tualatin Valley Fire and Rescue

DANIELLE: What's not to love? I love helping people. I love being able to go into what might be a terrible, chaotic, fearful situation for someone and know that we can make it better by the time we leave. It's so worth it. And I love the schedule, all my time off and the guys I work with.

Danielle and I wrapped up our work talk and then spent the rest of the afternoon talking and hanging out. Since I realized I might not see her in action firsthand, I asked her what it was like to go on a call.

Danielle's station responds to all types of emergencies—medical, car accidents, fires. It was a slow day at the station, which happens from time to time. Every now and then a whole twenty-four-hour shift will pass by without one call, and then on another shift there might be a dozen. While there's no way to predict what's in store, the crew has to be ready to jump at a moment's notice. If a Code 3 (high-level emergency) call comes in, they'll be dashing out the door in mere seconds. I asked Danielle to walk me through a fire call so we could see what it was really like.

 A FIRE CALL

Every fire we get called on is different, but here's an example of a house fire we went on recently. From the time that the call comes in, it's pure adrenaline and excitement. I go into such work mode that I don't think about anything else except the job that needs to be done.

We were the first ones on the scene, and when we got there, there was no smoke, nothing showing, so we got off the rig to investigate. The homeowner said that the windows in the back of the house had blown out.

Jeff is the fire officer, and his job is to assess the situation from the outside, so when we get there, he does what's called a 360, which means he walks around the building to see what's going on. In the meantime, I'm pulling hose and my partner is grabbing tools to break down the door.

When we get to the main door, everybody puts their mask on and we open the door. It's completely dark inside and it's full of smoke, and then we make our way in to find the fire, because we don't just go in spraying water.

Once we're inside, it's about fifteen to twenty minutes of, excuse my language, busting ass, and then at that point usually you have to get a fresh oxygen tank if the fire isn't out, and a truck company comes to start releasing smoke and toxic gases out through the roof. We'll set up a fan to start getting the smoke out, and once the fire is extinguished we start what's called "overhaul," salvaging whatever personal items we can from the house. After that it becomes a lot of grunt work. But my favorite part is finding the fire, fighting it, and keeping my eyes open for signs that the fire's getting dangerous.

People think we're crazy because everybody's running out of a burning building and we're running into it with smiles on our faces. I can honestly say I've never been scared. There are definitely awful things that can happen— I could fall through a floor or have a roof collapse on me—but I don't think about that when I'm going into a situation. I know the warning signs to watch for, and if the structure starts becoming unstable, then we would withdraw from it, so hopefully none of those things happen. But I can truly say that those fears don't cross my mind—it's just pure, 100 percent excitement.

what it takes

▸ Staying calm under pressure

▸ Being in great physical shape

▸ Working well within a team

▸ Courage and good judgment

By the time we wrapped up our conversation, the smell of the chicken and rice Dave was cooking for dinner had started floating in from the kitchen, so Danielle and I went into the dining room and set the table. Danielle, Dave, Bob, and Jeff had invited me to stay, so we ate at the table and talked and made jokes. Firefighters are nicknamed "the brotherhood and the sisterhood," and from the teasing and laughter at the table, I could see why. Danielle's four-person crew is very close and gets along extremely well. And they have to, because while one minute they might just be sitting together eating dinner, the next their lives may depend on one another.

Everyone felt bad that my ride-along had turned into a bust, so after dinner, we piled into the engine and took a drive out to an apartment complex that was under construction.

Danielle and her crew wanted to get a closer look at how the apartments were being built, so they can handle calls to the complex in the future as efficiently as possible.

I sat in the back between Danielle and Dave, and we all wore our headphones with microphone mouthpieces, since the sound of the engine is too loud to talk over. The banter continued on the drive, and even though I hadn't gotten to see any "action" during my day with Danielle, I was starting to feel as though I had a real understanding of why she loved her job so much.

By 9:00 p.m., I was starting to get tired, so I thanked everyone in the station and said good-bye. Danielle apologized for the slow day, but that's what some days are like when you're "on the line," and there's nothing wrong with that. I was just happy to get such an intimate glimpse of one of the most coveted professions around.

INTERESTED IN BEING A FIREFIGHTER? HERE'S DANIELLE'S ADVICE

▶ *You have to be physically fit, but that doesn't mean you have to look like Xena. We have girls who are five feet tall and tiny and they find a way to do it.*

▶ *Contact your local fire department and do a ride-along and see if they offer a cadet or volunteer program.*

▶ *As soon as you know you want to be a firefighter, start networking with women firefighters—relationships can be key in getting you in the door.*

in the field

Five More Careers in Emergency Rescue

emergency medical technician Emergency medical technicians, or EMTs, respond in ambulances to emergency calls. While they're not doctors, EMTs have to be skilled in basic life support, first aid, CPR, and other potentially life-saving procedures.

search and rescue worker When someone goes missing in the wilderness, search and rescue workers are called in to try and quickly locate the missing person. Search and rescue workers might also do disaster rescue, such as uncovering earthquake victims trapped in rubble.

bomb squad technician Bomb squad technicians handle emergencies that involve bombs, unstable ammunition, and chemical substances. In the case that a bomb explosion has actually occurred, bomb squad technicians play a key role in investigating the event.

dive team rescuer Rescue workers who specialize in water rescues, such as responding to a boat accident or rescuing a victim who's stuck in a submerged car are dive team rescuers. They might also rescue other divers in danger.

hostage negotiator Hostage negotiators try to ensure a peaceful outcome when a criminal has taken hostages. While hostage negotiators are trained in negotiation and mediation techniques, the best education is working as a law enforcement officer and getting experience dealing with people in crisis.

 ## you need to know about

Women in the Fire Service, Inc. (www.wfsi.org) is an organization that supports women firefighters. Check out their website for a ton of info about firefighting, the history of women in firefighting, a message board, and links to resources, articles, events, and job sites.

Nancy Pearl

librarian

the facts

Nancy Pearl, Librarian

▸ **what?** Librarians take care of the books and documents in a library, as well as deal with the public to help them interact with the library materials.

▸ **where?** Librarians work in public libraries, schools and universities, museums, nonprofit organizations, and historical institutions.

▸ **how?** Most professional librarians have at least a bachelor's degree, if not a master's, in library science.

▸ **$$$:** An average of $35,000 to $55,000, depending on whether you're working at a public or private library

▸ **dress code?** Casual to business casual

▸ **stress factor:** On a scale of 1 to 10, a 3

if ever there was a librarian who's achieved "celebrity status," it's Nancy Pearl. Nancy, who was the executive director of the Washington Center for the Book at the Seattle Public Library until her retirement in 2004, is a serious book expert and frequent guest on TV programs like the *Today* show and radio shows, where she talks about her recommended reads. She is also the author of several books herself, including *Book Lust* and *More Book Lust*. But perhaps Nancy's most interesting (and bizarre) claim to fame is that she has her very own action figure. Yes, you heard right: *action figure*. The librarian action figure, which can be found in kitschy boutiques around the country, is a little statuette of Nancy with a finger to her lips, as if to say "shush."

"A librarian is not solely a person who retrieves information—the public library really is the heart and soul of a community."

Nancy and I got together in a little coffee shop on a rainy day in Seattle, and the fact that several people approached us while we were talking, saying, "Aren't you Nancy Pearl?" and then introduced themselves like giddy fans, reconfirmed that she is indeed a celebrity librarian extraordinaire. Here are some highlights from our conversation:

ME: You knew you wanted to be a librarian from the time you were ten years old. What is it about being a librarian that appealed to you?

NANCY: I come from a family of do-gooders, people who really believed that you could change the world and make it a better place. And for me, the way that I understood even at ten that you could make the world a better place was by being a librarian, especially a children's librarian, and opening up the world of books and reading to kids who might be in unfortunate home situations or in other difficult places in their lives. Books have that unique ability in that you can both lose yourself and find yourself in the pages of the same book.

ME: So now, reflecting back, did you achieve your goal?

NANCY: Yes, I do think that librarians make the world a better place. A librarian is not solely a person who retrieves information—the public library really is the heart and soul of a community. I think that through recommending good books to read or through programming that they do, librarians make a library a living, breathing place.

ME: So what kinds of things do librarians in a public library actually do?

NANCY: I think one of the most exciting things is putting people together with good books. A lot of people come to the librarian and say, "I just finished this book, I loved it, can you find me another one exactly like it?" And the trick is to figure out what it is that they meant by "exactly like it" and find that book. Another important task is helping people find information for life skills, whether it's the address of the gas company or where to register to vote, that kind of thing. So all of that is accepted within the librarian's job description.

you asked . . .

"What, if any, are your regrets?" Molly, age 16

nancy answered . . .

"I think my general regret is that I let fear of the unknown stop me from doing things that I really wish I could have done. When my husband and I were first married, people of our generation were picking up and moving to a place in the world where they wanted to live without having a job there, and just sort of saying, 'Okay, we'll just go there and get a job.' We would never have done that . . . it was too scary. That sort of fear of just taking a leap is something that I really regret. I also believe at the same time that all of those wonderful things that have happened to me in the last decade or so happened as a result of everything else I had to go through. But generally, I think that fear is an awful sort of hang-up—it's a distraction in your life."

▶ Volunteer at the library in the teen section or get a job at a bookstore.

▶ Read books in all different genres.

▶ Keep a reading journal where you write your thoughts down about your favorite books and the impact they had on your life.

But I think that what a librarian ought to be doing a lot of is bringing the community into the library for book discussion groups, poetry readings, and author visits, and showing the public that the library isn't just a collection of dead books or books that only come alive when you read them. It's a place that breathes. My personal mission has always been to both deepen and broaden a user's experience with works of literature. So if somebody only reads fiction, for example, I will always look at the library in a more holistic way to try to get them out of that fiction section and show them that there are great books in other parts of the library.

ME: I *love* reading, but it also puts me to sleep, so it takes me a while to get through a book. How do you get all your reading in?

NANCY: It depends on the books that I'm reading. I think that books say to you, "Okay, this is how fast you should read me," so it's really hard to say how much time I spend reading. I've arranged my life at this old age of mine so that I don't do much else but read and write about the books that I'm reading. I think that reading is a choice that you make, and so you choose to read a novel instead of the newspaper or instead of a magazine or you choose to read a novel instead of play a game. My downfall is FreeCell on the computer, so I choose to read rather than playing a FreeCell game or something like that.

ME: What do you think are the most challenging things about being a librarian at a public library?

NANCY: Dealing with the public ... you're really a public servant. It's the public who pays your salary, and you owe them your best thinking and your courtesy, and sometimes that's very hard, as it is for anybody who's dealing with the public. There are actually a lot of similarities between retail and being a librarian. And so people tend to think of librarians as being sort of solitary readers who just sit at their desk or catalog books. And sure, there is that part of the library, but when you're working in a public library, you're on the desk a lot, you have to have good interpersonal skills and you have to be a people person. The people who use the library to find good books or information for making themselves a better person, that's the best part of society. And so you get to meet such interesting people.

what it takes

▸ A love of books and research

▸ Good people and
  organizational skills

▸ Being comfortable working
  with computers

ME: Are there any other stereotypes about librarians that you want to bust?

NANCY: I think one of the misconceptions is probably that librarians are stuffy and boring and don't read. And of course, there are some that are like that, but most aren't. Take teen librarians—they generally go into that field because they're really interested in teen books. They're people who have read those books and stand up for the rights of the teen in the library, and I think that's really important. When you have a teen librarian who is identified as such, that's somebody you can really trust, who knows what books are really good and who knows what you're going through.

then to now

Received MA in library
science from University of
Michigan

1998: Was named Fiction
Reviewer of the Year by
Library Journal

1998: Developed
breakthrough public
reading program, "If All of
Seattle Read the Same
Book"

ME: Do you make a distinction between your work and your personal life?

NANCY: Robert Frost has a poem in which he talks about when love and work are one, and I think that should be the goal. I've been fortunate enough that there's never been a separation between what I do in my work and what I would choose to do if I weren't in this job. I guess that's one result of knowing at age ten what I wanted to do. I've always just loved to read and escape into the pages of a book.

nancy's favorite authors for teens

▶ Sarah Dessen

▶ Deb Caletti, especially *Honey, Baby, Sweetheart*

▶ Pete Hautman, especially *Godless*

▶ M. T. Anderson, especially *Thirsty* and *Feed*

NANCY'S CAREER ADVICE

Take your work seriously, but don't take yourself seriously.

in the field
Five More Careers in Library Science

content manager Content managers create and manage the content of a website or online portal, keeping it up-to-date and providing information. Many content managers have some knowledge of HTML or other web languages so they can program the content themselves.

database administrator Just about every company tracks data electronically, such as customer and inventory information. Keeping

2003: *Book Lust* was published

2004–2005: Recipient of the Women's National Book Association Award

2004: Retired as executive director of the Washington Center for the Book at the Seattle Public Library

all of this data organized, secure, and accessible to the right people is the job of database administrators. These people set up, design, and maintain the databases, backing up information as needed.

information broker An information broker is someone who does research, like market research or patent searches. Some information brokers specialize in researching a particular kind of information, and all of them use the Internet and special online information databases to do their work.

indexer If you flip to the back of a nonfiction book, you might find an index listing references to names, terms, and concepts within the book and their corresponding page numbers. Indexers create these indexes to help researchers and others easily find what they're looking for.

taxonomist Originally taxonomy was a field of biology, and the job of taxonomists was to identify and figure out what family or "class" different organisms belonged to. Today it has a broader definition, and taxonomists classify different types of information and non-living objects.

 you need to know about

> A great website for anyone interested in working in a library is www.becomealibrarian.org. Here you'll find profiles of librarians, articles, info on scholarship opportunities, and advice on selecting a college and grad school.

For more on working with books, check out the independent bookstore owner profile on page 393.

networking, which is another word for making and nurturing professional connections with people, is an invaluable tool when it comes to exploring career paths and future job opportunities. Not sure how to network? Don't worry—here are a few of my trade secrets:

▶ Keep track of people you meet who might be good connections for you down the road. Put their names in a notebook and write down what they do, when and how you met them, and any other personal information or anecdotes they shared with you.

▶ Ask everyone you meet for a business card, and write notes on the back about the person.

▶ When you see people doing jobs that you want to learn more about, try to set up informational interviews with them. Informational interviews give you a chance to ask people every little detail about what they do, while giving you the opportunity to show people who you are. See the Lunch Break on Page 127 for more info.

▶ Don't let people forget you! If I meet someone I want to stay in touch with, I make it my job to stay on their radar so they'll remember me if I call to ask for a meeting or favor. A great way to stay fresh in people's minds is to send e-mail updates with big news (like a new job or a school graduation) or even send annual holiday cards. But don't overdo it—limit your contact to two times a year so you're seen as a go-getter and not a nuisance.

▶ Keep expanding your pool of connections by asking everyone in your network for the names of other people you could meet and speak with.

▶ Be memorable! When you meet people you want to add to your network, remember their names, shake their hands, and be super-professional in your communication with them.

Maureen Shirreff

advertising executive

the facts

*Maureen Shirreff,
North American
Creative Director for
Dove, Ogilvy & Mather*

▶ **what?** Advertising executives work for ad agencies, whose business is developing campaigns for products ranging from Diet Coke to Skechers. Creative execs like Maureen manage the way a campaign looks and feels, from concept through production, while account execs manage the relationship between the client and the agency.

▶ **where?** While both big firms and small boutique ad agencies are scattered throughout the country, the major players are based primarily in New York, Chicago, and Los Angeles.

▶ **how?** People in advertising have a BA in anything from English and philosophy to business and marketing.

▶ **$$$:** An average of $75,000 to $120,000 for an executive, plus bonuses

▶ **dress code?** Typical days are business casual, while meetings with clients might call for something dressier.

▶ **stress factor:** On a scale of 1 to 10, can reach an 8

one of the most talked-about ad campaigns in the past few years—the Campaign for Real Beauty from Dove, a global company specializing in personal care and cleansing products—features *real* women, with *real* bodies, *real* curves, and even *real* fat and cellulite, proudly strutting their stuff wearing nothing but white bras and panties. The message behind the campaign is to offer a "broader, healthier, and more democratic view of beauty for women and girls." Behind the scenes I found Maureen Shirreff, North American creative director for the Dove brand, working out of her office at ad agency Ogilvy & Mather in Chicago.

> "Until I was in my early twenties I had not a clue what I should be doing."

"I was kind of heavy when I was younger, so I always had body issues. When I started working on the Campaign for Real Beauty, I realized that in some weird way, it was helping me tackle some of that stuff. And here I am getting paid for it . . . how great is that?" Maureen says.

Maureen didn't always know she wanted to work in advertising. She found her passion by knowing her strengths and keeping her eyes open for a career that would allow her to express them all.

"Until I was in my early twenties I had not a clue what I should be doing. I knew I was creative, I loved to draw, I loved to do theater,

you asked . . .

"What is it that picks you up when things go wrong or you seem to be stuck?" Eri, age 13

maureen answered . . .

"Music. It's a wonderful thing that I need to have around me when I get stuck on a creative problem. I have an amazing sound system in my car, so I usually drive around and listen to Earth, Wind & Fire, Stevie Wonder, gospel music . . . it just does something to me. If your spirit can get lifted up a bit, it's amazing how you tend to look at obstacles differently."

I loved fashion, I loved architecture. I loved all these things, but I didn't know what job that would be a good fit with. My parents were really great about supporting me by saying, 'You're going to find it and it's going to find you.' That really came true for me," she explains.

Maureen's been in advertising for more than twenty-five years, so clearly she went down the right path. I asked her to break down for me exactly what she does as a creative director, and here's what she had to say:

"I'm responsible for the creative side of all of the advertising for the Dove brand—that includes television, print, and cause-related efforts. All of the messaging that the consumer hears about Dove usually comes through me. I supervise anywhere from fifteen to twenty creative people working on the advertising for different Dove products, and we do things like come up with creative ideas and work with the account folks to get our ideas approved, supervise the production for the ideas that we sell, work with photographers to shoot the print ads, go on production shoots for the TV ads, and work with editorial houses to finish commercials.

the breakdown

IN MEETINGS: 1–2 hours a day

ON THE PHONE: 1–2 hours a day

ONLINE: 1–2 hours a day

SITTING: Much of the day

PUBLIC SPEAKING: 1–2 hours a week

READING: 1 hour a day

"If you see a commercial for Dove right now, I would have done that, from the inception of the idea all the way through the production

then to now

| 1975: Graduated from Northwestern University with a BS in speech | 1975: Worked as a typist at O. O. Mallegy Co., Chicago, IL | 1977: Worked as bank teller at Water Tower Trust | 1978: Got first "creative job" as the art director for John Lucas & Co. | 1980–1983: Held various entry creative positions at Foote, Cone & Belding agency |

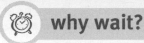
process. The only thing I don't do is actually deliver the commercial to the networks and push the button that gets it on the air, but pretty much everything in between, I'm involved in," she explains.

Because Maureen's business is an international one, she does a lot of traveling all over the world. She's out of town at least one week a month, which might not sound like a lot, but the time away generally makes her in-office days more full. For every trip she goes on, Maureen has to plan for it, get from point A to point B, have her meetings, travel home, and then fill in her creative team on everything that happened on her trip.

 paying your dues

Most people working in advertising start out in an entry-level assistant position. Expect to spend one to two years doing a lot of photocopying, finding scrap art, preparing presentations, and other support tasks while earning as little as $16,000 a year.

1983–1987:	1987: Rejected	1987–1993:	1993: Hired	2000:
Storyboard illustrator and junior art director at BBDO agency	by airline company to be a flight attendant	Was a freelance art director	as creative director at Ogilvy & Mather	Promoted to North American creative director of Dove at Ogilvy & Mather

She says, "There are parts of the travel that I really like, because when I'm away I can mentally focus on the bigger picture. I do miss my family a lot, although my children are now in high school and I think they're kind of used to it. When they were young it ripped my heart out. But what I love about it is that when you go into another office, you're there to get a job done and so you're really productive. You're also building relationships, which is the cornerstone of a global brand like Dove. I've got to have really strong relationships with Ogilvy folks in different offices and with clients in different parts of the world."

what it takes

▶ Creativity

▶ Thriving in a fast-paced environment

▶ Being open to constructive criticism

▶ The ability to think on your feet and handle pressure

I asked Maureen to tell us what the reality of working in advertising is versus what we might expect based on the Hollywood version shown in shows like *The Apprentice*.

"I think advertising is sometimes portrayed as this kind of villainous backstabbing environment where you're up for hours on end and you're fraught with despair because you can't come up with creative ideas. It's portrayed in a very tense, dramatic way, and yes, it has that, but there is so much joy there too. I don't think that gets a fair shake. Yes, there are a lot of ups and downs. You might come up with an idea and your creative director hates it or the client hates it. But when you are able to get something sold in and protect it so that it actually gets on the air and does what it's supposed to do, and you begin to sell product and people notice it, that's a pretty big high."

▶ *Don't beat yourself up if you don't know exactly what you want to do. Start by getting in touch with who you are as a human being and give life a chance to reveal itself to you.*

▶ *Network whenever you can.*

▶ *If you're interested in advertising, don't worry about being 100 percent sure what you want to do when you're first starting out. Take any job you can find at an agency and you'll eventually discover where you belong.*

▶ *Trust your instincts!*

in the field
Five More Careers in Advertising

traffic manager (entry-level job) Because there are so many stages of an ad campaign, traffic managers track schedules and budgets and control the flow of "traffic," making sure that production stays on track and deadlines are met. The traffic department is where many people start out, since it's a great way to learn what goes into creating an ad campaign.

media planner Advertisers pay big bucks for their commercials to be shown during a hit TV show or have a two-page spread in a magazine, and media planners are the ones who make it all happen by figuring out where to purchase advertising space for the products they represent.

account executive Account execs have to be good at dealing with clients, crunching numbers, and communicating with creative departments. Most account execs juggle only a few clients, and their main job is to manage the relationship between the agency and the clients.

copywriter Copywriting is often perceived to be one of the more glamorous jobs in advertising, because copywriters come up with the "tag lines" that become popular, like Sprint's "Can you hear me *now?*" They also write all the content of an ad, so they have to know how to write creatively and effectively about products using very few words.

research director In advertising, research directors analyze data regarding how efficient or effective an ad campaign is, conducting focus-group tests to find out how the consumer responds to different advertising strategies or trying to determine whether or not people are buying the advertised product.

 you need to know about

The Advertising Educational Foundation's website (www.aef.com) offers videos to download, case studies about different advertising campaigns, a list of must-read books, and career advice from the pros.

Dr. Nancy Knowlton

marine biologist

the facts

Dr. Nancy Knowlton, Director, Center for Marine Biodiversity and Conservation, Scripps Institution of Oceanography

▶ **what?** Marine biologists study the plants, animals, and organisms that live in the ocean.

▶ **where?** Most marine biologists work at marine research centers and often lecture at a university biology department. Not surprisingly, they tend to work in coastal areas, where they have easy access to the ocean.

▶ **how?** Marine biologists at the level of Dr. Knowlton or those teaching in a university need a doctorate, which involves a four-year degree in biology, a related master's degree, and a PhD in a specific area of marine biology. Marine biologists with a master's degree can teach at the high school level or at an aquarium.

▶ **$$$:** $40,000 to $45,000 a year for PhDs who are just starting out, and between $70,000 and $90,000 a year for more experienced marine biologists

▶ **dress code?** Casual to business casual (and sometimes a wet suit!)

▶ **stress factor:** On a scale of 1 to 10, an 8 (but Nancy says the stress is mostly self-imposed)

one of the top marine biologists in the world is Dr. Nancy Knowlton. She not only runs the Scripps Center for Marine Biodiversity and Conservation at Scripps Institution of Oceanography and the University of California, which she created in 2001, but she also directs a team of scientists researching coral reefs. Nancy has a beautiful office looking out onto the Pacific Ocean, and she can see whales spouting from behind her desk. In addition, Nancy has a part-time job at the Smithsonian Tropical Research Institute in Panama, where she has an office and lab as well.

"I have to say what really drives me is the sense of doing something that will make a difference a hundred years from now."

Nancy didn't always know she wanted to be a marine biologist, but she's always been a "science junkie."

"My first science love was really astronomy. My parents had gotten me a nice telescope when I was little, and I used to spend a lot of time looking at the planets. Then in tenth grade I took a biology course with a really wonderful teacher, and that's what turned me in the direction of biology rather than astronomy or other sciences," she explains.

A TYPICAL EXPEDITION

Last August I went on a cruise that went from Christmas Island to Palmyra Atoll, which is a series of very isolated islands in the middle of the Pacific Ocean south of Hawaii and right next to the equator. Christmas Island is inhabited by a fairly large number of people, whereas Palmyra Atoll is uninhabited, and there are islands in between that go from highly inhabited to fairly uninhabited. We were trying to figure out how the reefs change as you go from one island to another. Every day I would get up and go on a dive and collect pieces of dead coral to bring back to the boat.

In the afternoon I'd break the coral up into tiny little pieces, preserving all the animals and plants that we found, some for genetics and some for more traditional studies. Then in the evening we'd lay them all out in little cups. We would actually have hundreds and hundreds of cups of tiny animals all over the deck so we could photograph each one. Then we'd freeze them or put them in alcohol to study them when we got back. During that trip, we followed the same routine every day for almost three weeks. It was actually exhausting, because the diving is hard and you have to lug buckets and buckets of heavy seawater to the top of the ship. And the days were long—we'd be working from about eight in the morning to ten or eleven at night, and then we'd sleep for eight hours and get up to do it all over again. It's very physical work, but it's fun, too, because you see all these amazing organisms, and the physical activity is nice. Plus you're in this beautiful place where we'd see dolphins and manta rays, sharks and turtles, and all sorts of things in the water. It's quite spectacular.

Since marine biologists can specialize in many different areas, I asked Nancy to describe what her work is all about.

"I study coral reefs, so at least once a year, and hopefully more often, I go out in the field somewhere in the Caribbean, usually in Panama, and study coral spawning. Coral reefs undergo what's called 'mass spawning,' where all of the different colonies release their eggs and sperm into the water simultaneously once a year. This is a 'mega event' and it's very interesting biologically, so I go and study that because, although coral reefs are famous in the public eye, we actually know relatively little about the organisms that live there," she explained.

you asked . . .

"How the heck did you go through college without having your brain explode?"
Rosie, age 19

nancy answered . . .

"That's funny—I never felt like my brain was near exploding. I guess for me, college was hard, but it wasn't out-of-control hard. I know there were times that I stayed up all night to study for exams and write papers. I think the thing you have to do when you feel like your brain is on the verge of exploding is say, 'Okay, I'm going to do this this morning and I'm going to do this this afternoon' and break it into bite-size pieces. If you take it one piece at a time, it really helps with the exploding brain syndrome."

"One of the projects I'm working on is to figure out the family tree of corals and estimate how many species there are in coral reefs. The published estimates range from about one to ten million species, so there's a huge range, and they're horrible estimates. We really don't have a clue what's out there, and moreover, we don't have a real sense of what we're losing as reefs become more and more degraded. So one of the projects I'm working on now is trying to figure out what we're losing so we know how to focus our conservation efforts."

the breakdown

IN MEETINGS: 2 hours a day

ON THE PHONE: 30 minutes a day

ONLINE: 1–2 hours a day

SITTING: Most of the day

PUBLIC SPEAKING: 1–2 hours per week at most

READING: 1 hour a day

WORKING SOLO: Much of the time

When Nancy gets back from her research expeditions, the lab work begins, although at Nancy's level, it's mostly her team of scientists who analyze the samples she has collected in the field.

"I define the nature of the project, organize it, raise the money, and do a certain amount of the fieldwork. Then I organize the work, and at the end I'm usually the one who writes the papers that come out of the research," she explains. Nancy also fills her very busy days with directing the conservation center she created, raising funds, developing new programs, and handling administrative duties. She also does a lot of writing for academic journals and lectures both to scientists and the general public.

then to now

1971: Graduated from Harvard University with BA

1978: Received PhD in marine biology from UC Berkeley

1978–1979: Did a NATO postdoctorate fellowship in the U.K.

1979–1983: Was an assistant professor of biology, Yale University

With all that work, one can imagine that it would be challenging to find enough time in the day to get it all done. Nancy says that the more successful she's become, the more she is asked to do things. At present she is running approximately fifteen projects at the same time, juggling many different tasks to keep them all afloat and supervised. And while she says the travel is still exciting—in the past eight months alone Nancy traveled to Honduras, Taiwan, Panama, Japan, and Germany, to name just a few—it's also draining.

Still, the payoff is obviously worth it. Nancy's passion for her work came through loud and clear in our conversation. I asked her to tell me what keeps her going . . . what she really loves about her work.

"The core of what makes science fun is finding out something that you didn't know before. For a while I was working with a guy named Rob Rowan in Guam on the diversity of the little single-celled algae inside coral that are responsible for the productivity of reefs. In earlier work Rob had figured out that there were a lot of different species, and we were working on a project to understand what controlled all this diversity, and why you found some types in one place and different types in another.

 ## why wait?

▶ Rent a snorkel, mask, and fins the next time you're at an ocean or lake.

▶ Take biology and AP science courses in high school.

▶ Visit a nearby aquarium—many offer volunteer opportunities or special programs just for students.

1985: Became a staff scientist at the Smithsonian Tropical Research Institute

1996: Became professor at the Scripps Institution of Oceanography, University of California at San Diego

2001: Founded the Scripps Center for Marine Biodiversity and Conservation

2001: Joined the Advisory Board of the National Geographic Conservation Trust

paying your dues

After years of school, most marine biologists spend their first three to four years working in a postdoctoral position doing research under a more senior scientist.

"While we were in Guam, there was a major 'bleaching' event, which occurs when the water gets too hot and the whole symbiosis between these algae and the coral breaks down, so we went out there to figure out what was going on. It was amazing because we could look at the reefs and realize that the bleaching was differentially affecting the different types of algae—after five minutes swimming on the reef we knew exactly what was happening. It was extraordinary. It was almost like having a whole jigsaw puzzle in a box, shaking it up, and then throwing it on the ground and having it land assembled. It was a classic 'eureka' moment.

what it takes

▸ A love of research, the ocean, snorkeling, and scuba diving

▸ Attention to detail

▸ Being patient, extremely organized, and a good record keeper

"It's also great when you've worked hard on a project and you send it out for review and it comes back and it's been funded. Or if you give a lecture and people are really receptive and enthusiastic; that always feels good. Just feeling like you're making a contribution is a great feeling."

She added, "I'm also very proud of the center that I created, because it's transformed the Scripps Institution of Oceanography and has made conservation a really major part of the activities here. We've raised many millions of dollars and have trained a large number of students, and I feel like we're making a huge difference in terms of creating the next generation of scientists. I'm very proud of that.

"I don't consider myself in the ranks of Einstein or Charles Darwin, but in a more modest way, I've made a major contribution to marine biology, and I've made a major contribution to the institutions I've worked at. It's funny, some people are really driven by the recognition they get by being on the morning news or something like that, but I have to say what really drives me is the sense of doing something that will make a difference a hundred years from now."

NANCY'S ADVICE

▶ *Always make sure you enjoy what you're doing. You spend an awful lot of your life working, and if you love what you do, it doesn't really feel like work.*

▶ *Focus on the goal you're heading for, especially if what you're doing at the moment feels frustrating.*

▶ *For a career in science, it's important to do well in school. Take your studies seriously and get into the best college or university that you can.*

in the field
Five More Careers as a Biologist

botanist Botanists study plants, and depending on their area of expertise, they might focus on plant identification or how certain plants interact with animals and other living organisms in their environment. Botanists can work in botanical gardens, universities, private companies, or government agencies.

zoologist Also known as wildlife biologists, zoologists study all aspects of animals, from their behavior and biological structure to how they interact with their environment. Many work in zoos and oversee the care of the animals there, while others might study animals in their natural habitats.

biochemist Biochemists specialize in the chemical composition of living organisms, studying areas like reproduction and metabolism. Most spend their time doing scientific research for large biotech firms or government agencies, and though it's not an absolute requirement, most biochemists have an MD or PhD.

geneticist These scientists study heredity in living organisms. Most geneticists work in laboratories researching different genetic technologies, while others become genetic counselors who discuss genetic risks of hereditary problems, like some birth defects, with soon-to-be parents.

microbiologist Some organisms are so tiny they can't be seen by the naked eye. Microbiologists work in laboratories, using high-powered microscopes to study these organisms. They might work in the food and drug industry, within environmental organizations, for government agencies, or for large companies.

 you need to know about

The website www.marinebio.org is full of information relating to marine biology, including facts about different marine species, info on marine conservation and why it's so important, and a list of schools offering courses and degrees in marine biology.

Chiyo Ishikawa

museum curator

the facts

Chiyo Ishikawa, Deputy Director of Art, Seattle Art Museum

▶ **what?** Curators plan and organize exhibitions of art and other collections for museums—coming up with new ideas for exhibitions, figuring out how the art will be exhibited, planning how the event will interact with the public, and organizing tours, lectures, and interactive presentations.

▶ **where?** The majority of curators work for museums or at historical sites.

▶ **how?** Curators typically have a PhD in art history, and many specialize in a certain art style or time period.

▶ **$$$:** An average of $35,000 to $70,000, depending on the size of the institution

▶ **dress code?** Business casual

▶ **stress factor:** On a scale of 1 to 10, between a 6 and a 9 (depending on what's going on)

there's something intriguing about museums—they're full of so much history, the artwork on display is often worth millions of dollars, the atmosphere itself somehow feels . . . *creative*. The people behind the exhibits are called curators, and to find out more about what they do, I spoke with Chiyo Ishikawa, deputy art director and chief curator for the Seattle Art Museum. We met in Chiyo's office at the museum, which at the time of writing was being renovated under Chiyo's supervision. We caught up on a cool Friday afternoon.

ME: Can you tell us what you do at the Seattle Art Museum?

CHIYO: I'm the curator of European painting and sculptures in the museum, and that means I research our collection of art, present it through exhibitions, work with our conservation department if anything needs to be cleaned or restored, and present the collection to the public.

"Our most rewarding times are when we are down in storage looking at art objects and getting ideas."

I am also an exhibition curator, so that means organizing the exhibitions, either from our permanent collection or from work that comes in from outside the museum. We curators are ambassadors for the art, so when we do exhibitions, we have to raise money, market the exhibition, and train docents. We're kind of the point person for everything that reaches the public about the show.

When we're planning exhibitions or installations, a lot of my time is spent staring at a computer screen, or on the phone or in meetings, but I will say that our most rewarding times are when we are down in storage looking at art objects and getting ideas. It's a wonderful job. I've been doing it for sixteen years, and there's always something new you can do, even with a small collection like we have here.

ME: Do curators usually specialize in one area?

CHIYO: Yes. The training for somebody who wants to be a curator is to get a PhD in art history, and it's also helpful to have museum experience. The way it works in graduate school for art history is you start out generally and then you focus, focus, focus. So by the time you're writing your dissertation, it's about something pretty narrow. But what you ultimately end up doing depends on where you work. If I were at the Metropolitan Museum of Art, I'd focus on one little century or art from one region. But at a small, general museum, it's a lot of fun for me because I go from the dates 1200 to 1800. So yes, there is specialization, but at our museum we think about everything in a larger context.

ME: Are most curators people who grew up wanting to be artists?

CHIYO: It's more people who love art history . . . who love art and who love history. It's an incredibly different thing from being an artist. I think it helps to have done studio art—it really gives you empathy for the objects—but it's more of an engagement with looking at other things.

you asked . . .

"What is more important: success or significance?" Charlene, age 17

chiyo answered . . .

"I work for a nonprofit, so if we're talking about financial success, I'd have to say significance. For me, success is a feeling of satisfaction and love of your colleagues, and enjoyment and excitement about coming to work every day. People go into this profession for love—they have low salaries, they work really hard, they usually work much more than a forty-hour week. We get our satisfaction from people coming to our talks or giving tours in the gallery and having people thank us afterward. I think that museum curators uniformly would answer that significance is more important."

why wait?

- ▶ Take art history classes if your school offers them and get to know the works of the masters.

- ▶ Visit local museums and libraries to view art of all kinds and see what you're drawn to; inquire about volunteering or becoming a docent.

- ▶ Curate your own exhibit at school.

ME: So how did you know this is what you wanted to do?

CHIYO: When I was twelve, my dad was on a sabbatical. We bought a VW bus and drove around Europe off and on for six months. We went to lots of museums and churches, and I totally loved it. I didn't really realize how meaningful that trip was until I was in college, struggling with my desire to be a studio artist, and I discovered I was a lot more comfortable talking about other people's art than I was trying to come up with something on my own.

ME: What is it about museums that you love?

CHIYO: My dad used to be the assistant director of the Des Moines Art Center, and so growing up I was surrounded by art and by artists—they were just part of our world. I had so much fun going to little exhibition openings as a child, and I grew up knowing that art was special. So I think I had an inherent interest in it. Initially I wanted to be a dealer because I wanted to help artists, and then once I started graduate school, I saw how hard it was to write about

then to now

| 1969: First trip to Europe and exposure to great museums and art | 1979: Graduated from Hampshire College with BA | 1982: Began working on master's and doctorate | 1983–1985: Interned at the Metropolitan Museum of Art in New York | 1986–1987: Volunteer internship at the Museo del Prado, Spain | 1989: Received PhD from Bryn Mawr College |

contemporary art with any distance. I really wanted to have the ability to stand back and make judgments that I could be more confident about, and so I went back to the fifteenth century, and that's what I studied for the rest of graduate school.

ME: Do you ever look around and see what you're actually doing and think, "How cool is this?"

CHIYO: Yeah, I do feel really lucky. I work in a beautiful place, and that alone makes me feel kind of spoiled. Just being at a place where everybody is visually aware is wonderful, and it can be something as minor as seeing interesting clothes in the hallway which gives me a little lift every day, to looking at wonderful works of art that are coming into the collection. It's never routine here, and I love that. I also love that a big part of my job is seeing things in other cities, and that's certainly a big part of why people become curators—so they can travel. If you're going to work with objects, you really have a responsibility to know everything you can about them, and that often involves seeing where they come from.

ME: I didn't realize that travel was such a big part of your job.

 paying your dues

Many future curators spend one year as an intern while getting their PhD, where they might do things like researching, photocopying, writing, and attending meetings. Others might be a curatorial assistant until graduation, at which time they move into an assistant curator position.

| **1989:** Interned at the Museum of Fine Arts, Boston | **1990:** Hired at Seattle Art Museum as assistant curator of European paintings | **1994:** Promoted to curator of European paintings and sculptures | **2001:** Promoted to chief curator of collections, Seattle Art Museum | **2005:** Named deputy director of art, Seattle Art Museum |

CHIYO: I travel multiple times a year: once or twice to New York, sometimes to L.A., and to Europe at least once a year. When I was working on a Spanish exhibition, I was going to Spain for two weeks at a time, because you need to establish relationships in person and you need to see objects firsthand that you want for the exhibitions . . . it's where you get your inspiration. And every curator here always comes back from a trip with three or four good things—making a new collegial connection, hearing about an exhibition that might be good for us, promoting an exhibition that we might take to some other place. Personal contact is what really keeps you viable.

what it takes

▶ An acute visual sense

▶ A love of research

▶ An interest in putting things together in interesting ways

▶ Being open to new ideas

ME: Are there any tasks that are typical for a curator?

CHIYO: You think of the idea, you think about how you're going to communicate ideas through the art, and then you think, *Okay, I've got this plan, I want to talk with educators about it to see if I'm communicating it well, if it makes sense to them, and if not, how can I change it?* So those are kind of the ideal curatorial tasks, but there also are practical matters, like when a work of art that is being acquired was damaged in transit and you have to work with conservation to see what happened. There are also tedious things like submitting our budgets for the year. There can be talking to the public, giving lectures. Or a really fun part of the job is bringing works into the collection. It's a challenging job here at the Seattle Art Museum, because we don't have many acquisition funds and it's hard for us to compete with private collectors. But we work with donors who give things to the collection, and sometimes we identify something that we want and we raise money for it. One of the things I love about working here is that we're all dedicated to the same goal of making the museum better and making more people love art.

ME: Is the portrayal of the world of curators in *The Da Vinci Code* realistic?

CHIYO: All of the intrigue and sleuthing and people poisoning each other and stuff . . . we're a far more mundane world than that. I do think curating is a fairly romantic field, but it's also very tied to revenue projections and what level the art labels are hung so that they're not over people's heads. There are a lot of practical issues that are a part of it too. For me it's a good balance, because you get to stimulate your imagination as one part of the job and then you ground yourself and keep your head out of the clouds with other aspects. As far as *The DaVinci Code* is concerned, of course I like it when people become interested in art, but to me, there are so many fascinating and interesting things about Leonardo Da Vinci that don't involve murder and strange rituals.

INTERESTED IN BEING A CURATOR? HERE'S CHIYO'S ADVICE

▶ *Learn to look at art—training your eye is the fundamental skill that will sustain a curatorial career. When looking, always ask why. Why did the artist put that color there? How would the painting change if he hadn't? How does the background contribute to a portrait? Who is the main character in a narrative painting? This questioning attitude will lead to understanding the artist and will help the student or curator explain to others how the painting works.*

▶ *Learn other languages! Art historians need to read German and at least one other language. When conducting research in other countries, it's very useful to be able to communicate in the native language.*

▶ *Don't try to fit a mold, but really think about what you want to do and how you're going to get there.*

in the field

Five More Careers at a Museum

guest relations manager Most museums are visited by millions of people every year. Guest relations managers handle everything guest-related, including parking, admissions, maps, information centers, and programs and activities for guests, with a goal of making sure that museum visitors have a positive experience.

conservation scientist If you're a science junkie with a love of art, you might be interested in being a conservation scientist. They use their science background to research art artifacts by examining art to make sure it's authentic or conducting tests on artifacts to help museum conservators better preserve them.

exhibit designer Just as a set designer in a theater creates worlds for the actors to perform in, an exhibit designer in a museum creates the space for art exhibits. Exhibit designers figure out who will be visiting the museum and how to best create an exhibit to show off the work in a way that will be most comfortable for visitors.

gift store manager Most museums have gift stores that carry art prints, jewelry, books, and other goods reflective of the museum. Gift store managers interact with visitors from all over the world and are typically responsible for hiring and managing employees and keeping the store stocked.

archivist If you think of a museum as being similar to a library, then an archivist is the equivalent of a librarian. Archivists organize and catalog the information or material that is important to a museum, including photos, films, art documents, magazines, and computer disks.

For more art careers, check out the photographer profile on page 266.

Leanne Lusk

coast guard lieutenant

the facts

▶ **what?** The Coast Guard is the branch of the U.S. armed forces concerned with maritime law enforcement and safety, which means anything having to do with the coasts, ports, and inland waters of the United States, as well as international waters.

▶ **where?** The Coast Guard, whose motto is "Wherever America Needs Us," has units located throughout the United States, mostly in coastal cities.

Lt. Leanne Lusk, Assistant Enforcement Officer, Coast Guard

▶ **how?** Coast Guard officers need a bachelor's degree and must attend a seventeen-week-long Officer Candidate School (OCS) or, like Leanne, graduate from the Coast Guard Academy.

▶ **$$$:** Salary depends on rank. For officers like Leanne, it's anywhere from $40,000 to $100,000, depending on your level and number of years of service.

▶ **dress code?** Some type of Coast Guard uniform, depending on rank and the work. Leanne wears dark blue slacks and a light blue shirt, a nametag, and shoulder boards.

▶ **stress factor:** On a scale of 1 to 10, a 5

i interviewed leanne lusk, a lieutenant in the Coast Guard based in San Francisco, and while you might assume that Coast Guard jobs involve working at sea, Leanne works on land in an operational position. In Leanne's unit, the Coast Guard has three primary missions—homeland security, search and rescue, and law enforcement. Leanne's official title is assistant enforcement officer, and while her work encompasses a little bit of all these components every day, no two days are ever the same. Here are some examples of the kinds of things Leanne's job entails.

> *"I'm not someone that people would look at and think I'm a federal law enforcement officer. . . . I really like breaking out of that mold."*

▸ **planning for marine events**: Leanne puts together security plans for San Francisco marina events like Fleet Week or Tall Ships.

▸ **managing search-and-rescue boats**: Leanne manages seven small boat stations and four patrol boats within northern California, so any issues that come up regarding these boats and stations are her responsibility.

the breakdown

IN MEETINGS: 2–3 hours a day

ON THE PHONE: 2 hours a day

ONLINE: 3 hours a day

SITTING: Half the day

STANDING: Half the day

PUBLIC SPEAKING: Not daily, but often

READING: 2 hours

WORKING SOLO: 4 hours

▸ **developing training plans for stations**: Leanne comes up with training plans to help other stations run more efficiently.

▸ **coming up with security plans**: When presidential candidate John Kerry visited San Francisco, he wanted to go windsurfing in the bay, so Leanne met with the Secret Service and came up with a security plan for while he was on the water.

While a recruit who goes through boot camp graduates as an "enlisted person," Leanne got into one of the highly competitive military academies—the Coast Guard Academy, located in New London, Connecticut—and spent the next four years earning her BS in government and being trained as an officer.

When Leanne graduated in 1998, the protocol was that the first assignment for officers had to be on ships, but they've just changed the rules so that today new grads can move straight to a land job like the one Leanne's in now. I asked her to walk us through her early career journey:

"When I first got out of the academy, I went to work on a three-hundred-seventy-eight-foot ship out of Alameda, California. Our missions weren't locally based—we generally covered the Pacific Ocean, so I did several trips up to Alaska, where we did fisheries enforcement and search-and-rescue kind of stuff like you'll see on that *Deadliest Catch* show on the Discovery Channel. We also went down off the coast of Mexico and Panama to do alien migration 'interdiction,' which was dealing with people who were trying to illegally enter the United States by taking a boat to Guatemala or Mexico and then a bus

you asked . . .

"Did you know what you were doing when you were my age?" Annika, age 16

leanne answered . . .

"No. When I was seventeen I applied to colleges, planning to major in premed or political science. I didn't have any money for college and I was looking for a way to pay for it, so I talked to a recruiter and he told me about the Coast Guard Academy. I didn't think I had a shot in the world of getting in, because my high school GPA was a 3.85 when I graduated high school, and I thought I needed a 4.0. But I applied and got selected as an alternate. So I got into UC Davis and was planning on going there when I got a call saying that I had been selected for the academy. And that was it."

why wait?

▶ Visit a Coast Guard base near you and see if you can "get under way" with their crew for a ride-along.

▶ You can start the application process for the Coast Guard Academy as early as your junior year. It's competitive, so get good grades in high school!

into the United States. We also did counter-drug operations with people who run drugs on speedboats.

"That assignment was for two years, and we would generally get under way for three to four months, come home for a couple months, do maintenance on the ship, and then leave again for another three to four months. While I was onboard, I got qualified to drive the ship and bring a helicopter in for a landing on the deck. I also got qualified as a law enforcement boarding officer, as well as being in charge of all the weapons systems onboard," Leanne explained.

So do you have to be a thrill seeker to be in the Coast Guard? Leanne thinks so. Throughout her career she's done some fairly dangerous jobs, like boarding other boats. As she explained, you never know what you're going to find onboard—there could be dangerous drug runners.

Now that Leanne is working on land, it's not all high adventure all the time, but it's still pretty action-packed. Here is how Leanne described a day in her life.

then to now

1998: Graduated from the Coast Guard Academy with a BS in government

1998–2000: Worked on the Coast Guard cutter *Morgenthau* as a deck watch officer, gunnery officer, boarding officer, and landing signals officer

My workday starts at seven a.m., so I leave my house and get here between six forty-five and seven fifteen, depending on traffic. I used to have my own office, but now I share it with four other people. I work just downstairs from the command center, and I have a gorgeous view of the Bay Bridge out my window, so I look out at the water all day.

The first thing I do when I get here is check my e-mails and follow up on any issues that came up the day before. At eight a.m. there is a command briefing that goes over all of the cases that involve the Coast Guard. That usually takes about a half hour.

Then I come back to my office, and basically the rest of my day is spent putting out fires. I always have a list of projects that I'm working on. For example, if I'm putting together a security plan for events like Fleet Week or Tall Ships or something like that, I would be doing things like attending planning meetings. Like yesterday I had a meeting with the Red Bull airplane guys to plan the security and safety zones for Fleet Week. Or I might have other issues come up that concern our units. There's not a cookie-cutter type of day.

 what it takes

- ▶ A sense of adventure and public duty
- ▶ Being in good physical shape
- ▶ Working well with a team

For lunch, we have a cafeteria called a galley. It's $3.50 for lunch, and you can't beat that for an all-you-can-eat meal. But I usually end up bringing my leftovers in from the night before and working through lunch at my desk.

My workday officially ends at three o'clock, but I usually go home somewhere between five or six, and then I have traffic on the way home too. It's a long day, but there's a lot that goes into it and it's really rewarding. And once I'm home, it's not always over—I always make myself

2000–2003: Worked for the International Training Division, teaching courses in twenty-two countries

2003: Began working as assistant enforcement officer at Sector San Francisco

2004: Started working toward MBA at University of Phoenix

*available twenty-four hours a day. In my last position, I used to stand
a one-week duty that was a twenty-four-hour-a-day duty, where I was
available by telephone and I was briefed on any case that happened
in northern California for search and rescue, homeland security, law
enforcement, and any ships of interest coming into the port. One night
I had nine calls between one and five in the morning.*

Leanne told me about one of the more high-profile cases that she worked on. In November 2005 a woman threw her three babies into the San Francisco Bay. Leanne was out at dinner celebrating her step-mother's birthday when she got the call. She dropped everything and drove back to work to cover the operational aspect of planning the searches for the children, as well as meeting with the San Francisco Police Department's media people to coordinate press releases.

"It was a long night. . . . I was up until about two thirty a.m., went to bed, and got back up at four thirty to prep my captain and take him to the press conference. I just slept in my office on the couch. I was actively involved in the case, which ultimately became a homicide investigation, from the beginning all the way until noon the next day, when I got relieved so I could go home and finally get some sleep," Leanne says.

Like many women in this book, Leanne says one of her biggest challenges is juggling work and family life, especially since she's a new mom. She's a self-described go-getter and loves being dedicated to her job, but it takes an effort to make sure she has enough time for her husband and daughter.

But talk to Leanne about the Coast Guard and it's obvious that the benefits of the job clearly outweigh the downsides. "I love that I can retire when I'm forty-two years old because I'll have twenty years of active duty and I won't have to work another day in my life . . . my husband, too, because he's also on duty. We'll be able to watch our daughter's school events or whatever she wants to do; we'll be there to support her. She'll only be twelve when mom and dad will be home all the time," she says.

"I also love that when I come to work I don't know what that day will be like. It's really exciting, and I love being involved in the action. Particularly in the job I have right now, the stuff that you read in the newspaper or see on TV is the stuff that I'm actively doing."

I asked Leanne what it was like being a woman in the military, since traditionally it's been such a male-dominated career path. Leanne pointed out that out of all the armed services, the Coast Guard has the highest percentage of women. And she loves busting stereotypes about what women can and can't do.

"I'm not someone that people would look at and think I'm a federal law enforcement officer. . . . I really like breaking out of that mold. I know that I can get dropped in a country anywhere in the world and survive. . . . I know how to take care of myself," she says.

LEANNE'S ADVICE

▶ *To be successful in this career path, find an area that you're passionate about—search and rescue, law enforcement, engineering, driving ships and small boats, being involved internationally—and go for it!*

▶ *Don't think that a decision you make when you're seventeen or eighteen is going to affect the rest of your life. I thought I was going to go to the academy, serve my five years, and then do something else. But I've stayed here and it's been extremely rewarding for me.*

in the field
Five More Careers in the Military

aircraft launch and recovery specialist In the opening scene of the classic movie *Top Gun*, aircraft launch and recovery specialists are standing atop a huge aircraft carrier in the middle of the Indian Ocean. These specialists oversee the equipment that helps aircraft take off and land on an aircraft carrier.

medical care technician In the civilian world, medical care technicians could be compared to nurses' aides. In the military, they generally work in military hospitals, aboard ships, or in mobile field hospitals, administering first aid, taking pulse and temperature, prepping operating rooms, and feeding, bathing, and dressing patients.

emergency management specialist Emergency management specialists train for and plan responses to future disasters, as well as respond to various real-life emergencies, whether it be a terrorist attack or a natural disaster. There are emergency management specialists in all five branches of the military.

special forces officer Special forces officers have to be ready to do just about anything, anytime, anywhere. Their job is to be trained in many different skills, from parachuting and swimming to survival techniques, and they are in a "constant state of readiness" for the call to report for duty.

interpreter Interpreters in the armed forces interpret for people who speak foreign languages or translate other written languages into English. Unlike civilian interpreters, those in the military might help to interview or interrogate prisoners of war or translate foreign documents or messages that are intercepted.

Amy Friedman

TV network executive

the facts

▶ **what?** Television network execs oversee programming, development, or marketing and play key roles in creating the channel that you recognize when you flip on the TV.

▶ **where?** TV networks are primarily based in New York and L.A., although with the continual expansion of cable television, you'll now find them in other states, including Maryland (Discovery Networks) and Connecticut (ESPN).

Amy Friedman,
SVP/Creative Director,
Nickelodeon
Digital Television

▶ **how?** Many TV execs have a background in communications, English, or liberal arts from a four-year college, and then work their way up from the bottom, starting out as an intern or assistant.

▶ **$$$:** Anywhere from $50,000 to $200,000 a year and higher, depending on level and the size of the network

▶ **dress code?** Depends on the network . . . at Noggin and The N, it's casual.

▶ **stress factor:** On a scale of 1 to 10, usually a 5, sometimes a 2, and rarely an 8 (according to Amy)

amy friedman has a fancy title—senior vice president of development/creative director of Nickelodeon Digital Television— and she has been in the Nickelodeon family since graduating from college more than seventeen years ago. So when it comes to talking with an expert in television, there's no one better, and no one more inspirational. Here's what we talked about in Amy's office near Times Square in the heart of New York City.

ME: Is being a television executive something you dreamed of doing when you were younger?

"As much as I hate commuting, when I'm on the train, no one can reach me, no one can knock on my door. I have my cup of coffee, I have my scripts, and it's actually really fun."

AMY: From an oddly early age I knew that I wanted to be a writer on *Sesame Street*. I was six and my little sister was two, and she was watching *Sesame Street* and I said, "I like the writing on that show. I want to be a writer on *Sesame Street*." It could be that I was a good storyteller when I was little and my parents said, "You could tell stories."

ME: Wow . . . six years old! Let's talk about present day. Can you explain to us what exactly you do?

AMY: I am called the SVP of development/creative director of Nickelodeon Digital Television, which means Noggin and The N. My creative director side is all about look, feel, strategy. It's about how this brand fits into the world, what its logo looks like, who is it talking to, in what voice, what is our educational philosophy, what kind of programming are we doing, how does that differentiate us from what else is out there. A lot of that stuff happens at the very front end of brand creation and then is executed on a day-to-day basis.

And on the other side, as the SVP of development my job is to create new shows. And so we look at the world and we look at our channel and we say, "What's missing in this conversation?" And then we go out to the creative world, we tell them what our goals are, and they pitch to us. We listen to the pitches, we pick a few that we're going to make into scripts, and our job as development executives is to really midwife ideas. It's not to be the writer, but it's to help the writer make something appropriate for our brand. So let's say we took a hundred pitches and we made twenty scripts. We then narrow it down and make five pilots, which is the first episode of a

the breakdown

IN MEETINGS: Half the day

ON THE PHONE: 1 hour a day

ONLINE: 3 hours a day

SITTING: Almost all day long

READING: 1 hour a day, but should be more!

WORKING SOLO: 2 hours a day

"WALKING THE HALLS" AND CHECKING IN WITH PEOPLE: On and off throughout the day

show. Then we test the pilot and see how the audience loves it. If the audience loves it, our group hands it off to the production department and they start making episodes. Then we go off and find the next thing. Really, we are the "hunters and gatherers."

AMY'S (UN)USUAL DAY

Being a working mother is splitting yourself into two large clumps. Usually I wake up whenever my kids wake up, and I get them breakfast and get them dressed, and I really try to have an experience with one of them every morning. As a working mother, from when I leave my house at eight o'clock to 9:07 when I get in to Penn Station, there is something beautiful about it. When I'm on the train, no one can reach me, no one can knock on my door. I have my cup of coffee, I have my scripts, and it's actually really fun.

I get to work at nine thirty, and the day begins. On a typical day I might take a pitch at two different times during the day. At ten o'clock, I may take a pitch from an NYU film student who one of my development executives saw at a film festival. So I will sit with this person who's never done this before and hear a fresh new voice and try to help them think about what it would be like to translate their rawness into a commercial medium like TV. At eleven o'clock, there may be something called the "strategy meeting," and that's

amy answered . . .

"Oh God, yes. Especially as a working mother, if I'm going to leave my kids every day I'd better be having a lot of fun, because it's not worth it if not. I also believe—and it's a total cliché—if you do what you love, the money will come. I really think that that's true."

where I'm wearing my creative director hat. All the different departments of my company sit and say what is going on this week or what we need to do to change our schedule. Or we'll talk about how we as a company are going to get ahead of the curve and talk to the audience in an authentic way on different platforms. Sometimes those meetings are very satisfying, because either we solved a problem or we got out in front of the ball. Other days those meetings are really scary, because sometimes you can't solve the immediate problem. I actually find that puzzle really interesting.

Another meeting that I might go to is my development team's meeting. We may have all read a script in progress and one of the people in the team is having a problem with it. The agenda of that day is "something's wrong with this script and I don't know how to fix it," and we might all sit around and try to figure it out. There's a rule that there is no hierarchy in that meeting, so there are no bad ideas. So my assistant might have the solution to what's wrong with this script, or I do, and we debate and it's all good.

My next meeting may be with a writer—although this is rare now since I've become more management. But if it's a big project or one that I'm very passionate about, I meet with the writer. And that would be my project where I am sitting with a writer and trying to make a script as good as possible, and trying to figure out how can we relate to this character, what does each character want, are we letting our audience into this story? That kind of stuff.

 then to now

1986: Graduated from University of Pennsylvania with BA in American civilization and an MA in education

1987: Got job at Nickelodeon mixing slime for *Double Dare*

1988–1994: Served as writer, director, and producer/executive producer in Nickelodeon and Nick at Nite's branding group

At some point in there, on a good day I have a lunch date with a colleague. On a bad day, my assistant gets my lunch and I'm sitting on the phone trying to chew quietly so that nobody knows that I'm actually eating during a phone meeting. I would say 60 percent of the time it's a bad day, and 40 percent of my time I either take a walk and get my lunch and/or have a lunch date. I wish I had more lunch dates. . . . I think it enhances one's life.

At the end of the day I may have a pitch with a very experienced show runner who's done hit shows for either kids or adults, and that meeting is all about taking the person's expertise and actually trying to bring them to a teen place. It's the opposite meeting that I had in the morning.

Because I'm in a lot of meetings, I catch up on reading and work during my commutes and at night after I put the kids to bed. In a perfect world I would tell you that my assistant schedules two hours in the day to return calls and actually do work, but if you're looking for the truth, it doesn't happen, and that's why phone calls don't get returned for

1994–1998: Became creative director/executive producer of Nickelodeon's Creative Lab

1998: Moved over to be creative director of new network Noggin ✳ ✳

2000–2004: Executive produced The N's original series *A Walk in Your Shoes*

2004: Became SVP of development/ creative director at Nickelodeon Digital Television, serving Noggin and The N

what it takes

▸ A love of television

▸ Wanting to connect with an audience

▸ The ability to work in teams and think outside of the box

four days or they fall through the cracks. And that's why I end up watching shows I need to watch at night.

ME: Your day sounds exhausting. How do you have any energy for your personal life?

AMY: When I get home at night and walk through that door, I have to completely drop everything. That's one of the great things about being a working mom is that all the time with my kids is quality time. My babysitter cooks dinner. I never thought that I would be comfortable with that, but I have decided that I don't have to do everything, and what I'd rather do is eat dinner with my kids. And then for the next two hours, it is all about them. My time with my husband comes after they go to bed. We'll sit down and sort of decompress. And then it's back on the computer or reading scripts probably until midnight, and then the whole thing starts all over again at six a.m. the next morning.

ME: And the weekends?

AMY: Weekends? Zero work. From Friday at four thirty p.m. until Monday morning when I walk out the door, I don't do any work.

ME: Do you think your job is glamorous?

AMY: Yeah, most of me actually does think it's glamorous. I think that there is a branching-off point where one is often tempted to take more status and more money by moving to the management side of things, and you actually go further away from the creative, but I have maneuvered to stay close to the creative. So, on a relative scale, I really find it glamorous. What are the unglamorous parts of the job? My job is a lot of saying no to people and I find that really, really challenging. I think I've gotten pretty good at it, and people have told me that I'm the best sayer of no that they've dealt with. But I love it when a first-timer has a pilot that's competing with an old-timer and the first-timer gets their show picked up.

ME: What has it been like building The N into what it is today, knowing that you played such a huge role in it?

AMY: The simple answer is I feel like a mother. I feel like I have four children, and they are my daughters, Carly and Emily, and they are Noggin and The N. It's really funny. . . . I used to go to parties and people would ask, "Where do you work?" and I'd say, "Oh, I work at a little offshoot of Nickelodeon called Noggin, I'm sure you've never heard of it." Five years ago they'd say, "Oh, that's interesting." And now it's like, "Noggin? Oh my God, it's the only thing I let my kids watch!" I am thrilled and proud and also sort of in disbelief. I feel a little bit like the kid who grew up.

AMY'S CAREER ADVICE

▶ *Go with your gut creatively. I spent the first eight years of my career learning from my mentor, who taught me everything I know about branding. I rose up among the ranks and they really wanted me to run the promo department, and it just didn't feel right. So I said no to the promotion and a lot of people were shocked. But two weeks later, an opportunity came up to run the Creative Lab and make short films, and I knew I was ready for the change. I went with my gut, which was not necessarily the conventional way to rise in the ranks.*

▶ *Get a mentor—somebody who understands you, who will fight for you, and who will tell you when your farts smell.*

▶ *Get a craft. You cannot be credible if you actually don't know how to do one thing really, really, really well.*

promo producer Promos are like ads for a TV network, and promo producers are the in-house staff who develop, create, and produce the spots. Promo producers find new, creative ways to promote a network. They write scripts, create schedules and budgets, hire actors, and manage production and postproduction of the spots.

director of programming Directors of programming for a network plan out the broadcast schedule and figure out what episodes of which shows should air in which time slots to bring in the highest ratings. They spend hours each week poring over detailed ratings reports of the network and developing strategies to boost the ratings.

consumer products coordinator Most television networks create products that represent the network's shows—everything from T-shirts and backpacks to plush dolls and books. Consumer products coordinators work with designers and copywriters to manage their production, as well as managing the schedule and budget.

promotions marketing director Promotions marketing directors of a TV network plan and oversee promotions aimed at increasing visibility for the network, such as a sweepstakes for a behind-the-scenes tour of a show or an on-air contest to win a lifetime supply of Snapple.

executive in charge of production They've got some of the biggest job titles in the business, but what exactly do they do? Execs in charge serve as the liaison between a show and the network it airs on, writing up notes on scripts, doing rough edits, and even approving writers, actors, or other staff hired for a production.

informational interviews

when i was looking for a job in television news after graduating from college, I discovered this amazing thing called the "informational interview." An informational interview is a meeting where there is no job at stake. It's simply an opportunity to talk with professionals about their work, get tips on how to break into a company or industry, and most important, give people the chance to get to know and like you. A clever cover letter and a lot of persistence could just get you in the door.

As a twenty-two-year-old with very little experience, I managed to meet with the executive producers of ABC News's *20/20*, the newsmagazine *Day One* (no longer on the air), PBS's *MacNeil/Lehrer NewsHour* (now *The NewsHour with Jim Lehrer*), the head of broadcasting for UNICEF, and a small television production company called Globalvision. While nothing happened immediately, as a result of those initial informational interviews, I eventually got job offers!

Here are just a few advantages to informational interviews:

▸ You can do them anytime—even as a high school student.

▸ Most people are happy to sit down with you (if they can fit it into their schedule) and talk about what it is they do and answer any questions.

▸ Contacts made through informational interviews can be valuable job contacts down the road.

▸ By asking for an informational interview, you're showing people that you're motivated and serious about your interests.

The best place to start identifying possible interviews is with friends and family. Let people know what you're interested in and see if anyone has a connection to someone doing your hoped for career. You can also ask your guidance counselor if any alumni have the job you want—sharing an alma mater is a great way to get someone's attention. Lastly, don't be afraid to send a letter to someone you don't know and ask them for a meeting. If you're professional in your communication and the person you're writing to isn't too swamped with work, you've got a good chance of landing a meeting.

Here are some more "do's" and "don'ts" that will prepare you for successful informational interviews:

don't	*do*
* Address your query letter "To whom it may concern" or "Dear Sir or Madam."	* Address your letter to an individual, and make sure to spell his or her name correctly!
* Ramble on in the letter and forget to clearly state why you're writing in the first place.	* Be specific in your letter about what you're asking for—a half hour of their time for an in-person or on-the-phone informational interview.
* Demand that the person reply to your letter.	* Suggest that you'll follow up with a phone call in several weeks.
* Call the person every day and get frustrated that they haven't returned your phone call.	* Be patient and check in by phone no more than once a week.
* Show up late or unprepared for your informational interview.	* Come to the informational interview on time, dressed appropriately, and prepared with great questions (see below for examples).
* Take the fact that somebody offered you free career advice for granted.	* Send a personal thank-you note (handwritten is the best kind) to the person you met with.

Sample Informational Interview Questions

1. How did you get into this line of work?

2. What does your job entail?

3. What magazines do you read about your job? Are there any helpful organizations or websites I should know about?

4. What classes should I take in college?

5. Does your company offer internships?

6. What advice do you have for me about breaking into this career?

7. Can I get in touch with you down the road when I'm ready to look for a job?

Dr. Alice Wilder

educational psychologist

the facts

Dr. Alice Wilder, Director of Research and Development/Producer, Preschool Television

▶ **what?** Educational psychologists study how learning takes place and find ways to make it more effective. They do anything from coming up with ways to help a learning-disabled student get more out of a class to determining whether or not a new teaching tool impacts students' grades.

▶ **where?** Many educational psychologists work in schools, but they might also end up in hospitals, counseling centers, or even the world of preschool television.

▶ **how?** Many educational psychologists have doctoral degrees, which means being in grad school for up to seven years, but there are different job opportunities in educational psychology for all levels of degrees.

▶ **$$$:** An average of $25,000 with a BA, $40,000 to $60,000 with an MA, and $60,000–$100,000 with a PhD or EdD.

▶ **dress code:** Casual to business casual, depending on the day

▶ **stress factor:** On a scale of 1 to 10, a 7

until I worked with her, I had no idea that anybody did what Alice does. I met Alice while working for the hit preschool show *Blue's Clues* at Nickelodeon. One of the reasons the show has such a powerful impact on kids is because Alice takes the time to ensure that the content of the show makes sense.

To do this, she spends lots of time with preschoolers—acting out scenes from future *Blue's Clues* episodes, playing the same games that the characters on the show might play together, and seeing if the script is as interactive as the writers and show creators want it to be.

But wait . . . there's more. On any given day, Alice is juggling many other tasks. She might be writing an article for *Nick Jr. Family Magazine*, planning a presentation for a children's television summit, or even researching ideas for new educational programs.

> *"Something I love about researching with preschoolers is how silly they can be."*

Even though in Alice's line of work no two days are ever alike, I asked her to keep a diary for a day so we could peek inside her life.

 ALICE'S JOURNAL

7:00 a.m. Ugh. My alarm is going off. And I'm not a morning person. But I have to get up. I'm going to a preschool this morning to act out a new Blue's Clues *script. I'm hoping the script will work, because when it doesn't, it's a lot of energy to keep the kids' attention and think of things on the spot that I can change to make the script better. I love getting to play with preschoolers, but this morning is rough, especially since I was up late last night getting stuff ready. In my sleepy state, I flip on the TV, hoping for a "snow day" so I can go back to bed for a while, but there's no snow to be found, so I get up and get dressed. Today is definitely a "jeans day," since I'll be on the floor playing with preschoolers. If I had meetings with the network execs at Nickelodeon or a powwow with marketing or consumer products, I'd be in business casual or a suit.*

8:30 a.m. Head out the door. Since I'm not going straight to the office, I can't walk, so I jump on the subway and head downtown with hordes of* *other New Yorkers. As always, I've got my big blue bag in tow. . . . Inside it are things I never leave home without: a script or two, a schedule, a "to do" list, a pen and blank pad of paper (because there are just too many things I need to keep in my head), and my makeup so I can freshen up if I make it to the gym later that day.*

9:00 a.m. *Research time. I like sitting on the floor and playing. . . . I don't know why. Maybe because I'm short? Maybe because I've always liked to sit on the floor? I gather four or five preschoolers around me, tell them my name, and ask theirs. When we're doing this I try to notice something unique about each one of them—maybe one has something sparkly on her clothing, maybe another is wearing really cool sneakers—and talk about it with them, the idea being to make the kids feel as comfortable around me as possible. After all, I'm just a stranger coming in to read them a story. The tricky thing about researching with preschoolers is keeping them talking about the same thing I am, especially if they don't like the story.*

Once I start reading the story (which is the episode script in storybook form), I really get into it to make it more interesting for the kids. I act it out and play the part of different characters. If they like the story and are listening, it's easier. If they don't, it's going to be an exhausting forty-five minutes, and I'd better figure out what isn't working in the script. Something

you asked . . .

"What was the toughest obstacle you had to face in order to be who you are today?" Sarah, age 16

alice answered . . .

"Low self-esteem. When I was in college, I registered for a business course, and one of the requirements was a presentation in front of the class. As soon as I heard that, I wanted to drop the class. When I started at Blue's Clues *I used to whisper my notes in the creator's ear, not believing in the value of what I had to say. What helped me was going into schools every week and talking with preschoolers . . . the audience themselves. My voice had to be heard because it stood for them, not for me. My voice became respected on the show and in the industry because it had the integrity of representing the kids, and this gave me confidence. And now you can't keep me quiet, especially on matters of kids' voices being heard."*

I love about researching with preschoolers is how silly they can be. Like today, the script I was researching had a joke in it. We were transforming a wolf from "little" to "big." But instead of spelling "big," we spelled "pig." When the preschoolers thought about changing a wolf into a pig, they lost it . . . all-out belly laughs. They just kept laughing and saying, "Again! Again!" By this time I was laughing so hard I had tears rolling down my cheeks. It was so cool seeing them having such a good time and knowing it was educational, too (after all, we were teaching preschoolers spelling!).

the breakdown

IN MEETINGS: 6–7 hours a day

ON THE PHONE: 1 hour a day

ONLINE: Occasionally

READING: 2 hours a day

SITTING: Most of the day, unless at a preschool

READING: 2 hours a day

WORKING SOLO: Hardly ever

10:00 a.m. While the rest of my research team was working with other groups of kids, I tested the same script with some older kids, this time five- and six-year-olds. They totally got it. They were entranced in the story and screaming out answers as we played along. They made all of the connections. Today I brought the writer of the script with me so we could get a sense of what was working and what wasn't. It's kind of like "cheating," but in a positive way. We're just trying to find out what works before we spend the money and time to make the actual episode.

1:00 p.m. Back at the office. I have a quick debriefing with my researchers and then rush to a "story sketch" meeting for an upcoming episode of Blue's Room. In these meetings I sit down with the director, the producers, the writer, the storyboard artist, and the animation director. My job is to be the four-year-old in the room, to let people know how the episode works for the audience. Every episode of the show starts out as a script; the next step is for the director to draft rough sketches so we can figure out how the episode will actually look when it's on TV. Usually I try to have read through the script with the story sketches before this meeting, but today I haven't had a chance, since it's been so crazy. So I quickly try to read through it at the start of the meeting while people are talking about other things. It takes about two to three hours to go through the script, and I give notes about things I have issues with as we go along.

why wait?

- Be a teen peer counselor at a youth hotline.

- Volunteer at a hospital or clinic.

3:55 p.m. *The story sketch meeting has wrapped up, but the writer needs a few minutes of my time. He tells me that because of production needs, we have to make some additional changes to an upcoming script. He asks me to give any new notes today, because the storyboard artist has to start on it tomorrow if it's going to be done on time.*

4:30 p.m. *I gather my team together to talk more indepthly about what came up during research in the morning. Because we were all working with different groups of kids, we need to share what we each experienced. We talk about how the script went overall, what kinds of age differences we found, and whether or not the games worked. Once we've identified what the main issues are, we organize our thoughts and one of my analysts writes up our notes, checks the data, adds details, and prepares a memo for the writer.*

6:30 p.m. *I meet a friend after work, grab a bite to eat, and head uptown to Columbia University (my alma mater) to hear my "education hero," Jerome Bruner, speak. Aside from having a cool job, it's nights like this that make living in New York worth all the stress and hassle. His talk tonight was called "Educating a Sense of the Possible." After hearing him talk, I feel like I got a dose of inspiration that will last a year!*

10:30 p.m. *Ah . . . nighttime. I can't wait to get into my apartment. I need to take these shoes off and be comfortable. I don't care that it's ten thirty p.m. and I am just getting home and I have work in my bag. I need at least an hour or two of downtime before I go to bed—"me" time. I need to pay the bills, check my e-mail, clean, watch TV, return phone calls, and open the mail. I do all of these things at the same time. TiVo has changed my life, because I can still catch my shows even though I'm usually out four*

then to now

1988: Graduated from Skidmore College with a BA in psychology	1988–1989: Retail manager, Children's Workshop Toy Store	1989–1991: Program data analyst and coordinator, PBS	1991: Graduated with an MA in educational psychology, Columbia University

nights a week. I just can't seem to get to bed before midnight or one a.m. I want to . . . in fact, I need to. Every day feels as if there is not a moment of downtime. As I consciously enjoy the fact that I am not working and am relaxing doing something for me, I know that I need to get off to bed. Before I go to sleep, I figure out what time I have to get up in the morning (it changes every day, and for me, the later, the better!) and read a page or two of a book before I collapse in exhaustion. The last thing I do before I turn out the lights is my ten-minute meditation as I listen to Music for the Mind. I sleep well!

what it takes

▶ A passion for education

▶ A strong interest in research

▶ Strong analytical and communication skills

paying your dues

Want to be an apprentice to someone like Alice? You'll probably start out as a research assistant, where you'll be photocopying, taking notes in meetings, typing up notes, and coordinating research schedules.

1993:
Research intern, Nickelodeon

1993: Started working on doctorate, Teachers College, Columbia University

1995: Hired as the director of research and development/ producer, Nick Jr.'s *Blue's Clues*

1998: Received EdD in educational psychology, Teachers College, Columbia University

in the field

Five More Careers in Psychology

research psychologist These psychologists often work in universities, splitting their time between teaching and conducting research on things like memory, behavior, learning, and perception. Many research psychologists spend a lot of time writing articles about their research for academic journals and publications as well.

school psychologist Chances are you've crossed paths with a school psychologist before. School psychologists do things like deal with problem students, come up with ideas to support gifted and talented students, and work with teachers to make their classrooms more kid-friendly.

family therapist Family therapists are like marriage counselors, except they examine the whole family dynamic and the role each family member plays in any problems there may be. Family therapists usually have their own practice, and their patients come to their office for therapy sessions.

trial psychologist Featured in the John Cusack movie *Runaway Jury* (2003), trial psychologists are hired by prosecutors and defendants to help them strategize how to win their cases by giving them psychological insight into picking a jury, planning opening and closing statements, and figuring out a plan for the trial.

clinical psychologist Clinical psychologists work with mentally and emotionally disturbed people, or people going through a difficult time, and give them tools to deal with their problems. Some clinical psychologists work in hospitals or counseling centers, while others might have their own practice.

For more careers working with children, check out the nanny profile on page 378 and the teacher profile on page 364.

Jayne Morgan

accountant

the facts

▶ **what?** Accounting is the business of tracking the money that goes in and out of any company, organization, or wallet, and while many accountants file taxes and conduct audits, others use their expertise to develop financial plans for businesses and even run organizations.

▶ **where?** Accountants work in just about every industry—from Hollywood studios and hospitals to museums and government agencies. Others might be self-employed.

Jayne Morgan, Finance & Operations Director, NESsT

▶ **how?** Most companies require a four-year college degree in a field like accounting, finance, or business. Becoming a CPA (certified public accountant) means passing a special exam, and depending on the state's requirements, working a number of hours in accounting. Getting an MBA is a good idea for people with high career aspirations.

▶ **$$$:** $30,000 to $40,000 a year for entry-level positions at big accounting firms, and $60,000 to $150,000 plus for management and executives, depending on the company.

▶ **dress code?** Business casual at auditing firms and suits in supercorporate environments. At a nonprofit in Chile like Jayne, jeans it is!

▶ **stress factor:** On a scale of 1 to 10, a 7

when i interviewed jayne morgan, an accountant and the finance and operations director for the nonprofit NESsT in Santiago, Chile, she busted one myth about accountants right away. Contrary to popular belief, accounting really isn't about "math" per se. In fact, according to Jayne, the most complicated math an accountant will do is addition and subtraction . . . perhaps division on the rarest of occasions. As she explained, accounting is a "system" for tracking financial information. "You don't need to be good at math, but you do need to be good at following systems and procedures, and have the type of mind that likes to work within a rigid framework." She adds with a laugh, "Although I couldn't live without my calculator, and I can only use *my* calculator—that is one stereotype about accountants that's actually true."

"I couldn't live without my calculator, and I can only use my *calculator—that is one stereotype about accountants that's actually true."*

I asked Jayne how and when she knew she wanted to be an accountant, and she gave me her story.

"When I was in high school applying to colleges, I had no idea what I wanted to do. So my dad recommended that I apply to the business schools at all these universities, because no matter what you decide you're interested in, there's a "business" behind it. So if you're interested in medicine, you know, every hospital needs to be run—there's a "business" behind it. If you want to work in the movie industry, there are accountants and finance people behind every movie production. Once I was in business school, I really enjoyed accounting, because of that idea that it gives order to whatever business you're in," Jayne explained.

Jayne began her career like many accountants—working with one of the "Big Five" accounting auditing firms. Pricewaterhouse-Coopers recruited her out of college to be an auditor in their Chicago office, and in this competitive, entry-level position, she "audited" companies, meaning she reviewed their financial books, making sure

jayne answered . . .

"I had to give up a lot of evenings and weekends! To be successful, you cannot expect to work from nine to five, and you have to be ready to do whatever it takes to get the job done. Accountants work with a lot of strict deadlines, which sometimes means working long hours."

that everything added up and checking receipts for equipment against the equipment itself. She spent most of her time either on-site with clients or working in computer programs like Excel, which she used to add invoices and review documents.

"When you do an audit, usually you start with the physical documents like receipts or contracts or loan agreements. The first part of the process was to review those documents, and the second part was to enter the information into specialized accounting programs," Jayne says.

Accountants fresh out of college might spend a couple of years "paying their dues" as an auditor and then take their experience into the corporate world, where they might be hired as an in-house accountant for a company. Unless they're like Jayne. Then they might move to South America to run the financial side of a small nonprofit organization. I asked Jayne to explain what she does for the organization, NESsT (Nonprofit Enterprise and Self-sustainability Team).

 ## the breakdown

IN MEETINGS: 1 hour a day

ON THE PHONE: Less than half an hour a day

ONLINE: 2 hours a day

SITTING: Nearly the whole day

READING: 1 hour a day

WORKING SOLO: 7 hours a day

why wait?

▶ Get a job at a bank—many will hire high school students to work as tellers.

▶ Get comfortable using Excel—it's one of the biggest tools for accountants. (If you need help getting started, try doing an online tutorial.)

▶ Manage your own money matters. Create your own spreadsheet in Excel or try using a budget program like Quicken to keep your own "books."

"I work in a small international organization, and I'm not just behind my desk all day entering numbers into Excel. I'm using financial analysis and budgets to help support other people's programs. I play a big role in making sure that the organization is running properly, making sure our technology systems are working, helping with funding or hiring decisions, and so on. So it's human resources, technology, everything. . . . I really love my job, love the people," Jayne says.

what it takes

▶ Strong computer and analytical skills

▶ Paying attention to detail

▶ Being procedure-oriented

Because the accounting industry is so regulated by the federal government, and there have been a number of high-profile accounting scandals in recent years (does the name Enron ring a bell?), one of the challenges of being an accountant is staying up-to-date on changing regulations and the fast pace of the business environment. But when pressed, Jayne admits that while this

then to now

| 1997: Studied abroad in Madrid, Spain | 1998: Interned at Merrill Lynch in Boulder, CO | 1998–2000: Worked part-time job as forensic accounting assistant at RGL Gallagher in St. Louis, MO | 2000: Graduated from Washington University in St. Louis with BS in business administration |

is a challenge, she actually enjoys the continuing education, too. In fact, she likes pretty much everything about her job.

"There's definitely a certain satisfaction in being able to have everything in order so things can run efficiently, and being able to provide management with the information they need to make decisions about the company. No director of any company or nonprofit could make decisions without the necessary information, and one of the key pieces of information is financial information. So what I really like is being able to have accurate records of the past and use them to forecast into the future to help make decisions," she says.

According to Jayne, the job opportunities and the potential to rise up the ranks are enormous for people with backgrounds in accounting.

"People are really impressed when you put in your time with one of these accounting firms—it looks great on your resume. Accountants are in very high demand because in order to understand finance, you have to know what's behind the numbers, and that's what accountants know. So if you have a lot of experience in accounting, you can easily make a transition into other business areas."

JAYNE'S CAREER ADVICE

No matter what field you want to pursue, you need to cultivate your people skills and your networking skills. Even for accounting, you really need to be able to relate to your coworkers, deal with the clients, deal with the vendors. It's an important part of working life for anybody.

| 2001: Passed the CPA exam in Illinois | 2000–2001: Associate at Pricewaterhouse Coopers, in Chicago, IL | 2001–2002: Senior associate at Pricewater-houseCoopers, Santiago, Chile | 2002: Hired as finance and operations director, NESsT, Santiago, Chile |

in the field

Five More Careers You Can Have with an Accounting Background

financial auditor (can be entry-level career) Financial auditors examine the finances of a company or organization to ensure that everything the company reports about their finances is accurate. Many typically work for the "Big Five" accounting firms such as Deloitte & Touche and PricewaterhouseCoopers.

budget analyst Behind the budget of every company, organization, or government office is a budget analyst, who tracks budgets throughout the "fiscal" or financial year and creates new ones each year based on projected income and spending.

financial planner As pensions shrink, inflation rises, and people spend more than they're bringing in, financial planners are becoming increasingly important. They help companies, families, or individuals handle their money, whether it's setting up a retirement fund, figuring out if you can afford a new plasma TV, or saving to buy a house.

tax accountant While many tax accountants are busiest during "tax season" preparing tax returns, they support their clients year-round by handing things like audits or the complicated tax implications of a merger between two companies, as well as staying up-to-date on ever-changing tax regulations.

management accountant Management accountants typically work in large companies and analyze the structure of an organization as it affects the financial bottom line. They are always looking for ways to reorganize a company or reallocate resources so the company can be financially efficient.

you need to know about

Start Here—Go Places (www.startheregoplaces.com), hosted by the American Institute of Certified Public Accountants, is a great website to learn more about accounting, find out what courses to take in high school, and discover job and internship opportunities.

Severn Cullis-Suzuki

environmentalist

the facts

▶ **what?** While "environmentalist" isn't necessarily an actual job title you'll find at a company, environmentalists are people who aim to protect and improve the environment through their work, which might involve things like education, engineering, and research.

▶ **where?** Some work for nonprofit organizations or government agencies, while others might work in academic institutions or for environmental firms.

*Severn Cullis-Suzuki,
Environmentalist*

▶ **how?** Environmentalists should take science and biology classes in high school and get an undergraduate or graduate degree in some sort of social or environmental science.

▶ **$$$:** An average of $40,000–$55,000, but varies widely depending on the organization

▶ **dress code?** Casual to business casual

▶ **stress factor:** On a scale of 1 to 10, between a 5 and a 9

while there is no cookie-cutter career description of an "environmentalist," any way you shake it, that's what Severn Cullis-Suzuki is. Her father is world-renowned scientist Dr. David Suzuki, and his passion for nature and the environment clearly rubbed off onto Severn at a very young age. So young, in fact, that Severn spoke at the first-ever International Earth Summit in Rio de Janeiro in 1992. She was only twelve years old.

Since then, she has continued to speak out about the environment, using her voice and her passion to educate others about the plight of the earth and the need for people to improve their relationship with its natural resources. I talked with Severn about her work and what it means to be an environmentalist.

"One of the challenges...
is becoming so absorbed in the
problems that you forget to enjoy
your life. Burnout is a really big
problem in activist communities."

ME: We hear the word "environmentalist" used all the time. What is an environmentalist?

SEVERN: Actually, one of the things that I'm trying to do personally and professionally is to reevaluate what the term "environmentalist" means. I think one of the biggest problems that we have with respect to our environment is how we've really externalized it. How it's this thing that certain people deal with and we call them "environmentalists" or we talk about "environmental problems" or the "environmental movement." In reality, the environment is everything that surrounds us. It's the air that we breathe, it's the food that we eat, it's our health, it's our economic interactions. What I'm trying to do is redefine our relationship to our resources and to one another in a very grand way.

ME: How are you trying to do that?

SEVERN: The first thing is education. Right now I'm in school again and educating myself. I've been active in environmentalism for a long time, and after I finished my undergrad degree I was public speaking and writing and doing a lot of educational stuff. But I went back to school because I realized I wanted to learn more about different worldviews and different ways of managing our environment. Right now I'm doing a master's in ethno-ecology and studying with First Nations* here in British Columbia, learning about environmental attractions and the economy. That's the first step. Another step is to translate what I'm learning into my personal life, as well as teaching others what I'm learning about. I don't have a career plan or step-by-step process in my mind, but I do think that people who are interested in environmental studies, environmental engineering, and sustainability will have a lot of career options.

ME: You've done a lot of public speaking about the environment. Do you see yourself continuing to do that in the future?

* **THE LINGO: First Nations** is a term used in Canada to refer to the indigenous people of North America, sometimes called Indians or Native Americans.

why wait?

▸ Start an environmental club at your high school or in your community to raise awareness of issues you're passionate about.

▸ Read biographies of famous women environmentalists like Rachel Carson or Julia Butterfly Hill for inspiration.

▸ Start at home! Recycle, take shorter showers, turn off lights when you leave the room, and keep electrical appliances unplugged when you're not using them.

SEVERN: I think I'll always be doing that. I started when I was quite young, and it's just part of my role as a communicator.

ME: You were only twelve years old when you spoke at the Earth Summit in Rio. How does doing so much at such a young age impact you now?

SEVERN: I'm not sure. The Earth Summit was a pretty big event. I'd say that was probably the biggest speech I've given in my life. So it's kind of funny to have this precedent set right off the bat. But I find it a useful tool when I'm speaking today, because as a story it really captures people's imaginations. It shows the potential for anyone to make a difference, and people love the imagery and the idea of a child going to the Earth Summit and speaking to world leaders. It's almost like it has a life of its own.

ME: Your work and your life really seem to be one and the same. Is there any separation between the two?

SEVERN: It really seems that what my life is about and what my work is about are one and the same. I consider myself lucky in that regard. It's also kind of hard because some of the issues are kind of overwhelming, so it's difficult to not bring that into your personal life all the time.

ME: Can you talk more about that? What are the challenges of your work?

SEVERN: Well, one of the challenges that I'd say is true, not only for environmentalists, but also for activists, is becoming so absorbed in the problems that you forget to enjoy your life. Burnout is a really big

 then to now

problem in activist communities. I was just talking to my parents this weekend, and I was going on about how there is such heavy ecological pressure on our ecosystems right now and it's pretty hard to look up from that, and my mom reminded me that life is pretty good. There are always going to be problems . . . it's part of the human condition, part of being alive on Planet Earth. To forget about the positive is really part of the problem. So we've really got to work on personal sustainability as well.

what it takes

▸ A willingness to make changes in your own life

▸ Dedication and commitment to your cause

▸ A willingness to fight "uphill battles"

ME: When do you feel like you're having the biggest impact in your work?

SEVERN: It's really hard to measure when you're dealing with raising awareness or conveying ideas. But at the same time, whenever I reevaluate things and consider whether I'm making a difference, I come back to the realization that planting seeds in people's minds about possibility for change is a really important starting point, especially in the industrialized world, because our actions have incredible impact around the world.

And so starting with conversations and opening up new avenues of thought and realizing the impact of our actions is really important, but it's really hard to measure. Sometimes when I'm giving speeches I think, *Oh man, who am I to be giving a speech on what I think? I mean, this is just what I think.* So when I give talks, that's exactly what I say. I say this

2002: Graduated from Yale with a BS in biology

2002: Founded the Skyfish Project, an Internet-based think tank

2002: Took part in a twenty-one-city speaking tour across Japan

2003: Hosted documentary *A View from the Summet* for broadcast on Canadian television

2004: Enrolled at University of Victoria, B.C., for master's degree

is what *I* think, and then I ask the audience to think for themselves, and that's pretty much my main message. Think! Think about your actions.

Afterward young women will often come up to me, and they'll have a bunch of questions or they want to talk about what they're interested in or they'll thank me for being there. And that's why I'm justified in being up there. Because we should be speaking out. So it's pretty rewarding to get that feedback.

ME: I think that being able to speak out and inspire others is a real gift.

SEVERN: Yes, but we *all* have voices.

ME: Last question—have you ever thought about doing anything else?

SEVERN: I plan on doing *everything* else!

 SEVERN'S ADVICE

More than ever right now we need female voices, so don't be afraid to speak out. I think that one of the most important roles that youth can play is to raise all hell about what is happening to our future. I mean, what's happening today and the decisions that are going down and the lifestyles we are now living is really degrading the quality of life that we're going to have. We have everything to lose, so we have to bring attention to this. Who else is going to?

in the field
Five More Careers Working to Save the Environment

ecologist Ecologists study the relationship between people and other living organisms and the environment in which they live. Many work in academic settings, where they teach and do research, while others might work for government agencies or for-profit companies to ensure new products are environmentally friendly.

environmental educator If you're passionate about the environment and aren't afraid of speaking out, you might consider being an environmental educator. These educators usually work for government or nonprofit organizations, and they educate the public about environmental issues through lectures, hikes, and tours.

outreach director Environmental outreach directors usually work for nonprofits focused on environmental issues, and they develop campaigns to get public attention, form alliances with like-minded organizations, figure out ways to identify volunteers, and hold community events in support of the organization's cause.

environmental field specialist When a company's work potentially impacts the natural resources of the environment, environmental field specialists go out in the field to collect water and soil samples to research how the operation of the company is affecting the environment and then write up reports based on their findings.

fuel economy researcher As the price of gas continues to skyrocket, fuel economy researchers are becoming more important. They develop ways for people to rely less on traditional fuel, whether by creating alternative power sources such as biodiesel or by developing more efficient modes of transportation.

 you need to know about

The National Resources Defense Council (www.nrdc.org) is a nonprofit environmental action organization with more than a million members. On the website you'll find out about important environmental issues throughout the world and get involved as an online activist.

Anke Langenbach

veterinarian

the facts

*Anke Langenbach,
Veterinary Surgeon*

▶ **what?** Veterinarians are medical doctors who specialize in the care of animals, from Fido and Fluffy to livestock and even zoo animals. Vets do everything from tending to injured or sick animals and administering vaccinations to performing surgeries.

▶ **where?** Many work for small animal hospitals, where they deal primarily with people's pets, while a smaller percentage work in laboratories, zoos, or in their own private practice.

▶ **how?** Veterinarians must attend an accredited four-year veterinarian medical school program following undergrad and pass a number of exams. Most states also require a veterinarian to be licensed to practice.

▶ **$$$:** An average annual salary of $65,000 a year

▶ **dress code?** Lab coat or surgical scrubs

▶ **stress factor:** On a scale of 1 to 10, can range from a 3 to a 10

as a serious animal lover, there's always been a part of me that has dreamed of being a veterinarian. Veterinary surgeon Anke Langenbach said that she hears that a lot. For whatever reason, being a veterinarian seems like such a cool job to many teens, but a lot of people shy away from the career when it comes down to actually making the choice to pursue it. Perhaps it's because vet schools are so competitive? Perhaps it's because people are intimidated by the amount of schooling?

None of those reasons deterred Anke, who knew she wanted to be a veterinarian from a very young age. I recently had a chance to catch up with Anke to talk with her about her work.

> *"It feels so good to know that I put a new hip in and now this dog is going to be able to jump in the car or run again."*

ME: When did you know you wanted to be a veterinarian?

ANKE: When I was ten years old.

ME: Was there any one thing that sparked that interest?

ANKE: I always dragged home everything that was broken and needed help—earthworms, the neighbor's cats, frogs. I used to take frog eggs out of a dirty pond by this industrial area behind our house, and I raised them in the yard. My dad could never cut the grass— there were little frogs everywhere. I guess you could say I never thought about doing anything else.

ME: I think that's great. And now that it's what you're doing, is veterinary work what you expected it would be?

ANKE: No. When I went into veterinary medicine, it was certainly because I had a love for animals and a love for science, but I worked mainly with veterinarians who did this old English-type work, getting called out to the farm to help with a calf or something . . . large animal work. Then, as I went through veterinary school, I realized that's not really what I wanted to do.

you asked . . .

"How did you accomplish all of the work that you've done over the years?" Anastasia, age 13

anke answered . . .

"One task at a time, with lots of long hours and lots of coffee."

ME: So what kind of veterinary medicine did you end up going into?

ANKE: I'm what's called a veterinary surgeon. I went through veterinary school, and after that I did another four years of training to specialize in small animal surgery. So what I do is fix things that your general veterinarian doesn't fix, such as broken bones, torn ligaments, back surgery, hip replacements, and things like that. I work only on a referral basis. So people with animals can't just call me and say they need to see me—they have to go to their veterinarian, who would refer them to me.

ME: What kind of animals do you do surgery on?

ANKE: Mainly dogs and cats, but I also work with the local wildlife group and help them with birds and other wildlife animals such as raccoons and squirrels and bats, some owls. Tomorrow I'll do surgery on a little bunny. I do that for free on the side.

ME: Where do you actually work?

ANKE: I work within a big animal hospital in Virginia. It has an emergency clinic with about ten emergency doctors and lots and lots of technicians, a cardiology group, an internal medicine group, and a

the breakdown

ON THE PHONE: 2 hours a day

SITTING: 3 hours a day

STANDING: 8–12 hours a day

READING: 1 hour a day

HANDLING APPOINTMENTS: 3 hours a day

DOING SURGERY: 4 hours a day

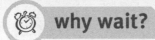

why wait?

▸ Volunteer at a local shelter or wildlife care center or get a job working at a kennel or in a veterinary clinic.

▸ Run a dog-walking or pet-sitting business and make money while you get experience working with animals.

▸ Take advanced biology classes in high school.

surgery group. I own the surgery practice, and I have two other surgeons that work for me.

ME: Well, I'm very impressed!

ANKE: *(laughs)* It's fun. . . . I enjoy what I do.

ME: How long does a typical surgery on an animal take?

ANKE: It depends on the case, but most take an hour or an hour and a half. There are some complicated procedures that could take a lot longer, though.

ME: Is there any one surgery that was really challenging or memorable that sticks out in your mind?

ANKE: There are lots of challenging cases. I had a case where a dog had been hit by a car and had broken its neck so badly that it couldn't breathe anymore and it had to be on a ventilator. So we fixed the neck, put in pins and rods and so forth, and then he was paralyzed for about half a year and now he's walking again, doing just fine. And that little terrier hates me *(laughs)*. He hates me so much, he chases me every time he sees me. But he's doing great.

ME: That's amazing.

ANKE: There are lots of cases like that, we see a lot of fun stuff, a lot of interesting, weird stuff.

Usually I get into work at around seven thirty a.m. after I drop my older boy off at the bus stop for school. The first thing I do when I get in is check on the cases that had surgery maybe the day before. Then the other surgeons and I get together with the technicians and the overnight people. I have appointments until about lunchtime, and I have a technician or two that help me restrain animals, take temperatures, take x-rays, and stuff like that.

In the afternoon we do surgeries. We have real operating rooms with real tables and anesthesia monitoring, just like for people. It's the same thing . . . it just looks a little different because everything is a little smaller. The surgery we do is mainly for cases we saw that morning. Usually I get home anywhere from six thirty to nine p.m., when all the work is done. I usually do some work at home on the computer at night, depending on what happened that day.

That's what my day looks like four days a week. On Wednesdays I'm home, and the other surgeons and I share weekend "on-call" duty with other vets at the hospital, because there always has to be somebody on call at night or on the weekends.

ME: It seems that there would have to be a sad side of your job too. How do you cope with that?

ANKE: It's hard. I think you get tougher as you get older because you have to start to separate yourself. We had a dog that passed away last night unexpectedly. He was very, very sick, but we thought he had pulled through, and then his condition took a turn for the worse. I spoke with the clinic at three in the morning and everything was fine, so I went back to bed. And this morning, he had passed away. So it's very sad . . . it's very tough. I think if you lose the ability to be sad about it,

then to now

1992: Graduated from Ludwig-Maximilians University, College of Veterinary Medicine, Germany

1994–1997: Residency in small animal surgery, University of Pennsylvania veterinary teaching hospital

1997–1998: Lectured at the University of Pennsylvania teaching hospital

then you're not right for the job anymore, because it gives you that extra edge to fight really hard. Of course, there are situations where you just can't help the animal. Sometimes an animal has cancer, and they're going to die, no matter what you do. It's tough. I always used to take everything home with me, and I still do, but I can deal with it a little bit better now than I used to. Thankfully in surgery, our situations are always very, very controlled and it's rare that we lose an animal.

ME: Let's talk about the best parts of your job. What do you love about what you do?

ANKE: Helping animals and helping the people that own the animals. It makes my day. I can never say no. My husband hates it—even in the middle of the night when they call and have something they need. I don't mind, I just go and do it. It feels so good to know that I put a new hip in and now this dog is going to be able to jump in the car or run again, or we'll do a sur-

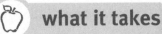

what it takes

▸ A strong background in biology, chemistry, and other sciences

▸ A love of animals

▸ Good grades in college—veterinary schools are competitive to get into

gery where the dog was three-legged lame, and now the dog can run and play Frisbee again. It's very rewarding, it really is. And most animals even seem to be thankful, which is weird.

ME: Besides the sadness involved in losing animals, are there any other challenges?

1998: Certified by the American College of Veterinary Surgeons

1998–2001: Associate surgeon at veterinary surgical referral practice, northern Virginia

2001–2004: Co-owned private small animal surgical referral practice, Washington, DC

2004: Founded own private practice in Virginia

ANKE: I sometimes think that veterinarians don't get as much credit as regular physicians do, even though we went through the same training. We often put more work in, but we don't get paid nearly as much as they do. The work we do is a lot like what a pediatrician does, because like them, our patients don't talk. We have to be able to know what the problem is through other means. And the fact that there isn't always health insurance for pet owners makes it hard because you're always seen as a businessperson, so you often feel bad charging for what you do.

ME: Is what we see on Animal Planet what it's really like?

ANKE: I think Animal Planet paints a very realistic picture of veterinary medicine, at least the hard-core work in the ER. But there are lots of people who work as veterinarians in other fields like research, in administrative forms, at universities, or in the private sector.

INTERESTED IN BEING A VET? HERE'S ANKE'S ADVICE

Don't give up. It's very hard work and it's very hard to get into vet school. So persist, and work really hard to get good grades. It's a very rewarding, wonderful career, so just go forward and try it out.

in the field

Five More Careers Working with Animals

animal trainer Animal trainers not only teach dogs to sit, stay, and come, but some train wild animals, from grizzly bears to elephants. Anytime you see a movie or TV show with a wild animal onscreen, you can be sure that an animal trainer is just outside the shot, coaching the animal's "performance."

animal conservationist Some of the most interesting animals on the planet—rhinoceroses, gorillas, tigers—are endangered. Conservationists work in zoos, research facilities, on nature preserves, and in nature to find ways to protect these species and bring attention to their plight.

zookeeper If you want to get up close and personal with cool, exotic animals and don't mind spending a lot of time on your feet, then check out this career. Zookeepers meet the zoo animals' nutritional and physical needs, as well as get to know the animals so they can monitor their behavior and emotional state.

pet therapist Everyone knows that cats and dogs are like therapy in the form of a furry companion. But what about when the pets themselves need a little couch time? Pet therapists deal with behavioral issues affecting pets, like separation anxiety, by using their background in animal behavior or psychology.

service dog trainer Have you ever seen a young dog wearing a harness and a vest that says "Dog in Training"? This dog was learning to be a service dog to work with blind or other disabled people. Service dog trainers get the dogs ready to start their new "jobs," as well as show the new owners how to work with their canine companions.

 you need to know about

The Association for Women Veterinarians (www.vet.ksu.edu/AWV/index.htm) is a national organization dedicated to supporting women veterinarians and encouraging more women to enter the field. Here you'll find resources, info on the history of women in veterinary medicine, and a list of must-reads for girls interested in being a vet.

For more careers in medicine, check out the physical therapist profile on page 372 and the nurse-midwife profile on page 251.

lunch break

how to research your dream job

with the internet at our fingertips, we can all become experts in just about anything. I truly believe that when it comes to career exploration and job hunting, the more information you can get your hands on, the better. Here are some of my research tips:

▸ Read the trade magazines for your industry. Trades are magazines geared at professionals, and just about every industry has one. For example, I used to work in children's television, so I read *Broadcasting & Cable* and *Electronic Media* every week, just to stay up-to-date on any news in the television industry.

▸ Google people you're going to be meeting with or want to approach about an informational interview. The more you can find out about that person, on both a personal and professional level, the better. When I worked at Cartoon Network and took meetings with animators, I'd always be impressed if someone came in and knew a little bit about me—it showed me that they'd done their homework!

▸ If there's a company or organization you're interested in learning more about, visit their website. You can usually read their mission statement, read recent press releases to learn about the kinds of work they're doing, read bios for top employees, and maybe even find out how to apply for a job.

▸ Do your own market research! If you're interested in pursuing a certain career, or maybe even starting your own company someday, do your own e-mail survey. With a push of the send button, you can be on your way to getting valuable feedback from people about your ideas or goals.

▸ Read anything and everything you can get your hands on that concerns your interests, from articles to autobiographies.

Holly McPeak

professional athlete

the facts

▶ **what?** A professional athlete is anyone who gets paid to compete in athletic and sporting events. In the United States, women are professional athletes in sports like soccer, golf, basketball, tennis, and of course, beach volleyball.

▶ **where?** They can live just about anywhere, although sometimes it's determined by their sport. During their season, WNBA players live in the city where their team is based, and many play in Europe off-season to make a living. Professional beach volleyball players like Holly have to live on the beach (sounds tough, huh?).

Holly McPeak, Professional Beach Volleyball Player

▶ **how?** There are no educational requirements to be a professional athlete, but they must have great natural athletic ability, passion for their sport, and a willingness to work hard.

▶ **$$$:** It depends on the sport. WNBA players earn an average of $55,000 to $80,000 a year, while a tennis pro can earn well over $100,000 in one match. Many professional athletes supplement their income by doing commercials and promoting their sponsor's products.

▶ **dress code?** Athletic gear. Holly's work outfit is a bikini!

▶ **stress factor:** On a scale of 1 to 10, a 2 when training and a 6 when competing

i had the chance to interview Olympic beach volleyball player Holly McPeak in Hermosa Beach, California, where she lives and "works," staying fit and training to be the best beach volleyball player she can be. We grabbed a drink at Coffee Bean on a sunny California day. Here are some highlights of our conversation.

ME: What were your career dreams as a teen girl?

HOLLY: Growing up, I knew that it was important that I do well in school, because I really wanted to earn a volleyball scholarship.

"I love the fact that you get out of it what you put into it, because no one's going to train harder than me."

Volleyball was my passion, and I knew it was also my vehicle to get into a good school and get a good education. I was able to get a scholarship, and I started at the University of California at Berkeley and graduated from UCLA. I got a good education, and my volleyball paid for it. My original plan when I started college was to be an attorney. I didn't think sports would actually become my career.

ME: So when did you realize, "Hey, wait a minute . . . I can actually earn a living by playing volleyball"?

you asked . . .

"Were the sacrifices you made for your career worth it for the success you've achieved?" Fallon, age 18

holly answered . . .

"That's funny, because I don't necessarily feel that I made any sacrifices. I worked my butt off, but I know that that's what it takes to succeed. Yes, I have to travel. Yes, I miss people's birthdays and things like that, but it's all part of the process of doing what I want to do to achieve my goals. So I don't feel like I made any sacrifices—I've just worked hard and stayed focused and followed my dreams."

7:00–8:30 a.m.: *Wake up, make breakfast for my husband, and take the kids to school.*

8:30–10:00 a.m.: *Work out at the gym.*

10:00–10:30 a.m.: *Grab a snack!*

10:30–1:00 p.m.: *Volleyball training, comprised of hard drills and repetitive training on the beach with usually three other people or a coach and my partner.*

1:30–4:00 p.m.: *Shower and do other errands, like grocery shopping, picking the kids up from school, dentist appointments . . . whatever I need to do in the afternoon. I use these couple of hours to do my "normal person" stuff—pay bills, clean the house, do laundry, that kind of thing.*

4:00–5:00 p.m.: *Slip in another hour of cardio workout.*

5:30 p.m.: *Shower and make dinner, or get ready to go out . . . whatever is going on that night.*

9:30 p.m.: *I'm physically and mentally exhausted and I'm ready to go to bed.*

HOLLY: I think it was my senior year at UCLA. I had just finished playing as a collegiate player, and I started to train on the beach. I had played beach volleyball my whole life, but never professionally. And I just fell in love with it. I love the fact that you get out of it what you put into it, because no one's going to train harder than me. I studied the game, and as soon as I started playing, I was hooked, and it just took over my life. I loved it. It was something that challenged me in every aspect—physically and mentally.

ME: How sweet is it that what you do for your job is so good for your life?

HOLLY: Yeah, I basically get paid to go to the gym and work out. I mean, I don't get paid specifically to do that, but it's a very important part of my job. I'm one of the shorter players out on the tour. I have to be fit, I have to be strong, and I have to make up for those short-comings in other areas. So staying healthy is very important for me.

ME: So do you have a volleyball "season" or are you training year-round?

HOLLY: Basically April through November we travel internationally or all over the United States almost every weekend. After the first or second weekend in May, I don't think we have a week off until November. It's a full schedule, and it keeps us busy. One of the things that I really appreciate is being home.

ME: How do you deal with traveling so much and still being on top of your game?

HOLLY: It comes with the territory. It's taking care of yourself while traveling, hydrating, eating well, and getting a good night's sleep. Those are all really important to me. I know I've done the work to train and I'm in shape. I just have to make sure I take care of myself while I'm traveling.

ME: Can you tell me what some of your biggest challenges are?

HOLLY: I think there's obviously pressure to compete. I have to do well to make a living. If I don't do well, I don't win any money and I don't pay the bills. But at the same time, one of the lessons I learned early on is that I can't think about the money while I'm playing the sport that I love . . . I just can't. I remember in my first season, I was

 then to now

1987:	1987:	1991:	1991:	1993: First	1996: Came
Played first	Voted NCAA	Graduated	Named	tournament	in fifth at the
professional	Freshman of	from UCLA	Rookie of the	win at the	Atlanta
beach	the Year		Year by the	AVP Phoenix	Summer
volleyball	at UC		Women's	Open	Olympics
tournament	Berkeley		Professional		with partner
and finished			Volleyball		Nancy Reno
in ninth place			Association		

playing a game that was for about a thousand dollars, and I was a starving student—a thousand dollars was a lot of money. And I focused on the money and my volleyball went out the window. So that was something I learned early on. I think it's a lot of pressure when you know you have to do well to make a living.

ME: So do you have some way of centering yourself to deal with that pressure?

HOLLY: I know I've prepared the best I can. The rest is mental. It really comes down to being mentally prepared and working together with your partner. I focus on what I've trained myself to do and just allow myself to play the best volleyball I can play.

ME: It seems like there would be a lot of perks to being a professional volleyball player.

HOLLY: Yeah, there are. We get to play in front of a huge crowd of people, and it's a very fun sport. We get to travel all over the world. And then there's competing in the Olympic Games—I don't think anything

2000: Came in fifth at the Sydney Summer Olympics with partner Misty May

2004: Won the Bronze Medal at the Athens Summer Olympics with partner Elaine Youngs

2004: Awarded Outstanding Achievement Award from the AVP

2004: Set the all-time win record for women's professional beach volleyball tournaments (72 wins!)

2005: First woman to break the $1 million mark in beach volleyball earnings

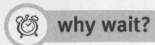

▶ If you're passionate about a sport, look into athletic scholarships at colleges.

▶ Coach a youth team in a sport you love.

▶ Get fit, eat well, and take care of your body!

can compare. And I've been able to do it three times. I've also been able to travel around the world various times and see lots of countries. I've been exposed to all parts of the world, all different cultures, and that's been great. And you get to meet a lot of amazing people.

ME: Is there any specific highlight you want to tell us about?

HOLLY: Getting on the medal stand at the 2004 Olympic Games was amazing for me. I've won seventy-two tournaments in my career, and all of those are superspecial, but to me, being on the Olympic medal stand was number one.

ME: What was it like?

HOLLY: It's a blur. It's something that I dreamed about as an athlete growing up. It was beyond. It was so special because I was up there with, in my opinion, five of the best volleyball players in the world. Two Americans who I really love, my partner who I love, and my two best Brazilian friends in the world. That was the podium. I couldn't have thought of a better podium. Except for us on top. That would have made it better. But otherwise it was a dream come true.

ME: What will you do when you're not able to continue playing volleyball competitively anymore? What's the next step?

HOLLY: There are a couple different directions I can take with my career. I can work for some of my sponsors in player relations. And I've been in the sport so long that I have TV opportunities to be a commentator. I'd really like to do that, because I'm a credible name and I'm explaining this sport to people who don't know it. I'd also like to help by working either within the AVP or in some grassroots programs trying to grow the sport and reach out to people who wouldn't normally be exposed to it.

ME: Those sound like pretty great options. What are some of the pros and cons of being a professional volleyball player?

HOLLY: I think that one of the big pros of playing my sport for a living is that I get to stay healthy and fit. A lot of people who work very hard in a career are behind a desk all day working crazy hours, and fitness takes a backseat. But fitness is part of my job—it's part of what I do. On the con side, I'm out in the sun. Skin cancer's a major fear with all of us, and we have to really protect ourselves from the sun. Another challenge that's specific to our sport is the fact that we have to play in a bathing suit, and I think that freaks out 99 percent of the women. I mean, what woman wants to stand in front of ten thousand people in a bikini? That's something that I had to deal with at the beginning. And yeah, we're really fit athletes, but at the same time, we have to feel comfortable in our body. For me it's a machine. I don't think of it as a sexy thing. This is my machine. Some people think the sport takes advantage of us by making us wear bathing suits to give the sport sex appeal, but that's not the case. If I had a choice in what to wear to compete, it would be a bathing suit, because it's the most comfortable, you can move the best in it, and it collects the least amount of sand. But I think it's also been a big lesson for me in feeling comfortable in my body.

what it takes

▸ A lot of drive

▸ A willingness to work harder than anyone else

▸ Natural athletic ability

HOLLY'S ADVICE

▶ *Don't let anybody set limitations on what you can do. When I first started playing, nobody thought I could do anything on the professional level because I was small and I hadn't made a big name for myself in indoor volleyball. But I believed in myself, I studied the sport, I watched, I trained as hard as I possibly could, and I followed my dreams.*

▶ *The opportunity to play a professional sport and get paid for it is one that everybody would like to have, so treat it special, respect it, always appreciate your fans, and always appreciate your sponsors who support you and allow you the opportunity to play a sport you love and make a living doing it.*

in the field

Five More Careers that Involve Sports

sports agent Just as actors and writers have agents, so do professional athletes. Sports agents work to get the best deals for their clients, whether it be multiyear contracts or hooking them up with sponsors like Nike. They have to be great negotiators and be willing to work long hours, especially when their client's sport is in season.

sports announcer Until recently, sports announcing had been seriously male-dominated, but today you'll find women sitting behind the anchor desk, reporting live from the sidelines or commentating with a play-by-play. They have to become a sports specialist, tap into their journalism skills, and get comfortable being on the air.

exercise physiologist Exercise physiologists specialize in knowing how exercise impacts the way the body functions. Some work in hospitals or rehabilitation centers to promote better fitness and health; others specialize in sports, and work with athletes to help them achieve the best performances they can.

coach Coaches are experts in their sports, and they coach athletes and athletic teams. At the school or community level, coaches might be volunteers, while others are former athletes who want to stay involved in their sport and find full-time opportunities at high schools or universities.

referee Referees enforce the rules, make calls, and assign penalties on questionable plays at sporting events. Women are popping up more and more as referees for women's team sports like basketball, soccer, and volleyball.

 you need to know about

The Women's Sports Foundation (www.womenssportsfoundation.org) is a national nonprofit promoting girls and women participating in sports. The website features profiles of top women athletes, information about sports scholarships and grants, and tons more.

For more fitness-related careers, check out the yoga instructor profile on page 323.

Joyce Roché

nonprofit director

the facts

Joyce Roché, President and CEO, Girls Inc.

▶ **what?** Nonprofit directors or presidents are the top-level execs at not-for-profit organizations, whose primary objective is to promote an issue or cause as opposed to making money.

▶ **where?** Nonprofits can be found everywhere.

▶ **how?** Many nonprofit presidents, like Joyce Roché, previously held high-level positions in the business world and decided to apply their skills to the world of nonprofit. Others work their way up or move from nonprofit to nonprofit until they reach the pinnacle, or create their own nonprofit organization.

▶ **$$$:** From $70,000 to $110,000 on average, depending on the size of the organization

▶ **dress code?** Depends on the nonprofit, but generally business or business casual

▶ **stress factor:** On a scale of 1 to 10, a 6

girls incorporated is a national nonprofit organization dedicated to empowering girls, and it offers programs for girls ages six to eighteen in more than a thousand sites across the country. Girls Inc. runs after-school, weekend, and summer programs, including Operation SMART, which aims to build girls' skills in science, math, and technology; and Project Bold, which "strengthens girls' abilities to lead safer lives."

Sitting behind the big desk in the president's office on Wall Street in New York is Joyce Roché, who joined Girls Inc. in 2000. As the president and CEO, Joyce is in charge of overseeing all aspects of keeping the organization thriving, and because she is so passionate about the work, it is a huge responsibility.

"There's very little separation for me between what I do in my job and how I feel in the rest of my life. It's almost like I've got a personal weight now to carry," Joyce says.

> "I think sometimes people think that the nonprofit world is not as challenging as the corporate world. Well, it's probably one of the most challenging jobs I've ever had."

That kind of commitment is what it takes to successfully run a large organization like Girls Inc. and continue to inspire the staff as well as funders. I asked Joyce to give us a sense of what she actually does on a day-to-day basis to accomplish these goals.

"I'm on the road a lot. I travel an enormous amount of time visiting local Girls Inc. affiliates around the country, speaking at events, meeting with foundations or corporations to try and raise funds. About sixty-five percent of my time is spent traveling, where I might be working from eight in the morning until twelve at night, because I could be doing a whole bunch of meetings and then a dinner. Sometimes it goes over into the weekend.

"If I'm not traveling, I probably get into the office about eight thirty in the morning, and I don't leave until seven thirty at night. When I'm here at the office, my work can run the spectrum. We're in

joyce answered . . .

"Absolutely. I think first, everybody has to define what success is for them, because it can be different. Then you've got to look at it and say, 'Hey, I've made it. This is what I call success.' I think where people get into trouble is when they look at somebody else and say, 'That's what successful looks like.' Even if you could mimic it, it may not feel good to you—it may not be the thing that makes you feel that you're getting the gratification of accomplishment, because it's just not yours."

the midst of planning a big luncheon that we're having here in New York, so I'm spending a lot of time on the phone with people that we've invited and answering questions about the event. Right after this interview I'm going to have a meeting with a consultant who's working on pension things, so that's kind of the operations part of the organization. We're also in the midst of creating a new strategic plan, so my COO and I will kick that off. On top of that, about half of our organization is located in Indianapolis and the other half is in New York, so I do a videoconference staff meeting every month. And as you can see, my work can vary quite dramatically in terms of what it is I'm doing on any given day," Joyce explains.

Joyce hasn't always worked in the nonprofit world. In fact, she spent about twenty-five years working in corporate America, where, among other things, she headed up marketing at Avon for nineteen years. But all the while, she was doing volunteer and pro bono work for

 then to now

Graduated from Dillard University, New Orleans, LA	Graduated from Columbia University, New York, with an MBA	1990: Named by *Black Enterprise* magazine as one of the "40 Most Powerful Black Executives" for the first time

nonprofits, and the idea of working for an organization that had a strong social responsibility element to it really appealed to her.

"I realized that I was having a lot of fun doing that kind of work, and that maybe this was the place I needed to be as opposed to looking for a corporation that had this as an element of who they were. So that was really my 'aha' moment. I decided that I might make a career change for the right organization, and I did. That's how I got here," says Joyce.

The switch seems to have paid off. Joyce says her job is extremely rewarding, although the work is not without its challenges. Here's how she describes the highs and lows of running Girls Inc.:

"I think sometimes people think that the nonprofit world is not as challenging as the corporate world. Well, it's probably one of the most challenging jobs I've ever had. This is running a big business. It just happens that the business we're in is the support and encouragement of girls. But we've got to raise money every day to make sure that we're doing that. We've also got to manage this building we work in, we've got to support the PhDs on staff who are researchers, support people in program development who train our local affiliates, and board members who come from all over corporate America. The kind of skill that's required to run an organization like this requires being

 ## why wait?

▸ Volunteer with a nonprofit in your community and see if you like the work atmosphere.

▸ Start your own organization, club, or group focusing on a cause that you're passionate about.

1997: Featured on the cover of *Fortune* magazine	VP of global marketing, Avon Products, Inc.	President and COO of Carson Products Company	2000: Joined Girls Inc. as president and CEO

the breakdown

IN MEETINGS: 5 hours a day

ON THE PHONE: 1 hour a day

ONLINE: 3 hours a day

READING: 2 hours a day

TRAVELING: A lot

able to manage a business as well as being a person who's passionate about the mission. So you really have a more difficult job because it's not singularly focused.

"The biggest challenges center around money. We know we've got a great organization and we know that the work we do has a positive impact on the lives of girls, but sometimes a foundation that has traditionally been a big funder will decide to fund something else instead. And now money that we were projecting for the next year suddenly doesn't exist. So that's tough—sometimes there just don't seem to be enough resources to do it all.

"On the other side, I love the satisfaction of knowing that everything I do every day is to keep the Girls Inc. organization vital and vibrant so that we can continue to do great things for girls in this coun-

what it takes

▸ Being passionate about a particular cause or issue

▸ Strong organizational and business skills

▸ Being a good networker and fund-raiser

try. And then I have the opportunity to see girls whose lives have been impacted by this organization, who are able to have the confidence to look at opportunities and say, 'I'm going to do this,' because they've got somebody saying, 'I believe that you can.' That's really wonderful," says Joyce.

JOYCE'S CAREER ADVICE

> ▶ Don't be afraid to go for it, whatever that "it" is that you think you want to do. And don't let others limit your decision to go for it either!

> ▶ Don't be afraid of making a change. Have the courage and the confidence to pursue your dream, but once you get into it, be flexible enough to say, "Hey, here's another opportunity." Most of us ultimately don't end up doing what we thought we were going to do when we set out. I'm a prime example.

in the field

Five More Careers Working at a Nonprofit Organization

grant writer The bulk of the income for nonprofits comes from grants made by foundations or corporations, but applying for and getting this money is a lot of work, including filling out tons of paperwork and extensive application forms. Grant writers specialize in applying for these grants and bringing in money for nonprofits.

communications manager How a nonprofit organization is perceived by the outside world directly relates to how willing people are to open their wallets to make donations. Communications managers are the public face of nonprofits, and they write and produce all communications material for the press as well as the general public.

office administrator Office administrators keep everything in the office flowing smoothly. They coordinate staff events, help hire new employees and get them set up, manage the office space, and make sure office supplies are in stock. In a nonprofit, office administrators play a large role because staffing is generally lean.

planned giving officer Planned giving officers help individuals make a legal plan for donating part of their estate to an organization. For example, a wealthy woman who supports the Susan G. Komen Breast Cancer Foundation will work with a planned giving officer to make sure part of her estate goes to the foundation after her death.

program officer Nonprofit organizations generally have a mission, like helping underprivileged kids, or in the case of Girls Inc., "inspiring all girls to be strong, smart, and bold." Program officers run the programs that the nonprofit offers, such as organizing cool activities at an after-school program for underprivileged kids.

 you need to know about

The *Chronicle of Philanthropy* is the newspaper for nonprofits. It offers information on the nonprofit sector through articles and online resources, including a job board, info about conferences and events, and updates on issues affecting nonprofit organizations. Visit the paper online at www.philanthropy.com.

For more careers as an executive, check out the business executive profile on page 348.

 # June Ambrose

stylist

▶ **what?** Fashion stylists get paid to make other people look great. They work with clients to help them create "looks" for themselves, whether it is a musician doing a music video or a celeb who'll be walking the red carpet. Other fashion stylists might work on fashion shoots for department stores or ad agencies.

▶ **where?** Stylists can live and work anywhere, but high-profile stylists to the stars like June have to live where the action is—L.A. or New York.

June Ambrose, Founder & President, Mode Squad

▶ **how?** Most stylists have a background in fashion and design, but it's not necessary to break into the field. What is necessary is tenacity, being extremely personable, and having an amazing sense of fashion and great networking skills.

▶ **$$$:** This is a make-it-or-break-it industry, and stylists can earn as little as $5,000 or as much as $500,000 a year or more.

▶ **dress code?** Cool, hip, and fashionable

▶ **stress factor:** On a scale of 1 to 10, an 8

if this book had been written twenty years ago, there wouldn't be a profile of a stylist because the career hadn't even been invented yet. You could say that June Ambrose is somewhat of a pioneer in the world of styling, which is a career built around helping celebrities, musicians, and other high-profile clients create their image. June was at the forefront of the field, marrying the worlds of music and style together in the early 1990s, when Sean "Puffy" Combs (now known as Diddy) was first getting his start.

Though she landed an amazing job in the world of investment banking fresh out of high school, June was miserable in the corporate environment and wanted to work in a more creative field. So she quit the firm and took an internship at Uptown/MCA Records, a hip urban record label that was giving birth to all kinds of new musical talent, including Mary J. Blige. As June describes it, it was the kind of environment where if you were in the right place at the right time, you were going to get big opportunities. And she did. June tells how she broke into the world of styling.

"Who you are as a person will separate you and individualize you in this industry that's so oversaturated."

"One day a manager for an artist walked into Uptown and said he was looking for a stylist. At the time, the fashion industry hadn't yet realized that music was a great platform to market and brand their clothing, so there weren't people "styling" musicians . . . artists kind of dressed themselves. Anyway, he said he needed a stylist, and I thought to myself, 'Oh, what's a *stylist?*' This manager knew that I was really fresh and young and he asked me if I had a 'book.' And I said, 'Of course I do, but it's at home, you know, I wasn't expecting to meet anyone today.' I was totally bluffing. It was a Friday, and he said he wanted to see my portfolio on Monday.

"I went home and called my friends and put clothes together, took pictures of my friends that I developed at a one-hour photolab, and put them in a photo album. When I showed it to the manager that

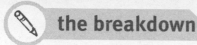

the breakdown

IN MEETINGS: 2 hours a day

STANDING: More than sitting

ON THE PHONE: All the time

READING: 2 hours a day

ONLINE: All the time (on BlackBerry)

WORKING SOLO: Half the time

Monday, he knew that I had thrown it together over the weekend, but he was impressed by the fact that I was so superenthusiastic about it, and he said, 'I'll give you a try.'

"I went to the shoot for the artist, and the publicist had said they wanted three different looks, so I showed up with three outfits. And he said to me, 'Is this a joke? You can't just come here with three options.' And I was like, 'How am I supposed to have options?' And he said, 'Well, girlie, figure it out. You got the job, now figure it out.'

"And I did. I found out about fashion showrooms, researched the market, started looking at movies differently, got every costume designer's books, read books on fabric and design and the technical trade, and I just soaked in everything there was to know about fashion and style," she explains.

you asked . . .

"What mistakes did you make along the way and how did you fix them?" Asia, age 14

june answered . . .

"Not managing my money when I first started out was one of my biggest mistakes. When I was younger, my credit got so bad that they shut me down and I couldn't even access my account. I was a wreck. But I learned enough to get a business manager who planned my life out for me, who set up my retirement funds, who made sure that every investment I made was solid, so if I broke my leg one day and couldn't do what I did, I had a way to sustain and survive. Another mistake I've made in the past is being afraid of rejection. . . . I think being afraid has held me back in some situations. But it's like being afraid to swim—you just have to jump into the water that first time."

Today June has her own styling company and management agency, the Mode Squad, which she started in 1994.

"I knew if I was going to excite my clients, I had to look the part and I had to reinvent myself and glamorize the work I was doing. At the time, it was this kind of grungy-schleppy job, picking up clothes and dragging them across the street, tons of hanger marks on the hands, cuts, scrapes, sleepless nights, no office, finding places to do fittings with the clients . . . it was tough. So I decided that I was going to start my own business and get my own office," says June.

The gamble has definitely paid off. Since starting her company, June has styled a ton of music videos for big-name talent like Missy Elliott, Ashanti, Ruben Studdard, Busta Rhymes, Diddy, and Macy Gray. She's also styled album covers, designed outfits for television appearances for celebs like Kim Cattrall and Kelly Ripa, and styled a slew of high-profile commercials, including Missy Elliott and Madonna's Gap commercial that got so much attention a few years back.

And while there are now more stylists working in the industry, including some former employees whom she trained along the way, June has worked hard to build herself as a "brand," referring to herself as an "architect of style." As she says, "Who you are as a person

then to now

Got a job at an investment banking firm fresh out of high school	1990: Landed an internship at Uptown/MCA Records in New York	Styled her first video for artist MC Quashan	1996: Styled Backstreet Boys European tour

will separate you and individualize you in this industry that's so oversaturated. For me, it was about branding. I thought about the branding of June Ambrose from a very early time in my career."

I asked June to walk me through the process of how she works, from the moment a new client picks up the phone to hire her through the styling for an event. Here's how June describes her job:

 WHAT JUNE DOES AS A STYLIST

When a new client calls me, whether it's a celebrity client or a corporate client, they'll usually ask to see a reel or portfolio of my work. My reel is divided into categories, like commercial work, advertising work, music video stuff, and so on. Some new clients want to see my reel, and some people don't ask to see my book at all—I'm known by reputation.

Let's say Gwyneth Paltrow is a client, and say she's four months pregnant and has a premiere to go to and needs a stylist. I'll get a call asking if I can send over a reel so Gwyn can approve it. So Gwyneth looks at it, she likes it, and then I go over and meet with her to do an interview profile. Because she's a new client, I need to know her likes, dislikes, colors, body silhouettes, complete measurements, what she doesn't like, what works for her body . . . the whole bit. If I'm styling for a TV event, my dynamic is a little different in terms of colors and patterns and textures. So I'll want to know more about the event—if it's a red carpet event, where she's going, what time of day it's taking place, what the weather will be like, and why she's going.

Then I'll have a fitting with her and we'll make "selects." We might nail down the accessories at the fitting or we might not. When I'm styling for an event, I like to have a day to fit and a day to troubleshoot before the event itself.

And that's it. When the event's over, I wrap my job up, get everything back to the showroom, figure out what was spent, tally up any other expenses, anything that was kept, and we reconcile the monies.

1999: Styled Diddy as cohost of the VH1/Vogue Fashion Awards

2003: Styled Gap commercial featuring Madonna and Missy Elliott

2004: Styled album cover for *American Idol* winner Ruben Studdard

Meetings with big celebs, high fashion, red carpet affairs . . . I asked June if she still got a thrill out of meeting celebs and being a part of that whole world. Her answer really surprised me.

"In terms of the whole celebrity thing, it's never been exciting to me to meet them. If you're going to be in this industry, you're not excited about that part of it, because my approach is that I'm an artist too, and these are my peers or this is my client. So for me to be enamored by, like, 'Oh, this is Michael Jackson,' just defeats the purpose. Because they're not looking for me to be that—that's what their fans are for. I'm the authority. So in order for me to be the authority and be respected, I go in with the attitude that I'm on the same level. When you're working with a client, they don't want to feel like they're working. They don't want to feel like they have to sign your T-shirt or the back of your hand. They want to feel like they're hanging out with one of their own and that you're getting a job done," says June.

what it takes

▶ A lot of moxie

▶ Strong networking skills

▶ A great sense of style

paying your dues

Many fashion stylists get internships or apprenticeships with established stylists, where they'll answer phones, schedule meetings, and run around getting wardrobes for shoots.

JUNE'S WORDS OF WISDOM

▶ *Think about your career like it's the Olympics. You have your gold medal, your silver, and your bronze. Are you going to be a gold medalist? Silver? Or a bronze? I want to be a gold medalist. And that's my fight.*

▶ *Do an internship that will ultimately lead you into the profession that you want to be doing. Figure out what area you want to go into and connect yourself with someone who can teach you the nature of that particular business.*

▶ *Humbly ask and you will humbly receive. If you wear your humility on your sleeve and approach people to ask for what you want, I guarantee you that the person will receive you.*

in the field

Five More Careers in the Fashion Industry

fashion designer Fashion designers start new trends and create the designs that ultimately end up on display everywhere from Saks to the Gap. They not only have to love fashion, but they must also know how to sew, understand textiles and fabrics, and have the skill to put garments together.

model Models are everywhere—on TV commercials, in the pages of magazines, on billboards, on the packaging of products. Some do magazine and print ads exclusively, while others do runway work. Since the work is freelance, it can be irregular and the hours long, sometimes in uncomfortable work environments.

handbag maker If accessories make the outfit, where would we be without handbag makers, who design everything from little cocktail clutches to beach bags? Handbag makers have a love of design, patterns, textiles, and sewing, and they sell their bags in their own boutiques or through larger stores like Nordstrom and Macy's.

fashion editor Fashion editors, or market editors, work at fashion magazines like *Cosmopolitan* and *Harper's Bazaar*, where they create the fashion spreads that we flip through each month. To stay in the loop, they attend fashion shows, sample sales, and designer parties.

fashion photographer There's more to photographing fashion spreads than snapping photos. Fashion photographers also handle all the logistics of a shoot—getting hair and makeup people on board, scouting locations, setting up lighting, and dealing with clients.

 you need to know about

The Fashion Institute of Technology, otherwise known as FIT, is the number one school for anyone interested in fashion design and styling. Check out their website for information about admissions and their program at www.fitnyc.edu. If you live in the New York City area, you can even enroll in summer classes at FIT as a middle school or high school student!

Kelly McCarthy

the facts

Kelly McCarthy, Video Game Programmer

▸ **what?** Behind every computer game is a staff of people who have written, designed, and programmed the games. Video game programmers write or "code" the computer language that makes games run on a computer.

▸ **where?** Programmers usually work for video game production companies, most of which are scattered throughout northern and southern California, although programmers and testers can work as freelancers anywhere in the country.

▸ **how?** Game programmers need a background in computer science and must be experts at programming the computer language of games, C++.

▸ **$$$:** An average of $62,500 for someone with a few years' experience to more than $200,000, depending on the level and the product

▸ **dress code?** T-shirt & jeans . . . supercasual

▸ **stress factor:** On a scale of 1 to 10, between a 2 and 3 when not on a deadline and a 9 and 10 during crunch times

i was really curious to take a peek at the life of a video game programmer from a woman's point of view and find out what goes on behind the scenes. I got in touch with Kelly McCarthy, who programs computer games in Los Angeles. To get a real sense of what her days are like, Kelly kept a diary for us. Here's what she wrote about:

 KELLY'S TYPICAL DAY

Today I got to work around ten a.m. and sat down in the office that I share with my lead programmer. Our studio has both cubicles and offices, with lots of windows that let in the sunshine. All around me is concept art for our game projects hanging around the public spaces for everyone to see. The atmosphere is relaxed and casual, and people dress in jeans and T-shirts and have toys and games in their offices.

"It does take a certain type of person to fit into this industry, but that type has nothing to do with being male or female."

The first thing I did at work this morning was start up my e-mail program and other computer programs that I use for my job, like Visual Studio. Then I read my e-mails, checked out a few new websites, and perused new messages on our developer message boards to see if there were any issues that concerned anything I might be working on.

you asked . . .

"What is the most difficult decision you've had to make to get where you are?" Elisa, age 13

kelly answered . . .

"The most difficult decision I had to make was at the end of my first year in college, when I still hadn't decided what I wanted to study. I had explored lots of other subjects when computer science came to mind. It sounded interesting to me, but I was afraid I would stand out and feel uncomfortable. I was really intimidated, but I gathered up my courage and attended a class one day, and found that it wasn't so bad and I really enjoyed it. Three years later I had a degree and a great job!"

Next I buckled down to work so I could get stuff done before lunch. Today I was debugging a program I was working on, which involves analyzing what our code is doing to figure out where it might be going wrong. When I'm debugging things, I can watch as the computer runs the game code, and stop it at any point to run it step by step to closely examine what's happening and change variables to make the game behave differently. Sometimes the problem I'm looking at is in code that I've written myself, but other times it's someone else's, which is even more challenging, because I have to try to understand what the other programmer was trying to do. Other mornings I might be helping to solve some technical issues that the designers and artists are running into or attending a project planning meeting with members of my team. Like most mornings, today there was a lot of running around between people's cubicles and offices, asking questions and viewing each other's work. Some people at work (including me!) even ride Razor scooters around the office to get from place to place quickly.

After lunch I headed back to the office, where I popped on my headphones and listened to some music. Electronic music is good for me to listen to when I'm in the zone—when I have a plan mapped out and I know everything I need to do. It helps me to just focus and do it. Sometimes

why wait?

▸ Start learning to program now! Start a blog or Web page and experiment coding with HTML.

▸ Play video games and take note of what goes into them from a design perspective.

▸ Try to get a position as a game tester—a lot of gaming companies hire teens for short-term testing gigs, and it's a good way to learn about the game industry environment and make contacts.

when I'm stressed out and under pressure, I'll listen to ambient music like Brian Eno or classical, which helps me calm down.

Today I needed to get down to some serious coding, which is basically writing the language of the game. Usually I come up with a plan for how my new code is going to work, and then I'll start building it, piece by piece, testing it along the way to make sure it's doing what I want. I'll end up running the game hundreds of times every week just to test it. Once I have the basics running, I'll let the designers try out what I have so far, and we'll refine the specification. We'll keep working until we get the right results.

I needed a caffeine break in the middle of the afternoon to give me a little push to get it done. I like to get up and stretch a few times during the day anyway and walk around to look out the window so my eyes can focus far away for a while. In general, though, I do okay sitting for most of the day. Our company gives us nice chairs that support us well, although a few years ago I did start having pain in my wrists from typing all the time. But that went away when I started using an ergonomic keyboard.

what it takes

▶ Attention to detail

▶ Stamina

▶ The ability to sit and stare at a computer screen for long periods of time

Not all of my time is spent working alone in a room writing code by myself, though. As part of my job, I'm really involved in the whole creative process of game developing. That means I get to work with artists, animators, and designers as we work toward one huge creative goal.

Today I worked until seven p.m., which is pretty typical. Sometimes I'm under deadlines that require me to stay later to wrap things up. I personally prefer to try to come in early when I have a lot to do instead of saving it until the late hours of the night. I play games at night sometimes—tonight I played Kingdom Hearts 2.

While creating fun games is really cool, the reality of our business is that we're building a product for our publisher. They shell out the millions of dollars it takes to make a game, and our company commits to making it for them. Since we're essentially spending their money, they

paying your dues

To start out, you'll have to land a job as an entry-level programmer, where you'll be working on small parts of the bigger game while you're learning the basics. Other entry-level positions include intern programmer, junior programmer, and game tester. Kelly, for example, interned during college at two different companies: Sunsoft of America and Black Ops Entertainment.

have a lot of control over what we do, and we have to meet our deadlines to deliver what they expect. And since each new game is expected to be bigger and better than the last, we are always having to find solutions to new problems. We need to meet our goals as a team, so if someone hits a roadblock, it becomes everyone's problem and we all band together to solve it. I find this very satisfying.

While it's true that women are still the minority in the game industry, it's not as bad as people think. It does take a certain type of person to fit into this industry, but that type has nothing to do with being male or female. It has more to do with possessing the knowledge, attitude, energy, and passion it takes to master the skills we use every day. It may be true that women have to prove themselves more than men do—you'll be under the spotlight and get lots of attention and people will be curious to see how you perform. As long as you can do your job, then you have nothing to worry about. The people I've worked with in the game industry are some of the most fun, interesting people I've ever met. We're smart, we're creative, and we're highly observant of the world around us. And most of us are still kids at heart.

KELLY'S ADVICE

You need to stay curious and keep actively learning every day. No book, school, or person will ever teach you everything you need to know. Ask questions, follow by example, and find your own solutions to problems.

in the field

Five More Careers in Computer Technology

computer support specialist Just about everyone who uses computers has technical problems at some point. Computer support specialists might work for companies like Apple or Dell and handle customer service issues, or act as in-house company support.

database administrator Most companies collect electronic data, such as customer and inventory information, and keeping this data organized, secure, and accessible to the right people is the job of database administrators. They set up and design the database, maintain it, and back up information as needed.

computer software engineer Every program on your computer, from your e-mail to your screensaver, was designed by a computer software engineer. They figure out what a new software needs to do, and then design, code, and test the program.

network specialist If you've ever "gone wireless" at Starbucks, then you've hooked into a computer network. Just about every company has a network powered by a main computer system and network specialists do everything from set-up to troubleshooting.

IT project manager If Internet technology (IT) firms were like movie studios, IT project managers would be the equivalent of producers. Project managers oversee the creation of IT systems for clients, managing the client relationship and handling the budget, schedule, staffing, quality control, and security.

you need to know about

Women in Games International was founded in 2005 to unite women around the world involved in the game industry. Sign up to receive their e-newsletter at www.womeningamesinternational.org and learn about their annual conference.

Cindy Guagenti

publicist

▶ **what?** A publicist creates and manages publicity for people like celebrities, musicians, or sports figures, or for events, like movie releases or concerts.

▶ **where?** Those who work with celebrities or for movie studios or TV networks are based in L.A. and New York. Some publicists work for big PR (public relations) agencies, while others might work in-house for a company or be self-employed, working exclusively with one or two big clients.

Cindy Guagenti,
Publicist, BWR
Public Relations

▶ **how?** There is no one set path to becoming a publicist, although many publicists major in public relations or communications in college. Most start out as assistants or in the mailroom at a big firm and work their way up.

▶ **$$$:** From $30,000 to $60,000 a year on up

▶ **dress code?** Business to business casual

▶ **stress factor:** On a scale of 1 to 10, between an 8 and a 9

if you're a fan of celebrity mags like Us Weekly, then you're already very familiar with Cindy Guagenti's world. Cindy is a big-time publicist in Hollywood, working for clients including Brat Pitt and Adam Sandler. If there's a rumor going around town about one of her clients, Cindy sets the press straight or provides a statement on her client's behalf. And there's so much more to what Cindy does, so let's get the scoop straight from the source.

ME: What does being a publicist mean?

CINDY: As a publicist, I create campaigns for my clients to publicize their projects, whether it be a TV show, a movie, or a record. That might involve things like setting up photo sessions, talking to magazines, conferring with the magazine on who the writers and photographers are, what the story is about, whether it's a "cover story," and so on. In a bigger-picture sense, we strategically plan out a client's long-term career, whether it's booking talk shows, handling personal appearances, travel, airline, hair, makeup, clothes . . . we're involved in all facets of creating and finessing our clients' public image.

"From the outside it seems like a lot of fun, but it's a lot of work and it's really high pressure because you have a lot of people to answer to."

ME: How did you get into publicity?

CINDY: I fell into it. I was one of those people who had no idea what I wanted to do. At the time, people I knew from high school were working in the mailroom of a record company, so after two years of junior college I applied and ended up working for the president and the VP of legal affairs who, on the side, was also advising John Lennon. I built a lot of relationships and moved around in different jobs learning different sides of the business, from PR and sales to product management and publicity. I ended up getting an offer at a large publicity firm as a publicist's assistant, and grew into junior

cindy answered . . .

"I worked hard, and sometimes it's hard to have relationships with people, with men, because you're traveling so much and you're out of town. And because you're working with high-profile celebrities, sometimes people don't think they're good enough, you know what I mean? It's never really said, but I think that's what they think. Lastly, I take my job seriously, but I also always try to have a sense of humor about everything."

publicity work. Eventually I ended up at the company I'm at now, and I've been here seventeen years.

ME: Wow . . . seventeen years. So you clearly love what you're doing.

CINDY: The glamour side of it really doesn't faze me anymore because I'm kind of used to it, but there are a lot of perks: parties, meeting people, free stuff by virtue of who you represent. But my greatest satisfaction is starting with someone new and growing with them and their career. For example, Adam Sandler has been a client since he was in his first *SNL* movie. When we started talking to Brad Pitt, he was on a TV show for FOX, before his break in *Thelma & Louise*. I did Benicio Del Toro's Oscar campaign for *Traffic*, which was cool because he'd never really done any press before. I launched Sarah Jessica Parker on *Sex and the City* back when not many people even had HBO. There are so many examples of stuff like that.

ME: It really does seem glamorous and exciting, especially the way publicists are portrayed in films and TV. Are we seeing the whole picture?

the breakdown

IN MEETINGS: 1 hour a day

ON THE PHONE: 6 hours a day

ONLINE: 5 hours a day

SITTING: Half the day

READING: 1 hour a day

CINDY: From the outside it seems like a lot of fun, but it's a lot of work and it's really high pressure because you have a lot of people to answer to. It's a lot of strategy and a lot of planning and you don't see that side on TV. Also, unlike managers and agents, where clients pay them on commission, with publicists, our clients pay us a monthly fee, so we're always on the line. It's a tough job, but it's a great job.

ME: What are some of the biggest challenges of your work?

CINDY: The hours. When you reach the level I'm at, you're on call twenty-four hours a day, especially with BlackBerries and cell phones. When I started in this business we didn't have those. Now we're reachable all the time. And in this work we have to do press things on the weekends and a lot of late nights—premieres, parties, a lot of events that you have to be at. And it's fun on some level, but it's not a party—it's work. People look at what we do and think it's cool that we get to go to the Oscars or this or that premiere. But what they don't realize is that when we're there, we're standing in a little area where they make the publicists stand. Sometimes we don't have shade or it's raining and we get yelled at by the police and the fire department to get back. On top of that, you have to stand on your feet all night running around—it's work.

ME: Besides being on hand at premieres and things, could you give us an idea about the tasks you might do? Is it a lot of phone work? Juggling a million things at once? Traveling?

CINDY: It's all of that. You're constantly on the phone talking to studios, TV networks, your clients, their managers, their agents, their lawyers, the press, the hair people, the agencies, the magazines, the photo editor. For one movie launch you might have to talk to many

 then to now

Attended two years of junior college	Got internship as assistant at PMK Public Relations, Los Angeles, CA	Worked at Andrea Jaffe, Inc., Los Angeles, CA

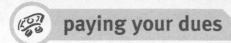

paying your dues

Most future publicists start off as assistants or even in the mailroom, and they move up by working hard and showing lots of drive. Entry-level publicists will do things like answer phones, update schedules, book meetings, and other assistant duties.

different people at the studio—one for travel, one for a press junket, one for a premiere, one to get you money for a stylist for a magazine shoot. It's a lot of phone work. It's almost like sales—you're really selling your client, especially if you're starting out with somebody new. But you're also finessing a campaign. When you're working with a major star, it's all about their image, like what magazine covers make sense for what the movie is and making sure it's the right photographer and writer and you're putting them on the right shows. For instance, if you have somebody in a comedy, you might not want them to do a very serious prime-time interview. So you have to really tailor each campaign to the client and the project.

ME: It sounds like there needs to be a lot of trust between you and your clients.

CINDY: I just love being with somebody for a long, long time because you end up knowing what they want to do, and you know what they did for the last movie, what talk show they did. You know, you become friends with them on a business level, too. You end up hanging out a lot.

ME: What's your travel like? Are you jet-setting around?

CINDY: I've tried to cut down, but I've traveled sometimes three weeks at a time on big international press tours. Right now it's closer to once a month. I always try to fly when I'm supposed to be sleeping, so I don't waste time. Some people do get private jets, but that's really high, high-profile people and that's mostly because they can't go through airports. Plus you can get in and out of anywhere really fast, especially if you're going city to city.

ME: Is there a lot of pressure in your job, knowing that in many ways you're responsible for a celebrity's public image?

CINDY: You're part of a team—there's the actor, there's the agent, and there's you. You're all working toward the same goals . . . you just have different roles. It's a very specialized job, and there's a real learning process. A lot of young girls start out and they just can't know what I know. That's why at a bigger company like ours, you'll usually start out as an assistant and you graduate to a junior publicist and then you're a publicist. By the time you're at that level, you've really learned the proper way to do the job.

what it takes

▸ Being very professional and trustworthy

▸ Handling very stressful situations with style

▸ Working around the clock

ME: So paying your dues is really important.

CINDY: I believe so. I'm sure there are lots of people who are on a fast track, but I really think you have to pay your dues.

ME: Publicity as a career must attract people who think they'll get to hang out with celebs all day.

why wait?

▸ Write a press release about an upcoming event at your school and try "pitching" it to a local newspaper to see if they'll write an article about it.

▸ Read the entertainment news and pay attention to how movie promotion campaigns work.

CINDY: Yeah, but you really can't be starstruck and do this job.

ME: Is there anything else you'd like to add?

CINDY: Publicity is a great job for somebody who has the right intentions and who's willing to put in the work. When I hire an assistant, she works long hours. My assistant gets there at nine and doesn't leave sometimes until seven thirty at night. She doesn't go to lunch. And she's done it for a while, too. You have to really, really, really want to do it. It's hard work, and the pay isn't great at the beginning at all, but if you really want to do it, then the rewards at the end of the day are great.

INTERESTED IN BEING A PUBLICIST? HERE'S CINDY'S ADVICE

▶ *Become a good writer—it's really important in this line of work.*

▶ *Get an internship at a PR firm—it gives you a great feel for the job.*

▶ *Get involved in the community that you want to work with as much as you can. If you want to work with actors, take a drama class so you can understand better what an actor goes through.*

---

in the field

Five More Careers in Public Relations, Marketing, and Communications

director of marketing Marketing encompasses advertising and public relations, and professionals are big-picture thinkers who try to figure out the best ways to "market" a company's products, brand, or ideas. Directors of marketing come up with strategies to expand their company's market and make the company more profitable.

corporate communications manager Corporate communications managers deal primarily with internal communications within a company, creating brochures, in-house websites, and other communications materials about the company's business and philosophy for employees, shareholders, or the public relations department.

public relations specialist Public relations specialists work within a corporation developing and implementing public relations plans for positioning a company to the media. They might write press releases, handle media queries, and fulfill requests for media materials from the public.

public affairs specialist Very similar to PR specialists, public affairs specialists work on behalf of government agencies and nongovernmental organizations, keeping the public informed about the activities of these organizations by holding press conferences, issuing press releases, and spearheading public affairs campaigns.

community relations manager If you've ever been to an author event at your local Barnes & Noble, it was probably organized by a community relations manager. They work for local organizations and businesses, managing how the public interacts with them and organizing community outreach efforts.

 you need to know about

The Public Relations Society of America (www.prsa.org) is the hub for public relations professionals in the United States, and the website has information about mentorships available to students. The PRSA recently launched the Communications Career Academy, which sets up programs in high schools to teach students about public relations work.

For more on careers in Hollywood, check out the talent agent profile on page 339, the actor profile on page 385, and the movie studio executive profile on page 60.

lunch break

paying your dues

many of the women I interviewed for this book mentioned how a lot of today's recent grads enter the workforce hoping, and sometimes expecting, to jump right into a big job, complete with high responsibility and a fat paycheck. They get the sense that many younger people today aren't as willing to "pay their dues."

Depending on the career you're looking to break into, paying your dues can be humbling, and yes, there can be all kinds of grunt work involved, like fetching coffee, typing up people's notes, standing over the photocopy machine for hours, and running personal errands. What makes it an even tougher pill to swallow is that many recent grads are entering the workforce more prepared than ever, because of internships and real-life work experience.

I know all about being impatient . . . it used to be my middle name. But as I've gone through my career and paid lots of dues along the way, I can look back and see that those early, less-than-glamorous job experiences went a long way in shaping me into the person I am now.

Here are some things to keep in mind when it comes to paying your dues:

▶ On-the-job experience can't be beaten when it comes to learning everyday "people skills," workplace etiquette, and the how-to's for handling office politics.

▶ People who are promoted too quickly run the risk of not having a strong enough foundation on which to build their career.

▶ Being eager to do your job and showing your bosses that no task is too menial for you will go a long way toward showing people you're a go-getter. Hard work and a great attitude don't go unnoticed, so be patient—it will pay off in the long run.

Heather Johnston

architect

the facts

Heather Johnston,
Principal, PLACE
Architects, PLLC

▶ **what?** Architects design and plan the structure for new or remodeled buildings—anything from tiny cottages to hundred-story skyscrapers. They identify their clients' needs, come up with designs, and oversee construction through completion.

▶ **where?** You'll find architects just about everywhere in the country, working for large architectural firms, boutique firms, or themselves.

▶ **how?** Architects must have a degree from a special five-year bachelor's program in architecture or a four-year degree coupled with a master's in architecture. After graduation, they must do a formal three-year paid internship at an architectural firm before taking the Architect Registration Examination (ARE) and becoming licensed.

▶ **$$$:** An average salary of $70,000

▶ **dress code?** Business casual at most companies, dressier at the bigger firms

▶ **stress factor:** On a scale of 1 to 10, a 6

to find out what goes on in the world of architecture, I interviewed Heather Johnston, founder and principal of nine-person Seattle architecture firm PLACE Architects. Heather gave me the inside scoop on her career, including busting one of the more prominent myths about architecture right away—that architects have to be great at math. Here's what Heather had to say about the "math myth" and some other misconceptions about architects.

"The whole notion that you have to be really, really good at math just isn't true. Sure, you have to do some math, but it's applied math. It's the fun stuff, it's geometry and spaces . . . it's not so scary. So I would encourage girls to be bold about that. And structural math? If you have the right attitude, it's really, really cool. I mean, in my structures class we did things like make bridges out of straws. How fun is that?

"I love being able to hang out with really smart people and hold my own."

"Another myth is that it's really glamorous and you get to jet all over the world and get paid boatloads of money. We don't. We try to dress like we do because we want people with boatloads of money to hire us. It's actually challenging—we have to have a nice enough car so the client isn't offended, but not too nice a car so they think you're charging them too much. It might seem really glamorous from the outside, but it's just not.

"The last myth is this whole idea that an architect is like an artist in a tower working alone—that we just imagine something and then it's built. It actually takes a lot of work and a lot of coordination with consultants, like mechanical and electrical engineers, to create something. There's a lot of teamwork, because we all have good ideas on our own, but when you put them together, sometimes unexpected things happen," she explained.

Heather's architecture firm, PLACE, takes on a mix of commercial, residential, and public work. At any given time they might be juggling a couple of jobs like building a new house, designing public housing, or even remodeling a garage to make it an office building. Since Heather runs the show, she oversees a staff of architects, but she is still very hands-on in most phases of a project.

"I don't do a lot of drawing anymore, maybe ten percent or twenty percent of my time is spent drawing. Other architects here might be doing eighty percent drawing, and only ten percent management and ten percent on the phone and working things out on an Excel spreadsheet," she says. Most of the drawing Heather refers to is actually work done on a computer, although the architects still do some actual sketching at PLACE.

To get a real sense of what an architect does, I asked Heather to walk me through the whole process, from the moment a phone call comes in from a prospective client through completion of a project.

AN ARCHITECTURAL PROJECT FROM START TO FINISH

When a new client calls up and says something like "I want to put a second story on my house," the first thing I do is talk to them on the phone and make sure they have realistic expectations of what it might cost and that the job is an appropriate thing for our firm to even consider. If it is, I'll go out and meet with the client. That part is always really fun, because I'll go out with my portfolio, and we'll sit down and talk about their dream and what they have in mind, and we'll look at the house and

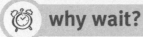

why wait?

▸ See if you can get an administrative internship with an architectural firm while you're still in high school or college.

▸ Get to know great spaces inside and out by volunteering as a docent at museums, libraries, and other architectural centers in your community.

take a bunch of pictures. Then I'll show them my portfolio and walk them through the five phases of an architecture project. If they choose to hire us, we would go through these steps to build their second story:

1. ***Predesign*** *is the first phase. When we get back from the interview, we'll look up the house on the building department's website and make sure that we know its exact dimensions, what the setbacks are, and what the building rules are. Also as part of predesign, we'll write a "program," which is a list of what the client is looking for, and we'll measure their house and make sure we have correct drawings to start from. Sometimes we gather conceptual information too, like if the people are interested in poetry or eclectic art or they like horses, or whatever it is. It's a lot of information gathering.*

2. *The **schematic design** is the phase that everyone thinks of when they think of an architect. It's where we do sketches of a design plan and we give it to the client. Then they think about it and get back to us and we sketch some more. We go back and forth with the client to develop the idea into two-dimensional finished drawings.*

3. *The next phase is called **design development** and **permit set,** where we submit for building permits as well as develop our schematic designs*

the breakdown

IN MEETINGS: 4 hours a day

ON THE PHONE: 1 hour a day

ONLINE: 3 hours a day

SITTING: Most of the day

READING: 2 hours a day

PRESENTING: Occasionally

WORKING SOLO: Half the day

into detailed plans. We try to get a contractor involved in this phase, because they give us validation that we're not crazy and that our design is actually doable.

4. *While the building department is reviewing our permit request, we put together the* **construction documents,** *and that's when you get into all the details of what the interior will look like. When the building department comes back to us and says "Yes, go ahead and build it," we issue a set of construction documents.*

5. *The last phase is* **construction administration,** *and it happens on-site where our contractors are building. We'll come out every week or two for a meeting and to check progress and talk about ideas, look at things that might change or whatever. Construction administration lasts six weeks to a year, depending on the project. In the end, hopefully everyone's still talking and we'll throw a party and our clients will move in.*

Like all careers, architecture has its ups and downs. I asked Heather to give me the lowdown on both.

"There's what we call 'driving the mouse,' which basically means drafting. In one construction set of drawings, there might be six hundred hours of drafting, and somebody's got to do it. It's not that bad, but it isn't necessarily glamorous. I used to say that was my job, driving the mouse. I'd just draft and draft and draft and draft.

"Another challenge is project management and dealing with clients—keeping everyone going in the same direction and moving along at the same time. Architectural design is very nonlinear—you try something, you come back, you try something else and you come back again. So people who are used to organized processes, like people

 then to now

1983–1985:	1987–1988:	SUMMER 1988:	1990–1991:
Interned as a carpenter at Cain Park Arts Festival in Cleveland, Ohio, during the summers	Worked various jobs as a carpenter and scene painter, Cleveland, New York, and Boston	Interned at Pei Cobb Freed & Partners, New York	Architectural intern, the Liebman Melting Partnership

Architects out of school begin their careers as paid architectural interns for three years. During this apprenticeship, they'll do lots of drafting, printing, copying, and helping out the architects with whatever they're doing.

who work in the software industry, or who run their own company, sometimes have a hard time with this forward-back-sideways and forward-back-sideways routine. That's the part of project management that we have to struggle with," she says.

"On the flip side, it's really awesome getting high-profile projects and saying 'Oh yeah, we built that' or, 'We're working on that.' That's cool. And I love being able to hang out with really smart people and hold my own. And then there's getting published—that's probably the most glamorous part. Getting published in *Architectural Record* last summer was one of my proudest moments. They profiled me and my firm for the "up and coming young architects" section, and there are pictures of some of our projects and a two-page interview with me. That was awesome," said Heather.

Heather knew what she wanted to be at a young age. She did stage acting as a child, but realized by sixth grade that she'd much rather design and build a set than be acting in front

what it takes

▶ A blend of creative and mathematical talent

▶ Being an organized, linear thinker

▶ Patience (to get through the three-year internship)

of it. By the time she was sixteen, she'd figured out that she wanted to be an architect.

"I just felt like I would never get bored with it," Heather says.

INTERESTED IN BEING AN ARCHITECT? HERE'S HEATHER'S ADVICE

▶ *Believe in your own power and intelligence, and at the same time, be open to learning from others. Architecture is a profoundly complex field and you'll always be learning, but people will be looking to you to have a clear vision and they'll value your opinion. Keep your eye sharp and trust your instincts.*

▶ *Get a well-rounded liberal arts education and then go to architecture school. If you have a feel for art and the humanities, it will only enrich the work you do down the road.*

in the field

Five More Careers in Architecture

drafter The plans created by other architects and designers for projects are often sketched, drawn out, and completed by drafters. They draw by hand or on a computer, and they lay out the different elements of a project, such as materials that will be used, where plumbing will be, landscaping ideas, and finishing touches.

industrial designer These designers design what goes inside a home—everything from office furniture to kitchen fixtures—making sure it's functional, safe, and usable. While many industrial designers design materials for homes and the workplace, they might also do things like transportation and environmental design.

construction manager Construction managers oversee the building of a structure, from hiring construction workers and finding the right building materials to making sure that the end product looks exactly like the architect and the client envisioned it. They must be available twenty-four hours a day and deal with any emergencies.

carpenter You'll find carpenters working on-site at most building projects, and their job deals primarily with building and installing structures ranging from walls and cabinets to the actual frames of a house. Many are self-employed and specialize in a certain area.

cartographer The next time you're on a road trip, consider that the map you're using to figure out your route was created by a cartographer. Cartographers create drawn or computer-generated maps, and they may work for government agencies, map companies, builders, or utility companies.

 ## you need to know about

The AIAS, or American Institute of Architecture Students (www.aias.org), offers info on pursuing a career in architecture, a guide to architecture schools, postings about conferences and events, and links to great websites about architecture.

For more on careers that change the landscape, check out the urban planner profile on page 306.

Christine Tucker

commercial airline pilot

the facts

Christine Tucker,
Captain, American Airlines

▶ **what?** Commercial airline pilots jet around the country, or the world, flying millions of people to their destinations at speeds of up to five hundred miles an hour. They not only pilot the plane during takeoff, flight, and landing, but are also responsible for checking their plane prior to each flight, monitoring weather reports, and developing flight plans.

▶ **where?** Most pilots work out of their "home base" and fly a regular route.

▶ **how?** Commercial airline pilots must have seven years' civilian flying or one year military pilot training with a five-year commitment under their belt, as well as having logged between one thousand and four thousand hours of flying time.

▶ **$$$:** An average of $30,000 to $70,000 a year (more for experienced pilots flying larger jets)

▶ **dress code?** A uniform provided by the airline, consisting of pants, a top, a sweater, a tie, black shoes, and a captain's hat

▶ **stress factor:** On a scale of 1 to 10, a 5 with an occasional 8

though their ranks are rising, it's still rare to find a woman in the captain's seat of a commercial airplane. In fact, in 2001 less than 5 percent of all commercial airline pilots were women. Among them is Captain Christine Tucker, who flies a Boeing 757 or Boeing 767 between San Francisco, where she lives, and New York City, Boston, or Miami for American Airlines. Because there are so few women commercial airline pilots, especially captains, I was curious to find out how she made it happen.

"When I was younger, we lived by Greater Pittsburgh Airport. We'd see airplanes overhead all the time, so I got interested in flying at a young age. Then we moved to a street where some of our neighbors were US Air captains, and their sons were learning to fly. That's when I realized, 'Wow, I could fly a plane.' One of the sons took me up for my very first flying lesson and showed me how I could do it. I also read an article in *Parade* magazine when I was a teenager on women airline pilots. After reading that I was like, 'Okay, I can do this.' I still have that article," Christine says.

> *"I really like that I have a lot of flexibility in my schedule. And you know, it is still really fun to fly."*

you asked . . .

"How long did you have to go to school, and did you like it?" Shelby, age 13

christine answered . . .

"To get in with a major airline, they typically want a four-year degree. My first two years I went to community college and got my associate degree in professional piloting and air traffic control. After that I went on to college in Pittsburgh and finished my four-year degree in business administration. You know . . . school's school, but the piloting courses, the flight engineer coursework . . . even the business classes, were all very interesting."

"Even today, it's still a big deal. People look in the cockpit, especially women, and say, 'Congratulations' and tell me how impressed they are with my accomplishments. *(Laughs)* I always feel bad for my male first officers because it appears no one's really paying any attention to them."

In preparing for my interview with Christine, I stumbled across this quote that some people use to describe what it's like to be a pilot: "Being a pilot entails hours of boredom interrupted upon occasion by seconds of sheer terror." Wow . . . quite a job description. So I asked her: Is it really true?

the breakdown

SITTING: The entire length of the trip

COMMUNICATING VIA RADIO:
The entire length of the trip

"Yes, monitoring the instruments might be viewed as a little boring, and yes, there are stresses involved, like being ready for an engine failure on takeoff or dealing with bad weather, but I wouldn't say it's necessarily 'boredom' with occasional 'terror.' That's kind of harsh," Christine answered.

So what does being a pilot really entail? What are they doing in the cockpit during a cross-country flight? How about when they're in another city between flights? I asked Christine to walk us through it.

A TYPICAL FLIGHT, A TYPICAL DAY

I get to the airport an hour before my flight, and the first thing I do is sign on to the computer so my company knows I'm there. Then I look at the flight plan from one of our dispatchers working out of Dallas–Fort Worth. He's the licensed expert who looks at the weather and talks to the other crews that have flown the route earlier so I know what kind of weather I'll have, what kind of turbulence to expect. The flight plan also includes a wind readout so I know the optimum altitude to fly in order to get the best fuel economy. I also check my flight plan for things like destination weather—visibility, wind, temperature—and most important, the amount of fuel I need to safely fly the trip.

After finalizing the flight plan, I go out to the airplane and help with the "preflight." Typically, the first officer starts preflighting the airplane an hour before a flight. Occasionally I'll do the exterior preflight, which means looking at the outside of the airplane—the tires, the structure, the tail—making sure that everything's fastened and all the nuts and bolts are there and nothing is leaking or out of place. I still get a sense of awe at how large this aircraft is that I'm about to fly.

Once we get inside the cockpit, we have to program the computer with our flight plan so the navigation system will give us proper guidance. We also check which taxiway is appropriate to get to the runway. Every departure is so different. There might be five different departure routes for one runway, so you have to be prepared for which one you're going to fly. This is really critical . . . you can't make a mistake. If you've got a certain departure plan, you'd best be on it because there might be an airplane on the other runway.

I fly the Boeing 757 and 767. The cockpits of both planes are identical, but the feel of flying them is a little different. The 757 is like a sports car—it's very responsive and powerful . . . I just love it. The 767 is more like a luxury liner, stable with even more power. There is an adrenaline rush every time you take off, partly due to the amazing performance and acceleration

paying your dues

as you roll down the runway. You constantly have your hands and feet on the controls in preparation for takeoff. Although all of our airplanes have autopilots, I usually hand fly the airplane up to cruise altitude.

Once I'm in the air and at "cruise altitude," I'll turn the autopilot on and sit back for around five hours and monitor the instruments and navigation. The flight over most of the United States from San Francisco to New York is beautiful when looking down from six miles up. As we get closer to the destination airport, we check the weather and begin planning our approach to the airport.

When we begin our descent, I'll hand fly the airplane for the remainder of the flight—why let the autopilot have all the fun? The air traffic controllers will have a planned arrival route, which is like a highway in the sky, to help keep other planes at a safe distance and flying the same direction as we are. They'll tell us what altitude to descend to and at what speed they would like us to fly. Then we'll start the approach, using an ILS or instrument landing system, which helps guide us and tells us things like if we're too high or too far left or right off course.

what it takes

▶ Staying calm in stressful situations

▶ A desire to travel and see new places

▶ A sense of safety and responsibility

If I'm flying into New York, we usually get in around six a.m. In most cases we have between fourteen and twenty-four hours off-duty to enjoy the sights and sounds of the Big Apple. In New York my airline provides a hotel downtown—it's not the Ritz or anything, but it's adequate, and I love my stay in the heart of the city. I can go shopping (remember, I am a girl) or out to the theater.

then to now

1980: Began flying in eleventh grade	**1981:** Started college and flew freight at night	**1984:** Graduated from college and started flying bank checks in North Carolina	**1985:** Hired by Air Virginia as a first officer flying metro liners

Christine's schedule can be brutal, especially when she's flying across the country. Because of changing time zones (it's a three-hour difference), her body never really has a chance to catch up with her. Here's what a typical trip from San Francisco to New York and back might look like:

Fly out of San Francisco: *Monday night, 10:00 p.m.*
   Pacific Standard Time (PST)

Arrive in New York: *Tuesday morning, 6:00 a.m.*
   Eastern Standard Time (EST)/
   3:00 a.m. PST

Go to sleep in hotel: *Tuesday morning, 8:00 a.m. EST/*
   5:00 a.m. PST

Force myself awake: *Tuesday afternoon, 2:00 p.m. EST/*
   11:00 a.m. PST

Force myself to sleep: *Tuesday evening, 11:00 p.m. EST/*
   8:00 p.m. PST

Force myself awake: *Wednesday morning, 6:30 a.m. EST/*
   3:30 a.m. PST

Fly out of New York: *Wednesday morning, 9:00 a.m. EST/*
   6:00 a.m. PST

Arrive in San Francisco: *Wednesday afternoon, 12:30 p.m. PST*

As you can imagine, Christine is wiped out after a trip like that, which is one reason why she's worked out a schedule that gives her a chance to refresh and have quality time at home with her kids. She

1987: Was hired at American Airlines at twenty-three years old as a flight engineer on a Boeing 727	1990: Became a first officer on a Boeing 727	1996: Became a captain on Boeing 727	2002: Became a captain on a Boeing 757/767 flying domestic routes

says it's always challenging to be away so much each month, especially because she has to make sure things at home are taken care of—the kids are set, the dog is fed, bills are paid, everything's in order. "It's not like you can just scoot back home and do something if you're flying across country . . . you're really gone for those days," she says.

But while the schedules for commercial airline pilots can be challenging, the flexibility is also something Christine says is one of the biggest perks of the job.

"I use my vacation time as individual days instead of taking a week off at a time—that way I'm home more. I'm typically working 'on reserves,' which means that I have a guaranteed twelve days off each month, but other than that I'm on call," Christine explains. "I really like that I have a lot of flexibility in my schedule. And you know, it is still really fun to fly."

Before we wrapped up our conversation, I asked Christine to clear up any misconceptions about pilots, and she said she thinks the biggest myth is that pilots make a lot of money and are overpaid for what they do.

"We're in charge of a hundred-and-twenty-five-million-dollar airplane, we have to take medical exams every six months, we have to go through check rides, or flight evaluations, every nine months, and our job can be taken away from us if we make a mistake. There can be stress involved, with no room for error. I have two hundred twenty people in my airplane who count on me to safely get them to their destination. But I can't imagine doing anything else. Professionalism is paramount in this business, but I love what I do. I leave work every day with a sense of pride and accomplishment."

CHRISTINE'S ADVICE

▶ *You have to be motivated to succeed. If you're motivated, organized, and want to see new places, then you can do it.*

▶ *Be persistent—flight jobs are hard to find.*

in the field

Five More Careers Working in the Travel Industry

travel agent Travel agents organize, plan, and book trips for people, whether it be for business or pleasure. Their job includes everything from reserving flights, cruises, and hotels to organizing tours and providing itineraries and maps for their clients.

flight attendant While some people think flight attendants are onboard to make the passengers' ride more comfortable by handing out pillows, their most important job is safety. They must ensure that passengers follow safety rules, and they assist in the case of an emergency.

air traffic controller The stress meter hits a ten if you're an air traffic controller, as they monitor all the aircraft in their airspace, communicate with pilots, and make sure that all the planes are flying safe distances from one another. Those at busy airports might coordinate the landing and takeoff of a dozen airplanes at any one time.

airline reservations agent Airline reservations agents take reservations over the phone for airlines and book the flights. They use a computer program to do their work and spend their whole day providing customer service.

flight mechanic Airplanes are checked over by flight mechanics before embarking on a trip, and they'll look over the whole airplane and use special lighting tools to look for cracks in the surface that would be invisible to the naked eye. Flight mechanics are also called in to fix any problems the pilot might sense prior to takeoff.

 you need to know about

Women in Aviation International (www.wai.org) is all about encouraging women to pursue careers in aviation. At this website you'll find articles about aviation, scholarship opportunities, conference information, and links to great sites just for women interested in flying. Bonus: You can even join as a high school student!

Mary Sue Milliken & Susan Feniger

chefs

the facts

Mary Sue Milliken & Susan Feniger, Owners, Border Grill and Ciudad Restaurants

▶ **what?** Chefs are professional cooks, but most do much more than just cook food. They often create the recipes and menus that are served in restaurants or private residences, oversee cooks, order ingredients, and figure out the cost involved in various recipes. Some also run restaurants.

▶ **where?** Chefs can work anywhere that food is served.

▶ **how?** A degree isn't a requirement, but a college background in hospitality or culinary arts is a bonus, along with experience working in the restaurant industry. Additional training at a place like the Culinary Institute of America will open up many opportunities.

▶ **$$$:** $20,000 to $40,000 for lower-level chefs at smaller restaurants; $60,000 to $100,000 or more for those in more prominent restaurants.

▶ **dress code?** A chef's outfit—usually a white chef's jacket, simple pants, and a white chef's hat

▶ **stress factor:** On a scale of 1 to 10, a 7

longtime chefs and restaurant partners Mary Sue Milliken and Susan Feniger own two restaurants in Los Angeles (Ciudad and the Border Grill) and recently opened a Border Grill in Las Vegas, have written several cookbooks, have hosted two cooking shows on Food Network, have a weekly Sunday-morning radio talk show, and even have their own brand of food called Border Girls, which can be found at Whole Foods Market. So I thought, who better than Mary Sue and Susan to tell us what it's really like to work as chefs and restaurateurs? Here are some highlights from our conversation.

ME: You're so much more than chefs—you run three restaurants, write books, have a weekly radio show. How do you juggle it all?

"The one thing you can count on in this business is that next year won't be the same as last year. The business and the atmosphere are constantly changing."

SUSAN: On a typical day I might start looking at e-mails at around nine thirty a.m., something like that, and then I usually try to go into the restaurant somewhere around ten or ten thirty. I may go to downtown to Ciudad, I might go to Border Grill in Santa Monica, or I might get on a plane and go to our restaurant in Vegas. I check in with the chefs and walk through the restaurant to connect with the people there. I may end up sitting down with one of the chefs to talk or maybe going over what specials we're switching over to. Then usually right before lunch I'll taste the specials.

During the lunch service, I try to be working on the floor at one of the restaurants, either looking at the food coming out of the kitchen, which is called "expediting," or talking to customers. If it's busy, I'll jump in. Then I'll end up in meetings in the afternoon—sometimes it's kitchen meetings, sometimes it's financial meetings with the whole team. In the afternoon we might be doing an interview or a demo or a TV thing. Then dinnertime comes and I'm usually involved with the tastings, working on the floor, connecting with customers, watching food coming out, and maybe even doing office paperwork. We've got a big benefit coming up in less than a month, so right now I'm putting together auction packages and menu plans, figuring out a prep list for it, and so on. Tomorrow I'm meeting with the chef at the Beverly Wilshire Hotel to plan for the event. And then at nine or nine thirty p.m. I may meet friends for dinner at the restaurant or head out.

ME: Wow . . . that's a packed day. Is your routine any different, Mary Sue?

MARY SUE: I think I do more planning and I work a lot on the radio show, figuring out what we're going to talk about this week, writing new recipes that we're going to try out, or testing recipes. I also go to the Santa Monica Farmer's Market and see what foods are new and interesting there, research what's happening in the food industry, and do a lot of big-picture planning, like trying to figure out how we're going to sustain this business while staying true to our philosophy.

you asked . . .

"Would you say that through your success, your job has allowed you to contribute something to the benefit of this world?" Brittani, age 16

mary sue and susan answered . . .

"Absolutely. One of the benefits of being in the restaurant business is that it gives us the venue and the opportunities to give back to the community in a way that many businesses can't do other than by just giving money. Giving back is a big part of our culture and our company, and it's something that we get our staff involved in so that they can see what an incredible opportunity it is.

Mary Sue & Susan's favorite charities? Share Our Strength (www.strength.org) and the Scleroderma Research Foundation (www.srfcure.org).

ME: I wanted to ask you about that. It seems that a lot of restaurants are here today, gone tomorrow, but you've both been very successful at keeping restaurants in business. Is it stressful knowing that your industry is so unstable?

MARY SUE: Well, the one thing you can count on in this business is that next year won't be the same as last year. The business and the atmosphere are constantly changing. We just try to stay connected to what our business and the people here need. The people who work for us are really what make the whole thing work.

ME: Besides that fact that the restaurant industry is so tough, what are some of the other challenges of being a chef and running a restaurant?

SUSAN: It's long hours, and in some ways you're always on call. If you're at the restaurant and you're planning to leave and something goes wrong, you always have to be ready to just jump in, no matter what. You also have to be able to juggle a lot of things at one time. You have to be able to handle situations that for many people would be very stressful. In one night you might have someone not show up for work, someone else give their notice, a toilet overflow, a ton of people waiting at the front door for a table, and half of your produce order doesn't arrive. You have to be able to juggle all that.

 the breakdown

IN MEETINGS: 1–2 hours a day

ONLINE: 1–2 hours a day

SITTING: 1–2 hours a day

STANDING: 4–6 hours a day

TALKING TO STAFF & CUSTOMERS:
All the time

MARY SUE: And you can look at that as a challenge, or you can look at that as an opportunity to be really creative. You'll need to figure out what kind of specials you can make with only half the produce that you were expecting, and that's actually fun in some ways. I think that's a part of what attracts people to the industry—that you get totally immersed in the job because you're so busy and there are so many challenges.

ME: What do you *love* about your job?

SUSAN: You get to wear a uniform every day—that's a great thing.

MARY SUE: That's true. *(Laughs)* You don't have to decide what to wear to work anymore—that is a big perk.

SUSAN: Plus, you know, you can have friends come in and the restaurant feels like an extended arm of your home, so that's a great thing. There's also a camaraderie that happens within the restaurant business, with staff as well as with customers that come in, and you build these extended relationships because it's a very social, giving environment.

MARY SUE: I also think a huge perk is that you get to eat. And not only do you get to eat, but you get to make recipes that you like over

 why wait?

▸ Every restaurant in town is hiring—if you're sixteen or older, go get a job and see if you like it!

▸ Take a cooking class. Many supermarkets offer free or inexpensive classes that are open to all ages.

▸ Cook as often as you can at home and experiment with all kinds of recipes. Start by closely following recipes and then begin adding your own personal touches.

 then to now

| Mary Sue graduated from Washburne Culinary Institute and Susan graduated from the Culinary Institute of America | 1978: Mary Sue and Susan met while working at Le Perroquet in Chicago | 1981: Opened first restaurant, City Café, on Melrose Avenue, L.A. | 1985: City Café moved to larger space and changed name to CITY | 1985: Opened Border Grill in old City Café space |

paying your dues

Even with a degree from a culinary institute, most chefs start out working in a variety of positions—from prep cook to dishwasher—to learn all aspects of cooking and work their way up the ladder.

and over. If you love to cook at home and you make a dish a hundred and fifty times, you and your friends and family would be so sick of that dish that you wouldn't even like it anymore. But if you're cooking in a restaurant, you can make it a hundred and fifty times in the first month since you're serving it to different people, and you can really figure out how to make it better each time. So that's a huge perk.

ME: Would you say that your work is creative?

MARY SUE: Yes. It's like a puzzle every day—you walk in and see what's ready to be eaten and what's not going to be good by tomorrow if you don't figure out what to make with it, so you have all kinds of creative opportunities there. Or when you're opening a restaurant and your budget is tight . . . you have to be creative then, too. When we opened City Café, we didn't have any wine buckets and we were opening the next day, but we had no money. One of our partners found these really cool marble crocks at Pic 'n Save for $2.99 each. She bought twenty of them and we sandblasted them in the back alley

what it takes

▶ A love of tasting and smelling food!

▶ Being able to handle pressure

▶ Creativity and ability to think outside the box

▶ Endurance . . . it's long hours on your feet

of the restaurant . . . they ended up looking fantastic. So you have the ability to be creative in lots of ways—in the way you create the atmosphere, in the way you create the menu. It's all a way of communicating who you are. . . .

SUSAN: . . . down to what the staff uniforms are going to be, what kind of silverware, what kind of china and glassware, how the menus are going to look—you've got all these different avenues besides the food where you're able to explore your own creativity. It's exciting and it keeps someone who's driven and creative really challenged.

ME: When you first got into this career, would you ever have dreamed that you'd not only be chefs and own your own restaurants, but that you would be writing books . . . even starting your own line of food?

MARY SUE: Not at all. But Susan and I were both really passionate about teaching and educating people about food, what they're eating and how they eat. So we started teaching cooking classes to people, and every time we'd teach a class people would say, "Oh, you should be on TV" or "You should be on the radio." And you know, they were right. We really do enjoy it and it came very naturally to us, which was lucky.

MARY SUE AND SUSAN'S ADVICE

▸ *Trust your instincts, but don't be afraid to ask anyone in sight when something is baffling you. Your colleagues and role models will generously share ideas and advice that is more valuable than any education.*

▸ *Get in there and do the grunt work. Start as a dishwasher, be a prep cook, work in the kitchen—really try to experience it. Even though the work that you do over time might change, the hours and the commitment are the same, so you have to be really passionate about it.*

*in the field

Five More Careers in the Restaurant Industry

sommelier Would you believe there's a career in knowing which type of wine goes best with different meals? You might find *sommeliers* (French for "wine waiters") working in fancy restaurants, and their in-depth knowledge of wine helps them make recommendations.

hostess Hosts and hostesses are usually the first people you see when you walk in a restaurant. They have to be serious multitaskers, taking reservations, answering phones, seating people, and acting as the public "face" of the restaurant, all at the same time.

pastry chef Many consider baking to be an art, since it takes skill and creativity. Pastry chefs might whip up delectable desserts for a French restaurant, bake three-tiered wedding cakes, or create crois-sants and scones for their own boutique pastry shop.

server This is one job that never gets boring. Servers have to be good at juggling information, dealing with all kinds of people, staying cool under pressure, and multitasking—keeping track of who wants extra butter, whose steak is too rare, and who is missing a place setting.

line cook Without line cooks, chefs' creations would never go from ingredients to finished meals. Line cooks make the food on the menu, and they must be consistent in re-creating the chef's special-ties time and time again—the restaurant's reputation depends on it.

 you need to know about

Women Chefs & Restaurateurs (WRC) was founded in 1983 by top women chefs with a goal of "promoting the education and advancement of women in the restaurant industry." At the WRC's website, www.womenchefs.org, you'll find information on internships, books to read, links to resources, and a free downloadable newsletter.

Melissa Block

journalist

the facts

Melissa Block, Cohost, All Things Considered, National Public Radio

▶ **what?** Journalists report the news for television or radio stations, newspapers, magazines, and websites.

▶ **where?** As a journalist, you can live and work just about anywhere. Many work for a specific news outlet, while others work freelance and submit stories to various media for publication or broadcast.

▶ **how?** Most journalists have at least a four-year degree in English or journalism or a master's in journalism.

▶ **$$$:** An average of $22,000 to $47,000 a year

▶ **dress code?** Casual for print and radio journalists and business for on-air TV journalists

▶ **stress factor:** On a scale of 1 to 10, between an 8 and a 10 ("A bad day can be pretty stressful, but it's all relative," says Melissa.)

if you tune in to your local public radio station on a weekday afternoon, chances are you'll hear the voice of Melissa Block. As cohost of National Public Radio's two-hour news show *All Things Considered*, Melissa not only sits in the big anchor chair and introduces news pieces, but she also interviews special guests and reports on breaking news and human interest stories from the field. Since I'm a news junkie, it was exciting to peek into Melissa's life and hear about what goes on behind the scenes at NPR. Here's our conversation.

ME: The news industry seems so competitive. Was it tough to break in?

MELISSA: I don't think it was as hard then as it is now. I hunted around for a job for a bit, but found my niche at NPR, even though I hadn't worked in radio before. It just turned out to be such a great place to work. . . . Here it is twenty-some years later and I'm still here.

> *"I don't necessarily need to know what the answers are—I need to know what the questions are that need to be answered."*

ME: Did you know that you wanted to work in journalism when you got out of college?

MELISSA: I was a little torn. I got into law school but deferred for two years in a row, because by the time I got in I had started working in journalism. So part of me thought journalism was the industry for me, and part of me thought that law would be interesting. I remember having a conversation with the admissions person at Yale Law School, and when I asked her if I could defer for a third year she said, "You know, it sounds like you're very happy doing what you're doing. Maybe you don't need to go to law school." And I realized she was right.

ME: Let's fast forward to the present day. I realize your days are probably very different depending on whether you're in the studio hosting or on the road reporting. Could you walk us through what each day might look like?

in the studio . . .

I have a young daughter, so my day starts with trying to squeeze in a little time with her. That's part of this whole equation—how to balance having a family and having a job that's satisfying to you. So morning time is spent with her, having breakfast, making lunch, as well as trying to read as much of the paper as I can.

9:00–10:00 a.m.: *I get to the office and I'm reading, reading, reading as many papers and websites as I can. I need to get a sense of what's going on in the world.*

10:00–11:00 a.m.: *We head up to a staff meeting at ten o'clock every day to kick ideas around for that day's show. The best shows for me are the ones where I feel like I'm invested and have a stake in the stories and when I've brought something to fruition on the air. There's a lot of back-and-forth from all the staff in the meeting—from interns all the way up to the executive producer and the hosts—and we get some sense of what each host's assignments will be for the day.*

11:00 a.m.–3:00 p.m.: *I'm reading and preparing for interviews, doing interviews, and writing introductions to stories.*

3:00–4:00 p.m.: *We're doing preproduction for the show, like recording some elements that are taped in advance. We have a very early deadline. Going on the air at four p.m. is a pretty punishing thing when your day starts at nine thirty—it doesn't give you a lot of time to get things ready. There's a sort of funny acceleration. There's a point where you look at your watch and go, "Whoa, it's two thirty," and the day sort of accelerates from there.*

4:00–6:00 p.m.: *We go on the air. During the show I'm doing live interviews, reading introductions to reporter pieces, and handling the live broadcast of the show. Assuming we haven't made any mistakes or things haven't changed newswise, the day is more or less done after the broadcast of the show.*

7:00 p.m.: *I get home.*

on the road . . .

The days when I'm on the road can really vary. Sometimes I'm working on stories that we've planned well in advance, and other times I'm responding to something that happened. For example, after Hurricane Katrina hit in August 2005, we were heading down to the Gulf Coast of Mississippi the next day with no preparation. We were just trying to get on the first airplane there and get as close as we could. It can be something like that. Or it can be something like a trip I took to Nebraska to interview the poet laureate, Ted Kooser, or next week I'm going to talk with Bruce Springsteen. It can be a huge range of things, which is partly what makes the job so great.

When I'm on the road, I go out with a crew—my producer and an audio engineer. When I was a reporter in New York, I did all my own stuff, but now that I'm hosting we go out as a team. If I'm reporting on a breaking news story like in Mississippi after Katrina, we'll file the report from the road through a satellite phone or computer. Otherwise, if it's a longer-term project, we may bring the tape back and have time to put it together back in the studio.

you asked . . .

"How does what you do for a living affect other parts of your life?" Anna, age 20

melissa answered . . .

"I like thinking about the fact that my daughter, who's now almost four, hears me on the radio and it's just a part of her life. I like the notion that she's growing up knowing that women do this, that her mother does this, and that it's a possible career choice. It is a squeeze, though. I don't have a job where I can get in at ten and be home at five and have dinner and not have to work at night. You do bring work home with you and there's a lot that you don't leave at the office, so that's a choice. It's a choice I've made gladly and it's a wonderful thing that I'm doing, so I don't regret it. But it is a trade-off."

IN MEETINGS: 1 hour a day

ON THE PHONE: Maybe half an hour

ONLINE: Constantly

SITTING: Unfortunately, almost all the time

PUBLIC SPEAKING: Every day on the radio

READING: Constantly

WORKING SOLO: Half the day

ME: Do you have a lot of choice over the stories you get to work on?

MELISSA: Yes. I think the feeling is that the best stories are the ones that the hosts have a natural curiosity about, which isn't to say that I'll only do stories that I pitch or that are my idea, but there's less translation involved if it's coming from me. That said, I've also done a zillion interviews that have been pitched by our staff members.

ME: How do you become an expert on all the topics you're reporting on?

MELISSA: I think the first thing you have to do is realize that you're never going to become an expert. (*Laughs.*) I see my role as a surrogate for the listener, and the listener's not an expert. I don't necessarily need to know what the answers are—I need to know what the questions are that need to be answered. Obviously it can help if I'm well informed, and I certainly try to be, but sometimes the most interesting interviews come when I'm thrown into something that I haven't had a chance to really prepare for and I'm just reacting more spontaneously

 then to now

1983: Graduated from Harvard University with degree in French history and literature

1984: Was a Fulbright scholar at the University of Geneva

1985: Started working for NPR setting up interviews for *All Things Considered* host Noah Adams

to. I think the main skills are being a fast reader and a quick study, having a general curiosity about things, and not being afraid to ask dumb questions, because they're probably not dumb. They're probably what everybody else is wondering and hoping somebody will ask.

ME: How do you go about booking your interviews and reporting on stories?

MELISSA: Usually the producer sets up the interviews. I'll jump in if it's somebody I know or somebody I want to establish a connection with first. But usually it's a producer doing most of the legwork and research.

ME: And after you've interviewed someone and you're putting together a story, are you sitting down and writing the script for air?

MELISSA: Yes. The producer and I work pretty closely—sometimes the engineer, too—to think about structure. Usually right after an interview is the best time to talk about it because it's fresh in your mind, and often there is some moment from the interview that stands out very clearly in your mind as something to preserve.

 why wait?

▶ Join the staff of your school newspaper, yearbook, or radio station.

▶ Get an internship at a local radio or TV station . . . many will hire high school students.

▶ Become a news junkie—stay up-to-date on local, national, and world news by reading the newspaper and online news, listening to NPR, and watching national and local broadcasts.

1994: Moved to NYC to report for NPR

1999: Her report investigating rape as a weapon of war in Kosovo was cited among stories for which NPR News won an Overseas Press Club Award

2003: Became cohost of *All Things Considered*

paying your dues

> To work in national news, many people start out at a TV or radio station in a smaller market, sometimes working as a production assistant (PA) or freelance reporter. The field of journalism is notorious for low starting salaries, but your pay will increase with your experience.

There's sort of a way that everything fits together, and the challenge is trying to figure out the most logical sequence for a story to flow. In TV news, you can rely on the pictures, but with radio, you can't. So we let the ambient sound that we record on the road do a lot of the talking for us. But the rest is in the writing, and it needs to be as descriptive as possible. I do all of the writing for my pieces.

ME: What did it feel like to hear your voice on national radio for the first time?

MELISSA: The first national piece I did was a story about a green card lottery for immigrants. It was a scary, weird thing to hear my voice on the radio. I think anyone who's ever listened to their own answering machine recording sort of does a double take and says, "That's not what I really sound like, is it?"

ME: What is the biggest challenge of your job?

MELISSA: There is a constant time pressure of being on a daily deadline with a two-hour program. That and having to juggle a lot of things in your brain at the same time. I mean, I may be doing several interviews in one day—one on the White House press secretary resigning, one on the twentieth anniversary of Chernobyl, and then maybe something frivolous like a guy who grows the biggest tomato in Texas. You have to keep all of those balls in the air at the same time.

ME: What do you love about your job?

MELISSA: It's such a privilege to have access to people and to situations that a lot of other people don't have access to. You know, being in the Yankee locker room right after they've won the World Series and getting doused with champagne— that's an amazing place to be. And it's great to be able to take that and say, "Here's what I saw, here's what I heard . . . let me tell you about this." What an incredible thing to be able to sit down with a daughter whose mother was killed in the attacks on the World Trade Center on September 11, and talk to her about the fact that they haven't found her mother's body and how the family is dealing with that. I just consider that a real privilege of the job. It's a pretty intimate thing, and that's a real joy.

what it takes

▶ Good communication and analytical skills

▶ The ability to work under tight deadlines

▶ A willingness to pay your dues

INTERESTED IN JOURNALISM?
HERE'S MELISSA'S CAREER ADVICE

▶ *Volunteer in your local community—jump in and do as much as you can. Whether it's for your local public radio station or community newspaper, there's nothing better than hands-on experience.*

▶ *Be someone nothing is lost on. Take everything in, be a good observer, and write like crazy.*

▶ *Keep improving your writing. Keep a journal and learn your voice.*

▶ *Read like crazy. Read authors whose writing you feel passionate about and figure out why their writing resonates with you.*

in the field
Five More Careers in Broadcast Journalism

assignment editor Assignment editors on news programs work with the staff to come up with story ideas and then assign them out

to reporters, hosts, and crews. This can be a highly stressful job, since assignment editors have to keep tabs on who's working on what and make quick decisions about breaking news.

news producer After assignments are handed out, news producers coordinate the production of news segments, working with a camera or audio crew and journalist to make the story happen. They research stories, find interview subjects, oversee the recording of material, and help package the story into complete news segments.

beat reporter Beat reporters are journalists who cover one aspect or "beat" for the news, usually carrying their own recording equipment for interviews, writing their own copy, and producing the final radio news segment. For example, a beat reporter who specializes in education will cover local or national education stories.

booker Many TV and radio news shows rely heavily on on-air guests, and bookers are the ones who research potential guests, contact them and/or their publicists, and "book" them for an upcoming show. They might also prep the interviewer or show host, as well as prepare the guest for what to expect on the program.

news graphic designer TV news uses on-air graphics—maps, diagrams, titles—in news stories. News graphic designers use their expertise and computer design programs to create these graphics. Those working for twenty-four-hour news channels like CNN and MSNBC might create the news crawls on the bottom of the screen.

 ## you need to know about

The Project for Excellence in Journalism sponsors the website www.journalism.org. Here you'll find links to articles and books about journalism, an annual report on the State of the News Media, resources, ideas, and job postings.

For more on careers in journalism, check out the magazine editor profile on page 289.

Lauren Faust

animator

the facts

▶ **what?** Animators make cartoons—television shows, commercials, online shorts, or even personal indie films. They do many different jobs, such as designing characters or backgrounds, drawing hundreds of frames to create the illusion of movement, or creating storyboards to plan out the action.

▶ **where?** While independent animators can work almost anywhere, the hubs for the industry are New York and L.A.

Lauren Faust,
Supervising Producer,
Cartoon Network Studios

▶ **how?** There are no firm job requirements for animators, beyond a talent for drawing, although a degree in animation from an art school may make it easier to land a job.

▶ **$$$:** From $26,000 to $150,000 a year, depending on level of experience, the studio, and whether animating for a TV show or a movie

▶ **dress code?** Can you say "cut-offs, T-shirts, and flip-flops"?

▶ **stress factor:** On a scale of 1 to 10, 5 on a good day, 8 on a bad day

animators have to be great at so many things to do what they do—be great artists; have an incredible imagination; be smart, funny, and creative; and have a unique way of looking at the world. Lauren Faust, who I met when she was an animator on *The Powerpuff Girls*, is all of the above.

The term "animator" as a job title is pretty broad, because like many fields in entertainment, creating an animated show or movie is usually a group effort. For a half-hour animated TV show, there's a whole team of people behind it—from the artists who designed the characters, to the storyboard artists who blocked out the action, to the background designer who designed the "scenery" for the cartoon, to the director who timed out the show. People in all these jobs would be considered "animators," and that just scratches the surface.

"Don't be afraid to promote yourself. People won't notice you unless you put yourself directly in their sight."

Lauren has worked on a number of projects at Cartoon Network, including *The Powerpuff Girls*, and most recently as the supervising producer and story supervisor for *Foster's Home for Imaginary Friends*. For *Foster's*, Lauren is involved in lots of high-level action, including story planning meetings, production meetings, and writing and storyboarding episodes, pretty much all at the same time. No two days are the same, and Lauren constantly has to shift gears from one moment to the next, wearing her artist hat for one meeting and her producer hat for another, sometimes back-to-back.

I managed to cajole Lauren into keeping a diary for us for a few days. I thought it would be a great way to see what the work of a supervising producer for an animated TV show was really like. Here's a peek into her journal:

february 13

10:00 a.m.–12 noon: *Met with a composer to review music for a project of mine in development. It's the very first song for the microseries—very exciting!*

12:30–1 p.m.: *Quick lunch with my boss, Craig. We discussed a script outline from a freelance writer.*

1:00–2:30 p.m.: *Reread the outline we discussed at lunch to think about how to make it stronger. I felt it was very funny, but it was missing a solid character arc, and there was not enough at stake to make the story exciting.*

2:30–3:00 p.m.: *Read and returned e-mails. Returned phone calls. There are several blogs and forums on animation that I check regularly to catch up on news in the animation industry. Usually when I'm checking e-mails, I do this, too.*

3:00–4:30 p.m.: *Prepped my own story outline for a script I am about to start writing.*

4:30–6:00 p.m.: *Reviewed notes for the freelance outline with Craig and another writer, Darrick. We discussed our different thoughts and decided what direction to take.*

you asked . . .

"*How long have you known what you wanted to do with your life?*" Jean, age 16

lauren answered . . .

"*I've loved drawing, art, and animation ever since I can remember, but it wasn't until I was fourteen that it occurred to me that you could make cartoons for a living. Still, at that point I only added it to the list of things I was considering for my career, along with teaching and zoology. A couple years later I visited Walt Disney World with my family, and they had an animation exhibit, which included a glimpse of a working animation studio. As soon as I saw it, I just knew that was what I had to do!*"

february 14

9:00–10:30 a.m.: *Read and returned e-mails.*

11:30 a.m.–12:30 p.m.: *Revised the script outline from the freelance writer. Implemented the notes we discussed yesterday.*

12:30–2:30 p.m.: *Had lunch and visited a friend's art show!*

the breakdown

IN MEETINGS: 2–3 hours a day

ON THE PHONE: 20 minutes a day

ONLINE: 30 minutes a day

SITTING: Practically all day

READING: 1 hour a day

WORKING SOLO: 5 hours a day

2:30–3:00 p.m.: *Finished script revisions and turned in for approval. Craig was happy with it.*

3:00–4:00 p.m.: *Nap (seriously, I needed one).*

4:00–6:00 p.m.: *Sat down to start my own script. Wasn't able to get anything down, but I took down some notes and did some drawings of ideas for possible gags and sequences. Hopefully they'll fit into the final script.*

february 15

10:30–11:00 a.m.: *Got in late today. Ran into an old friend I worked with on* Powerpuff Girls *who had been working in Europe for the past two and a half years. Besides saying hello and catching up, Craig and I wanted to gauge his interest in writing scripts for us. Hopefully we can secure him— we've always liked his work!*

11–11:30 a.m.: *Turns out I was locked out of my office! I had to wait for someone to let me in. Talked about Disney movies with the other writers while waiting.*

then to now

1992–1994: Attended California Institute of the Arts

1993: Layout artist, Rough Draft Studios

1994: Animation assistant, Turner Feature Animation

1994–1996: Animator, Turner Feature Animation

1996–1998: Animator, Warner Bros. Feature Animation

why wait?

▶ Talent counts for more than experience, so hone your skills—take drawing and writing classes as often as you can.

▶ Draw *all the time!*

▶ Rent DVDs of great animated movies like *Toy Story* and *Cinderella* and watch the extra features for the behind-the-scenes scoop on how the films were made.

11:30 a.m.–12:15 p.m.: *Read and returned e-mails and phone calls. I was hoping to receive notes on the outline I sent to my bosses in Programming in Atlanta. It has been three days and I haven't heard back from them. They usually send the outline back right away if they like it, so I'm worried they will have heavy changes. Unfortunately, worrying about it is giving me some monster writer's block for my own script.*

12:30–1:30 p.m.: *Lunch with friend I ran into earlier, Craig, and our producer, Vince.*

2:00–4:00 p.m.: *Sat in on editing session with Craig. Episode was slightly too long. I made some suggestions to help cut down.*

4:00–5:30 p.m.: *Met with a development exec from Atlanta and a coworker to discuss* Kotatsu, *an acquired property from Japan that Cartoon Network has asked me to help develop as an animated series. Good meeting. There are plans to meet with cowriter Kevin next week to proceed with the bible, which is basically a proposal or summary of a show.*

7:00–9:30 p.m.: *Dinner with a former colleague. Discussed the animation biz.*

1999–2003: Storyboard artist/writer, Cartoon Network Studios

2003–NOW: Supervising producer/story supervisor, Cartoon Network Studios

2004: Nominated for an Emmy Award

2005: Nominated for an Annie Award (the highest honor for excellence in animation)

paying your dues

Most animators start as production assistants or storyboard clean-up artists, and they stay in these positions for one to two years. They'll be expected to do things like make copies and scans, organize artwork, hand out memos, prepare materials for artists, and implement story or drawing notes made by a director.

february 16

10:00 a.m.–12 noon: *Read and returned e-mails. Also, an animator came by with a question about a scene. I finally got word from Atlanta on my outline. It was approved! In fact, they were quite happy with it and had only one minor adjustment. Turns out my boss had approved it on Tuesday, but the e-mail did not get through to any of us. I've been worrying for the past two days for no reason!*

12:30–2:00 p.m.: *Lunch.*

2:00–6:00 p.m.: *I was supposed to be writing, but the writer's block has continued, even though my outline was approved. I wrote some things I was unhappy with and put aside. Then, in hopes of stirring up some inspiration, I spent some time drawing some new characters I have to introduce in this episode. Sometimes that helps me to figure out how to write for them. Not much luck. I have a lot of drawings, but very little writing to show for it.*

february 17

9:30–10:30 a.m.: *Read and returned e-mails.*

10:30 a.m.–12:30 p.m.: *Supposed to be working on my script, but I still have that nasty writer's block.*

what it takes

▸ A great imagination

▸ Natural artistic ability

▸ Being comfortable working solo

12:30–2:00 p.m.: *Lunch.*

2:00–3:30 p.m.: *Story meeting. A freelance script was turned in a few weeks ago, and I felt it needed work, but Craig was much more unhappy with it. Darrick is going to be revising it, so we discussed our plan of attack to fix it.*

4:00–6:00 p.m.: I spent the end of the day suffering with more writer's block. The fact that it's late afternoon on a Friday isn't helping. I sure hope I have better luck next week!

writer's block update

In the following two weeks, I managed to write forty-six pages of the eighty-eight-page script. Thankfully, the first half of this one-hour special was approved with very minimal notes. Sometimes a couple of days of letting my brain breathe does the trick . . . that and the all-encompassing fear of missing a deadline!

in the field

Five More Careers in Animation

in-betweener Because animation is literally bringing inanimate objects to life, each frame of an animated project has to be either hand-drawn or drawn on a computer so that the movement we see on our TV is smooth. In-betweeners are the people who do all the drawings in between key poses to make the transitions smooth.

background artist Live-action shows are filmed on location or on a set, but the background of an animated project has to be designed from scratch. Background artists look at photographs, art, and movies to get inspiration and then draw and paint the background, giving animated characters a "world" to live in.

character designer Whoever your favorite animated characters are, behind their cool look is a character designer. Character designers are responsible for designing all of the animated characters in a show, making sure that the design is consistent with the creator's vision and the show's style.

animation timer Bringing characters and objects to life is part of an animation timer's job. They act out what their characters will be physically doing and make notes on timing sheets on how many seconds each movement should take. This tells the in-betweeners how to translate the desired action through the drawings.

storyboard artist Before any film, TV show, or commercial is produced, a storyboard is created to visually plan out what the end product will look like. In animation, a storyboard artist draws out each scene, detailing the action, sound effects, and dialogue. When it's finished, a storyboard might resemble a graphic novel.

 you need to know about

Animation World Network, or AWN (www.awn.com), calls itself "The Hub of Animation on the Internet." This site has everything from interviews with leading animators and job postings to animation business directories and thousands of links to animation resources, as well as a free monthly online magazine called *Animation World* magazine.

lunch break

i'm not sure if you've noticed by now, but just about every woman profiled in this book considers her job to be highly stressful. Yet these women not only kick butt in their jobs, but they love the work they do to boot. How do they keep it all in balance? Here are tried-and-true stress-beating techniques from some of the women I spoke with:

▸ walking, writing in a journal (actionist Jessica Weiner)

▸ looking at photos of family (movie studio exec Alli Shearmur)

▸ listening to music, specifically R&B and gospel (advertising exec Maureen Shirreff)

▸ meditating and going on silent retreats (sheriff Lupe Valdez)

▸ scheduling "meetings with herself" to slow down and catch up (business exec Claudia Poccia)

▸ reading soap opera updates online (engineer Tamara Hayman)

▸ spending time with family (recruiter Bo Kim)

▸ hanging out with her dogs (firefighter Danielle Aust)

▸ hiking, skiing, and gardening (nurse-midwife Michelle Grandy)

▸ playing video games (video game programmer Kelly McCarthy)

▸ practicing yoga (yoga instructor Miriam Kramer)

Susannah Grant

screenwriter

the facts

Susannah Grant,
Screenwriter and Director

▸ **what?** Screenwriters write the screenplays or movie scripts for every film that gets released, as well as for thousands of movies that never actually get made. They might adapt novels or other stories, or come up with an original concept to write about.

▸ **where?** Screenwriters can work anywhere, although many choose to live in L.A. or New York to be closer to the action.

▸ **how?** Writing . . . a lot! According to Susannah, "No one cares where you studied, if you studied, or whom you studied with. All they care about is whether or not you have something to say and can say it in a way that's either artistically accomplished or (more likely) commercially promising."

▸ **$$$:** Anywhere from $5,000 to more than a million dollars a year

▸ **dress code?** Anything they want

▸ **stress factor:** On a scale of 1 to 10, wildly and unpredictably between a 1 and a 10 (according to Susannah)

i know there are lots of aspiring screenwriters out there, so I wanted to profile someone whose films we've seen and who's work we really connect with. I was lucky enough to hook up with Susannah Grant, an extremely successful screenwriter whose writing earned her an Oscar nomination for *Erin Brockovich*. Susannah also wrote the screenplays for *Ever After* starring Drew Barrymore, *28 Days* with Sandra Bullock, and *Charlotte's Web*, starring Dakota Fanning and Julia Roberts.

> *"I try to focus on the things that are harder for me before I indulge in the stuff that's easy."*

I talked with Susannah about how she got into screenwriting, what it feels like to work in Hollywood, and what she loves about her job. Here's our conversation—in screenplay form, of course.

INT. DEBBIE'S OFFICE IN SEATTLE. LATE MORNING.

Debbie dials Susannah's number and waits as the phone on the other end rings. She checks the clock to make sure she's calling on time.

After three rings, Susannah picks up the phone.

INT. SUSANNAH'S OFFICE IN SANTA MONICA, CA.

Screen becomes split screen so we can see both Debbie and Susannah talking.

DEBBIE

Hi, Susannah! It's Debbie Reber calling.

SUSANNAH

Hi, Debbie!

DEBBIE

Is this still a good time to talk?

SUSANNAH

Yes, it's perfect.

DEBBIE

Great. Do you mind if I put you on speakerphone so I can record our conversation?

SUSANNAH

No problem.

Debbie pushes the orange speaker button on her phone and gently sets the handpiece down in its cradle while pushing "record" on her tiny handheld recorder.

DEBBIE

All right . . . we're set! I would love to start by hearing in your own words what exactly you do as a screenwriter.

SUSANNAH

I try to create and communicate stories through the film medium that move people, that make them think, that challenge their ideas of who we are. I spent a lot of time watching films when I was growing up, and it always felt like it was a positive force in my life. Now I like to write stories that will have the same impact and comment on the world around us.

you asked . . .

"How have you managed to keep going and believing in yourself and your dreams even if other people gave up on you and stopped believing in you?"
Mandy, age 18

susannah answered . . .

"It's difficult working in a field where people are judging you on some level. And it's easy to think that if they don't like the writing, then there's something wrong with you. So before I expose my work to anyone else, I decide for myself how I think I've done. And if I don't think I've done as well as I could, then I don't turn in the script yet. Once I get to the point where I can look myself in the mirror and say, 'I did a good job this time, regardless of whatever anyone else thinks,' then I put it out there. It's a very conscious thing I do, because you can make yourself crazy hoping for validation from others."

DEBBIE

What is it about films that you love so much?

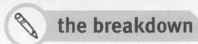
SUSANNAH

I think there's something really powerful about sitting in the dark with a couple hundred people and having a significant emotional experience. There's something that happens in the air when you're all laughing together or you're all moved at the same time. I like to be a part of creating that for people.

DEBBIE

What are some of the movies that really inspired you when you were a teen?

SUSANNAH

The one that really rocked my world was *Network*. I watched that when I was thirteen or fourteen and it just blew my mind. But it was always more about the experience than the movies. *(laughs)* My friend and I created the "dreadful movie club," and the two of us would pick the worst movie in the paper and go and see it and have a fantastic time.

DEBBIE

So did you know you wanted to pursue a career in screenwriting after you graduated from high school?

SUSANNAH

No. I majored in English in college. After college I thought I would be a journalist or an actress, so I lived in New York and pursued both for a while. Along the way I tried to write a screenplay, but I just couldn't quite figure it out. Eventually I reached a point where I looked ahead and I just couldn't see a career in journalism or acting working for me. So I abandoned both and I moved out of New York. I ended up in San Francisco, where I had a job I didn't like very much and a boyfriend who I really liked a lot. When he finished law school, my boyfriend decided to travel around the world for a year, so I asked him if I could borrow his computer. The plan was I would meet him in Paris in six months. I tried writing a screenplay again, and for some reason, it all came together nicely and I had so much fun doing it. And then I went to Paris to meet up with the guy and he had met a Swedish model in Thailand and fallen in love with her. So our relationship was completely kaput, but I had a screenplay and a passion that I really liked.

DEBBIE

Can you break down for us how the process of writing a screenplay works for you, from the seed of the idea through the completion of the movie?

THE SCREENWRITING PROCESS

the pitch The first step is getting a job and signing on to write something. The ideas for your screenplays will either come from you as a writer or they'll come from somebody else who has an idea. The screenwriter articulates the idea so that somebody who's going to be paying you to write it can get a sense of what they're paying for up front. That's called "pitching." It's going into a room and saying, "Here's the movie I want to make with you," and then talking them through it, trying to give a sense of how the movie will feel. And ideally they say, "That sounds great, let's go ahead and write the script."

writing the script They pay you half your fee up front and the other half when you deliver the first draft, and you contractually get three months to write that first draft. I usually take one month to just think and make notes and an outline and stuff like that, and then the rest of the time will be writing it. But I don't just sit down to write it until I know what I'm going to be writing. During the writing you're pretty much alone and doing your own

then to now

| Graduated from Amherst College with BA in English literature | Worked as a fact checker for *Rolling Stone* magazine | Attended American Film Institute (AFI) | 1992: Was awarded the Nicholl Fellowship in Screenwriting | 1994: Staff writer on *Party of Five* for FOX | 1995: Wrote the screenplay for *Pocahontas* |

thing. . . . I really love doing the first draft because then it's just mine. Usually you do a second draft and often a third. If everything goes smoothly, after a couple of drafts we'll have something that everyone feels good about, and then it becomes the studio producer's job to turn it into a movie.

making the movie The writer's involvement in this stage varies. Sometimes turning in a final script is the end of your involvement, but more often than not I get what's called "meaningful consultation" in the production. I can't approve or disapprove anything, but if somebody suggested a director or actor who seemed completely wrong for the project, I would at least be listened to. But that's something that comes with a certain amount of experience—early on in your career, it's not going to happen. Once a director's on, you tend to do more work on the script with the director, because getting it ready to shoot is different from getting it ready to just be read. Once they start shooting, if you had a good relationship with the director, you're often welcome on the set, and that can be fun and it can also be very tedious. Making a movie is a lot of long hours with nothing happening, but it is fun to watch it initially.

postproduction of the movie After the filming, which takes about three months, the producers create a "rough cut" or rough edit of the movie, and if you've been intimately involved with the director, sometimes he or she will bring you in to consult on the cuts of the movie as it gets edited, but that's not a given.

movie is released The movie comes out and you go to the premiere, and that's fun. And then you read the reviews and sometimes they're good, sometimes they're not. I try not to read the reviews; instead, I make sure that by this time I'm writing something else.

timeline In a fast-track scenario it can take two years from when you first decided to write something to it being on the screen. Sometimes it can take decades.

1998:	2000:	2000:	2005:	2006:	2007: Made
Wrote the	Wrote the	Nominated	Wrote the	Wrote the	directorial
screenplay	screenplay	for an	screenplay	screenplay	debut with
for *Ever*	for *28 Days*	Oscar for her	for *In Her*	for	her original
After:		screenplay	*Shoes*	*Charlotte's*	screenplay
A Cinderella		*Erin*		*Web*	*Catch and*
Story		*Brockovich*			*Release*

DEBBIE

You've had such a successful screenwriting career. What's your secret?

SUSANNAH

I've had really good luck and I've worked extremely hard, and writing only gets better the more you work at it. There's no point at which working more on a script is actually damaging. The easiest thing for me is writing dialogue that reads well, so I try to focus on the things that are harder for me before I indulge in the stuff that's easy. And I think that level of rigor has probably helped me professionally.

DEBBIE

Do Hollywood takes on screenwriting portray a true picture?

SUSANNAH

It's true that screenwriters are sort of the low woman (or man) on the totem pole. But on the flip side, screenwriters are the only people in the film industry who don't need someone else's permission to work. So for example, if you've gotten into a position where nobody thinks you can write anything but silly comedies, all you need to do is write a drama and prove everybody wrong. You can write yourself out of any professional hole if you're willing to work hard enough.

DEBBIE

Do you need to have an agent in this biz?

 why wait?

▸ Write, write, write.

▸ Visit Drew's Script-o-Rama online (www.script-o-rama.com) and download free screenplays of your favorite movies so you can see how the script was translated to film.

▸ Read books about screenwriting, like William Goldman's *Adventures in the Screen Trade*.

SUSANNAH

Yeah, you really can't get your ideas in front of studios without an agent.

DEBBIE

What would you say is the best part about your job?

SUSANNAH

Since I've had children, I'd say that the best thing is the flexibility and that I can work when I want to—it's the biggest luxury you can imagine. Also, if you get a certain amount of success, it's a job that pays really well. I really like working with funny, creative, crazy people and there just don't seem to be as many rules as there are in other professional environments. Lastly, I get to work on something that I love—movies.

what it takes

▸ A love of writing and the movies

▸ Extreme self-motivation

▸ Good networking and people skills

▸ No shortage of good ideas

DEBBIE

What film are you most proud of?

SUSANNAH

Obviously *Erin Brockovich* is the one that people have responded to most strongly. I really do like that work—I love the person, I love the movie it ended up being. I have a real fondness for the ones that fail, too. But my favorite one is always the next one I'm working on.

DEBBIE

Do you do a lot of research when you're writing a movie?

SUSANNAH

I tend to, because if you're going outside of your own experience and you want to be able to write about it with any sense of knowingness, you have to get to know the details of it. Details are everything.

DEBBIE

And how about your characters . . . how do you find their voices?

SUSANNAH

When I was little my sisters and brother used to tease me because I always had some strange dialogue running in my head, and every now and then a line of dialogue in some strange accent that made no sense would sort of blurt out of my mouth. It's just something I have always done. I also read a lot because I think that reading gets your brain stimulated on many fronts. And when I actually get to writing something, I listen to the music I listened to when I was an adolescent because it helps me bring out my emotional side.

DEBBIE

I know that you've got to run, so I'll let you go. But before we say good-bye, is there anything else you'd like to add?

SUSANNAH

Just that along with the hard work, discipline is really important. A lot of people say that they're screenwriters, but they don't ever get around to finishing something. Being disciplined and finishing and going back and reworking things . . . it's an essential part of the process. Everybody can do it, but the writers are the ones who actually do.

DEBBIE

Perfect note to end on. Thanks so much for letting us peek inside your world, Susannah. Bye!

SUSANNAH

Thanks for including me in the book! Good-bye!

Susannah and Debbie both hang up the phone. Screen goes black.

If you're a teenager interested in becoming a screenwriter, the most important thing I can tell you is this: Don't write screenplays. Not yet. The screenplay form is so full of mechanics that it's almost impossible to find your voice as a writer within it. And all that matters as a screenwriter—as any kind of writer—is voice. So write something else, anything else—poems, letters, stories. Write lots of them. Eventually you'll feel your way to who you are as a writer. You'll notice where your sensibilities lie, what you're good at, what you need to get better at. The more rigorous you are in discovering what you have to say in this world, the greater the odds are that once you write a screenplay, (a) it will be time well spent, and (b) someone will buy it.

in the field

Five More Careers Working as a Writer

novelist Novelists create amazing worlds in their heads and write about them in ways that keep the readers glued to the page. Like screenwriting, writing fiction books takes a lot of self-discipline—novelists do most of the work all alone, hunched over a computer or typewriter and transferring their ideas and thoughts onto the page.

playwright While screenwriters write for celluloid, playwrights write for the stage. And whether it's a one-act skit or an opera, playwrights take into consideration the venue of their play and create material that will translate well in a theater.

technical writer As computers and technology become a larger part of everyday life, the technical writing field continues to boom. These writers might write brochures about new products, directions on how to use computers and software, or press releases and articles explaining complicated concepts in ways that the layperson can understand.

freelance writer Freelance writers usually work from home, and they might write anything from magazine articles to marketing materials for a big company. Like most self-employed people, freelance writers are always looking for their next job, even as they're working on a dozen projects at once.

columnist Columnists don't get paid to report the news objectively, but rather present their strong opinions and perspectives to the public. Well-known columnists might be syndicated in major newspapers all over the country, while others might have a monthly column in a magazine.

 you need to know about

Creative Screenwriting is a magazine aimed at screenwriters, with great articles about the trade, interviews with screenwriters, resources, and updates on news relating to the biz. Check it out at your local bookstore or read more about it online at www.creativescreenwriting.com.

For more on writing in Hollywood, check out the TV show creator profile on page 2.

Michelle Grandy

nurse-midwife

the facts

Michelle Grandy,
Certified Nurse-Midwife,
Maternal-Fetal Medicine,
University of Washington
Medical Center

▶ **what?** Nurse midwives are nurses who've taken additional coursework to become certified as a midwife, which means they specialize in caring for pregnant women, delivering babies, and providing postnatal care.

▶ **where?** Most midwives work in hospital settings, while others are at birthing centers or start their own practice.

▶ **how?** Nurse midwives need a four-year bachelor's degree in nursing or a related field, as well as a master's degree from a certified nurse-midwifery program.

▶ **$$$:** An average salary of $80,000

▶ **dress code?** Casual to business casual while in the office or clinic, and scrubs while delivering a baby

▶ **stress factor:** On a scale of 1 to 10, between a 6 and an 8 (depending on the day)

i wanted to interview someone in the medical profession for this book, and I just loved the idea of talking with a midwife, because unlike many jobs in medicine where people are responding to an emergency, illness, or disease, midwives are dealing with something that's positive—pregnancy and childbirth.

Michelle is a certified nurse-midwife who works out of the Maternal & Infant Care Clinic at the University of Washington Medical Center. I met with her in her office at the clinic.

ME: How does a midwife do things differently from a doctor?

"Everything can be total chaos around me, but I can see my way through the logical steps to get us to where we need to be."

MICHELLE: Midwifery focuses on a holistic view of pregnancy and childbirth. I think a lot of times medical professionals see pregnancy as more the physical piece of it, and some of the other pieces get left behind. But pregnancy, the birth, and parenting changes everything about a woman—it changes every relationship she has, including the one she has with herself, it changes her emotional state, her spiritual state. And so for a lot of women who have normal, healthy pregnancies, the physical piece is small in comparison to this whole other journey that's happening.

Physicians see high-risk pregnancies all the time and so they're kind of expecting that at any moment a pregnancy can become a problem. And of course that's true, but why would you spend your energy thinking about that when it's 80 percent or 90 percent likely that everything's going to be totally fine? And while as midwives we always have in our mind all of the high-risk things that can happen in a pregnancy, if a woman presents to me as normal, my expectation is that she is normal and will continue to be normal through this journey, unless she shows me something different. In which case we'll take those other paths to find out what's going on.

ME: How do you help women through this "other journey" they're on?

MICHELLE: Part of it is giving them time—I have twenty to thirty minutes for each appointment. And I think the other part is being "open." When I sit down with a pregnant woman, the first thing I say is "Hi, how are you?" And then I say, "Tell me what questions or concerns you have." And then I just wait in silence for those to come forth. And if she says, "I don't know . . . everything's fine," I might give another open-ended question, and then wait. I'm leaving the space open for her to talk. And if she truly is fine and she truly doesn't have anything to say and everything's totally cool, which happens a lot, then I always have an agenda of things to talk about, based on where she is in the pregnancy, and things to check in with her about. But I'll always give her the space to talk first.

ME: What is it like when you're actually with a woman who's in labor and about to give birth?

MICHELLE: I have the ability to remain calm in very stressful situations. I think that tends to be the characteristic of lots of medical providers. Everything can be total chaos around me, but I can see my way through the logical steps to get us to where we need to be. Although

you asked . . .

"How have you pushed past all the problems and obstacles life has thrown at you to be where you are today?" Joanne, age 15

michelle answered . . .

"My biggest obstacles centered around financing my education. My family didn't save any money for me to go to college, so I had to go off of loans and scholarships and whatever I could get. Getting good enough grades so that I could qualify for whatever monies were being given out by the school was really important. I stayed motivated by being passionate about the work and feeling like I could make a difference."

a woman who's having a normal labor is not "chaos," for her it's very intense, it's very painful, and the sensations are very strong in her body. I'm also keeping an eye on everything that could go wrong, and signs that problems might be coming down the road. Is the baby doing okay? Is it doing well enough that I think it's going to be okay for the next hour or two or three or however long I think it's going to take us to get to the end of this journey? That's always something I'm tracking. How is the father of the baby doing? Has he eaten lately? How's his energy store? And whoever else is in the room supporting her, are they getting what they need? At the same time, I also hold positive energy and confidence in the woman's ability to deliver the baby—"I know you can do this."

ME: When did you know you wanted to be a midwife?

MICHELLE: When I was in college, I was studying to be a nurse, and I had a semester on obstetrics nursing with a great professor, and the idea that pregnancy is a "normal process" connected with me. There are few types of ways to work in medicine where you're actually dealing with healthy people, so I liked that a lot. Then, when I was working as an OB nurse, I'd be giving women in labor great support,

then to now

1987: Graduated from Seattle Pacific University with BS in nursing

1987–1989: Worked as a nurse at the Veteran's Administration Medical Center in Seattle

1989–1995: Worked as a nurse in labor and delivery, postpartum, and the nursery, Northwest Hospital

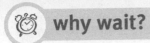

why wait?

▸ If you have a close friend or family member who is pregnant, see if you can attend the birth as an observer.

▸ Contact a local birth center or women's health clinic and ask about observing a midwife for the day.

▸ Read books about midwifery, like *Spiritual Midwifery* by Ina May Gaskin.

being right there with them and coaching them, and then I'd have the physician walk in at the last minute, catch the baby, and get all the money and all the glory. I thought, *I'd like to do that.*

ME: What's the reality of the job that girls should know about if they're interested in being a midwife?

MICHELLE: It involves happy, fun experiences most of the time. But there are lots of times when it's hard and stressful, too. And there are times when things don't go well or the baby dies. I mean, that does happen. It doesn't happen a lot, but a lot of people say, "Oh, how wonderful to be a midwife," and on my good days I say, "Yes, it is wonderful." But you do get those life and death moments, those scary moments where the woman is bleeding and you're the one standing there and trying to manage it. You have to be able to think ahead really fast.

what it takes

▸ Staying cool under pressure

▸ A nurturing nature

▸ Being a good listener

1996: Received master's in nursing from University of Washington

1996–2003: Worked as a certified nurse-midwife at Providence Everett Medical Center

2003: Began working as certified nurse-midwife at University of Washington Medical Center

2003: Joined faculty at University of Washington School of Medicine

There are two different kinds of days in my work. One is a "clinic day" where I'm scheduled from eight thirty a.m. to five p.m., with an hour break in the middle of the day. I have clients scheduled every half hour during that time, unless it's a new client, and then I see them for an hour. With each client, I go in, spend twenty to thirty minutes with them, then come out and do some charting, which is writing down everything that happened during a visit on that client's chart. Then I move on to see the next client.

Typically, things happen—people are late, somebody talks a little longer, somebody has more extensive problems—and then things back up. When things get backed up, that can cause some stress. So sometimes a lunch that is supposedly an hour is really only fifteen minutes, or I'm supposed to be out at five p.m. but things got busy, and I didn't have a chance to do my charting, so now I have to do that at the end of the day. That happened more when I was new—I would take too long because I couldn't think as clearly about problems. Now that I've been a midwife for ten years, it happens less and less.

On my "call days," I'm on call for twenty-four hours, so I will be with anyone in our group who is in labor. We usually have between twenty and thirty women due to deliver a baby each month in our practice, and they don't come one a day. I'll have one twenty-four-hour shift where not much is happening, and then I'll have another where I have three women in labor and I'm kind of going from room to room to be with them.

During a labor, I'll come in and out of the labor room depending on where the woman is in the process and what she needs. If she has three or four people in there all attending to her every need and she's coping really well, at a certain point during her labor I'll be there less. And as the labor progresses and things get more intense, I'm there almost constantly. After the birth I usually stay until the baby starts breastfeeding and everybody seems settled, and then I'll leave because the nurses will take over and get the woman everything she needs—food, a shower, a bath for the baby. Then one of the other midwives or I will see the woman every day that she's in the hospital and talk about going home—what to expect and any concerns she might have.

* in the field

Five More Careers in Healthcare

chiropractor Chiropractors study the spine and nervous system and look at their impact on overall health. Unlike doctors, chiropractors approach healing from a less "medicalized" perspective, and they use healing tools like massage, electrotherapy, and ultrasound therapy.

physician's assistant Physician's assistants, also known as PAs, work closely with doctors in hospitals, clinics, or private practices doing different procedures that a doctor might typically do. They might take medical histories, perform physical exams, draw blood for testing, give shots, dress wounds, and make diagnoses.

lab technician Hospitals never rest, and lab technicians work around the clock in hospitals, testing blood, tissue samples, and body fluids to help doctors diagnose their patients.

ER doctor Doctors who specialize in emergency care have to be ready, willing, and able to handle any problems that come through the emergency room door, and they never know what illnesses or injuries their next shift might bring.

anesthesiologist These medical doctors specialize in administering anesthesia to patients. Much of the work of anesthesiologists involves putting people "under" for surgery, and then monitoring the patient throughout the operation to ensure that they are stable and pain free.

For more careers in health and medicine, check out the physical therapist profile on page 372.

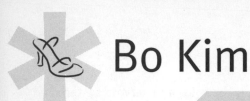

Bo Kim

recruiter

the facts

Bo Kim,
Managing Director,
Major, Lindsey & Africa

▶ **what?** Recruiters or "headhunters" find job candidates for specific openings and try to get their candidate hired into the position. Many recruiters specialize in hiring for a specific industry.

▶ **where?** Some recruiters are employed by a corporation and recruit staff for their own company, while others work for recruiting firms, who act as a third party between the hiring company and the candidates.

▶ **how?** There are no specific educational requirements for recruiters, although most have at least a four-year degree, as well as a background in marketing and sales or an industry they specialize in.

▶ **$$$:** Most recruiters work on commission—earning a fee paid by the company or a percentage of the candidate's salary when a candidate is placed.

▶ **dress code?** Casual to business, depending on the firm and the day's meetings

▶ **stress factor:** On a scale of 1 to 10, between a 7 and an 8

when it comes to big recruitment firms, Major, Lindsey & Africa (MLA) is one of the best. In fact, it is the world's largest legal search firm, and it has offices around the world. I had a chance to interview Bo Kim, a managing director at MLA's Chicago offices, where she specializes in placing associates at law firms. Bo shared with me what it's like to do her job.

ME: So, what exactly does a recruiter do?

BO: I do legal recruiting for a search firm, so basically what we do is try to find qualified attorney candidates to fit into law firm or in-house counsel positions. There are two parts to my job—there's the candidate side, where we're always trying to find qualified candidates, develop relationships with them, and target them to appropriate needs, and then there's the client side or law firm side, where we're trying to develop client relationships to make sure that we have a steady stream of jobs that we're working on.

"What I earn is directly proportional to what I put in."

ME: How did you get into this career?

BO: I fell into human resources. When I first graduated from college, I did sales for about six months or so, and I just really felt like it wasn't the right fit for me. I was an account rep, so I was in the field all day long, doing fourteen, fifteen appointments a day, basically pounding the pavement. So at that point, I decided that I didn't care what I was doing, as long as I was sitting behind a desk and working indoors—I was tired of being out in the snow and sleet. So I started working for a mortgage company doing loan processing, and I realized that I'd gone too far in the other direction, and I really didn't enjoy work that was so paper intensive and not having contact with people. So I started a job search and ended up working for a temp agency doing staffing, and that's where I first got my start in recruiting. Now I've been doing recruitment for over ten years, and I really enjoy it. I was a little apprehensive when I started in this position, since it's very sales-oriented and it's commission-based, so there's no financial stability. It's what you make of it, and I enjoy that aspect. I like that what I earn is directly proportional to what I put in.

ME: I didn't realize that some recruiters work on commission . . . so you only get paid when and if you place people into positions?

BO: Yes, if you're doing recruiting in-house on the corporate side, which I used to do, then it's a salaried position. But working for a search firm, it's 100 percent commission, so that was probably the biggest leap of faith for me to take. It's sort of a hard pill to swallow when you're not used to it.

ME: So if your job is to place lawyers into different law firms, how do you go about finding lawyers to work with?

BO: I spend a lot of my day doing research online. I use online professional research tools, and also go onto firms' websites and research people who I think might be a fit for whatever openings we have. I also do a lot of cold calling, which is calling candidates that I don't know to try and develop relationships. I also network and stay active in different professional organizations, getting my name out there, getting recognized, developing relationships. Then I have to do things on the client side as well, like maintaining client relationships, making sure that we're the first company they contact when they have new needs,

you asked . . .

"What do you believe success is?" Tawnee, age 16

bo answered . . .

"To me, success is very individual. I think different people have different ideas of success for themselves. I ultimately think it's being proud of what you've accomplished and being satisfied with what you do on a daily basis."

trying to stay current with the legal market. I try to spend at least a portion of my week doing research on different law firms and their practice areas. I also have lots of meetings, whether I'm learning more about clients and their needs, interviewing candidates, or meeting here with the staff. The position involves a fair portion of writing, too, which is different for me because I've never had to do much of it. I write cover letters when I submit candidates to different law firms, outlining their qualifications and why they're a fit.

the breakdown

IN MEETINGS: 2 hours a day

ON THE PHONE: 3 hours a day

ONLINE: 2–3 hours a day

SITTING: Most of the day

PUBLIC SPEAKING: On occasion

WORKING SOLO: A lot of the time

ME: I would imagine there's a lot of social stuff too, like nurturing relationships over lunch or drinks?

BO: Yes, absolutely.

ME: As you're describing this to me, it reminds me of the role of a talent agent.

BO: Yeah, it's very similar. I just happen to be dealing with the law.

ME: Can you tell me about your work atmosphere?

BO: The people that I work with in this office are great. Everyone is extremely smart and well-credentialed, and it's actually a pretty relaxed environment in our office. We don't have a strict dress code. If I have meetings, I'll dress business casual or whatever's appropriate, but if I don't and I'm in my office all day long, I could be in jeans and sneakers and that's fine.

ME: What are the hours like?

BO: Our office hours follow law firm hours, so they're nine to five, but my hours will vary depending on if I have meetings and what time they're at. It's definitely not the kind of position that requires you to be in the office ten, fourteen hours a day. On the flip side, there is quite a bit that I'll do from home, whether it's making phone calls, talking with candidates, or checking e-mails. It's a bit like a real estate agent in that you're kind of never off duty.

ME: What is the best part of your job?

BO: The most satisfying part of my job is being able to help people with their careers and placing them in the position that's right for them and gives them the potential they want. You make that fit and everyone's happy.

ME: What is the most challenging aspect?

BO: The challenging part is the cold calling. Getting on the telephone and calling people that you've never spoken with and trying to get them to talk to you when they're extremely busy at work is by far the hardest part of the job.

ME: So how do you get better at it?

BO: You just have to grit your teeth and do it, and the more you do it the more comfortable you get with it. I think that the cold calling is what separates people at the beginning, whether they can do this job or not. Because some people just can't overcome that hurdle. I had some sales experience coming into this career, so that's helped me quite a bit. And I've done a bit of recruiting, so in that respect I'm accustomed to calling people, and it wasn't so bad for me to get over that hurdle. My personality tends to be pretty outgoing, and I typically don't have a problem approaching strangers. For me, if I don't want to do something, I just do it—I just get it over with. It seems like the more you put something off, the worse it gets.

ME: What type of characteristics does someone need to be successful in this job?

BO: They have to be very self-motivated, because this is not the type of job where someone is going to stand there and say, "You need to get this and this done." You have to be able to set goals for yourself and be able to meet those goals. You definitely can't be a shrinking violet—you need to be outgoing and put yourself out there and introduce yourself to people. And you need to have good communication skills, both written and oral, and be a good listener.

ME: How do you balance work and life?

BO: There are some people in my office who live and breathe work. They think about it all day long, they never shut off their computer, never shut off their BlackBerry. That's just not me. I'm the type of person who's like, "I don't have a heart in the cooler. . . . I'm not doing a transplant." There are very few things that really will implode if you don't get it done right now, so I guess for me, it's important to prioritize and keep perspective.

ME: How long might it take you to find the right person for a client?

BO: It really varies. Sometimes it's as fast as a couple of months, and sometimes you'll never find the right match. On average, I'd say three to six months.

ME: How many law firms or clients might you be working with at a time?

BO: An average of fifty clients who have active needs.

ME: And how about on the candidate side?

BO: Most recruiters work with between fifty and a hundred candidates, but you're probably only working through the interview process with five to ten candidates at a time.

ME: And candidates work with only one recruiter at a time?

BO: We'd like them to work only with us, but that's not always the case.

ME: What happens if you're cold calling a candidate and they've already established a relationship with another recruiter. Do you move on and try to find someone else?

BO: Yeah, sometimes, or maybe we'll try to convince them to work with us instead. Recruiting is a very dog-eat-dog business.

ME: Ah . . . so you have to be a little competitive, too.

BO: Definitely.

 BO'S ADVICE

Fight for what you want. I've never sat back and expected things to be handed to me or given to me. I've always anticipated the difficult work and I worked hard to get there.

in the field

Five More Careers in Human Resources

human resources manager Human resources managers work in almost every company, large and small, handling everything having to do with the relationship between the employees and their employer—from helping two colleagues work out a dispute to dealing with benefits like stock options.

payroll processor There is a lot of paperwork involved in making sure people get paid—there are hours to calculate, taxes to be taken out, benefit plans to be deducted. Many companies contract this job out to companies employing payroll processors, who enter data and file paperwork to ensure all payroll issues are handled properly.

benefits specialist Benefits specialists manage the information related to employee benefits like vacation and health insurance, and they make sure employees have the benefits that they want. They not only have to be good with numbers, but they must also stay up-to-date on changes in the law that might impact their company's benefits.

training manager Whether a company is training employees in new technology or holding mandatory workshops on discrimination in the workplace, training managers figure out what kinds of extra learning opportunities the employees of a company might benefit from, and then set up the appropriate programs.

organizational development consultant These consultants are typically brought in to work with a company undergoing a major restructuring or reorganization. They look at a company from a human resources perspective and make recommendations of changes that will benefit both the company and its employees.

Amanda Koster

photographer

the facts

Amanda Koster,
Freelance Photographer

▶ **what?** Professional photographers are paid to take photographs—from wedding and editorial photos to magazine photos and fashion shoots.

▶ **where?** They might work for magazines or companies as in-house photographers, while many are self-employed and work out of their own studios as freelancers.

▶ **how?** There are no strict educational requirements, although most photographers take classes to learn about lighting, development techniques, and other skills. Most photographers work as an assistant or apprentice to an established photographer to learn about the job.

▶ **$$$:** An average of $25,000 to $50,000 on up, depending on the kind of photography

▶ **dress code?** Casual

▶ **stress factor:** On a scale of 1 to 10, a 5

it's taken her several years, but photographer Amanda Koster has found herself in the enviable position of having created her ideal work situation. While she has spent much of her career doing free-lance editorial photo work for magazines and newspapers, Amanda has slowly been weaving in the kind of work that drew her to the field of photography in the first place—photo projects that enable her to share powerful perspectives of the world with others through photography.

"In many ways it has been my tenacity that has led me to where I am today."

Amanda splits her time between her separate work worlds, and she shared her journal with us for two very different days in her life. Here are her entries.

AMANDA'S JOURNAL

april 25, seattle, wa

Today I woke up at five thirty a.m. I have an assignment for Sunset magazine, so I'm heading to Dungeness National Wildlife Refuge on the Olympic Peninsula, an amazing park near where the subject lives.

Like any morning before a shoot, today I did my normal rush around the house to gather all of my gear and information. For this kind of shoot I travel light with portable gear, my favorite way to work. Photographing outside feels the best to me, and though the morning is hectic, I look forward to meeting my subject and working outside today.

My assistant arrives around six a.m. She knows exactly how my gear should be packed and does a double check. We laugh about how early it is, have a little tea, and load up the car, heading north on I-5 by six thirty. We have to race to catch the ferry and just make it by three minutes. Once we are crossing Puget Sound on the ferry, the view of the Olympic Mountain Range is beautiful . . . it felt great to be out of the city.

Our subject, Gordon, was waiting for us at the park when we got there. I usually like to talk with people before we start shooting to get an idea of how comfortable they are with being photographed, if they've done this before, and if they have any ideas. I also like to do some location scouting by walking around with my assistant and finding good spots to photograph, keeping in mind the direction of the light, everything that's in the background, and how busy the location is. Today we discovered the perfect spot.

We photographed Gordon for about a half hour. I tried photographing from many different angles, since things in any shoot—the light, the conversation, and the energy—are constantly changing. I also have to be very sure that Gordon is comfortable at all times in order to get the best results.

While I was shooting, my assistant was taking meter readings, making sure bugs didn't crawl into my camera bag, that the drizzle didn't touch my gear, and that no hikers ran over my lenses.

We wrapped up the photo shoot and were on our way home by noon. My assistant drove so that I could make phone calls, write lists . . . just think. We stopped for lunch, caught our ferry to the mainland, and dropped the film off at the lab to be processed on our way back to the studio.

We're in my office by three o'clock. We listen to Youssou N'Dour's amazing album Egypt, while my assistant works on some scanning and Web design and I return a few calls, check my e-mails, and get back in the office groove. It seems as though there are always twenty e-mails to compose and fifteen calls to make at any given moment.

you asked . . .

"When did you decide that this is what you wanted to do with your life?"
Kayla, age 12

amanda answered . . .

"I was studying to be an anthropologist, and I thought that taking pictures of my research would be a great way to get myself ahead as an anthropologist. When I graduated from college, a friend of mine asked me to come to Ethiopia with her. I'd never been to Africa before, and I went and took all of these photos of kids in Ethiopia, brought back the photos and showed them to people, and no one believed I had actually been there. Everybody said, 'I thought everyone in Ethiopia was starving to death. These kids aren't starving—they're wearing winter jackets, and they're smiling and they have chubby cheeks.' When I realized how powerful photos were as a way to teach people about the rest of the world, that's when I knew what I was meant to do."

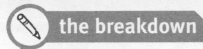

the breakdown

(AN OFFICE DAY)	(SHOOTING DAY)
IN MEETINGS: 2 hours a day	IN MEETINGS: 1 hour a day
ON THE PHONE: 2–8 hours a day	ON THE PHONE: 30 minutes a day
ONLINE: 3–6 hours a day	ONLINE: 2 hours a day
SITTING: All day	STANDING: Most of the day
READING: 2 hours a day	READING: 1 hour a day
WORKING SOLO: All day unless assistant is in	

By five thirty, my assistant heads out, while I stick around to finish up a few more things. I've always got e-mails coming in from people in other time zones, so I handle them as well. E-mails from Western Europe and New York usually get me up early, while those from other countries keep me going late into the night. It doesn't bother me at all—I like to feel connected to the planet.

As I walk home, it's like I can feel the entire time zone unwinding. The sun is setting and there are fewer cars on the streets. People are smiling more, moving a bit slower. The cats are out, eyes closed, very still. I love this time of day.

After I make dinner, I sit at my kitchen window, eat, and do some journaling, still seeing traces of daylight in the sky. An airplane flies by and I think of Saturday, when I will leave for Morocco and I too will be on a plane that high.

april 29, fès, morocco

Today I am in Morocco. This is one of seven days where I am photographing a project called "Moroccan Women's Music Project: Voices of Women in Islam." Our goal is to create a CD of musicians performing, as well as a multimedia collection of photographs, video, and sound for an exhibition that will tour with the CD release.

I woke up around five a.m. to pack up my gear before breakfast. Our team was leaving right after we ate, driving to the town of Taroudant,

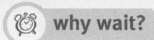
> ▶ Start taking pictures now! Photograph things that interest and excite you.

> ▶ Take a photography class in your school if it's offered.

six hours away. With me was the production team—a videographer, my photography assistant, a producer, a sound engineer, two musicians, a coproducer, a linguist, a translator, and a fixer—as well as our driver.

I first got involved in this project while attending a panel discussion about traditional Moroccan music in Brooklyn, where I encountered Zeyba Rahman, the chairperson of the World Music Institute. I was so inspired that I approached her with an idea for a photography exhibition that could travel with the CD release and concerts. I thought it was important that people had the chance to see the women they were hearing.

Luckily, Zeyba saw the merit in my idea and asked me to be a part of the project. Looking back, I can see that this is how much of my work happens. In many ways it has been my tenacity that has led me to where I am today.

The musicians were waiting for us when we arrived in Taroudant, dressed in their traditional clothing, smiling and chirping amongst themselves. After nearly a year of preparations, it felt amazing to be there with them. The women were wearing the most amazing blue-colored jellabas (Moroccan women's outerwear). Underneath the jellabas they were wearing their traditional clothing, which we thought would preserve all aspects of this particular tradition for the photos.

We got set up and the women started performing their music with a simple chant. The chant began to build on itself, the rhythm speeding up and new instruments being introduced. The music creates a sense of contemplation and divine focus, and as a result, I found myself in a

then to now

| 1993: Graduated from Southern Connecticut State University with BS in art history, anthropology, and religious studies | 1993: First traveled to Ethiopia | Took photography courses at International Center of Photography, New York | 1994: Was a photography intern at Medical Media Services at Yale University |

contemplative state, which made photographing interesting. I found that the more I invited this feeling in, the more I was able to follow the music, the chanting, and the exchange going on among the musicians. This kind of connection is important for my work. Whether I'm photographing the CEO of Microsoft, a woman who was widowed by HIV/AIDS, or a Moroccan musician, the connection must be there.

We had some technical challenges today, because the musicians perform inside dark rooms and they are constantly moving, so I had to push photography to the limit with the ASA, motion, depth of field, and focus. I have the feeling focus will suffer throughout this project because there was always such limited light. However, over the years I have learned to just let go and appreciate what I get.

The women I was photographing were awesome. I tried to remember when certain things would happen in the various songs so that I could anticipate a movement to photograph. For example, there was one woman whaling on a small clay drum. I wanted to make sure I could shoot underneath her because the action was wild and her expression was so intense. The drummer knew what I was doing, and when she hit the drum, she smiled, like she knew I wanted to capture that. Once we established that, we collaborated and I got the shot. The best part about it was none of us skipped a beat. The music stayed on course, the song continued, and no one even realized the silent conversation that had occurred.

 paying your dues

Many photographers spend several years working as a photographer's assistant, which is basically a paid apprenticeship. Photographer's assistants are the right-hand person to a photographer, and they learn the ropes while doing things like running errands, booking photo shoots, making copies, managing portfolios, and answering the phones.

1995: Became freelance "stringer" photojournalist for the *New Haven Register*	**1995:** Established own company, Amanda Koster Photography	**2001:** Launched body image project called "This Is Beautiful"	**2005:** Went to Kenya as a mentor and instructor with Bridges to Understanding

what it takes

▸ A keen creative eye

▸ Excellent networking skills

▸ Passion and a clear vision

We wrapped up recording and shooting around six o'clock and worked together to load everyone's gear into the van. Then we went to one of the women's homes for dinner, where we hung out in a typical Moroccan living room—very long and narrow with couches and cushions along the perimeter of the room and tables in the middle. We all (musicians, musicians' family, and crew) sat together, sipping our tea and eating our dinner, laughing, singing, talking a little . . . mostly just attempting any form of communication.

After dinner it was time to go. We all stalled a bit—no one wanted to say good-bye. I hugged every woman good-bye, hugging Amineh, the one I connected with the most, last. I saw her tears and next I felt mine. She affected me. I appreciated her and she appreciated me.

After the crew said good night, we were quiet—we have all been affected by the women of Taroudant. Sometimes after an experience like that, there really are no more words. We quietly waved one another off to our hotel rooms, and Maggie and I settled in. We cleaned up for bed and talked a little about the shoot, but were very silent inside. As I lay down and began to fall asleep, I thought about Amineh's tears welling up in her big black eyes . . . a picture I will never take. There are millions of photos to take, but the ones I remember the most are the ones I see without a camera. These are the photos that I experience, I feel. These are my favorite photos of all.

▶ *I see a lot of people freaking out when they try to take pictures for the first time. They're really worried about whether or not the pictures are going to be good enough before they even take one. So why not just take the pictures? I guarantee you'll find pictures that you love on that roll of film.*

▶ *Come up with a mission statement. When I got back from my first trip to Ethiopia, I realized what my mission was as a photographer: to use photographs to teach people about the rest of the world.*

▶ *Make sure you always listen to your instincts and follow your heart. No matter what job you have, you have to deal with your finances, the phone . . . everything else. So why not pick a job that you absolutely love, so when the phone rings you really look forward to answering it?*

in the field

Five More Careers Working in the Fine Arts

gallery director Galleries are like small museums that showcase works from various artists, except unlike pieces in a museum, the items in a gallery are generally for sale. Gallery directors look out for new talent to showcase in their spaces and play a key role in executing and promoting an exhibition.

portrait painter Painted portraits used to be a familiar sight hanging over fireplace mantels, and while they're not as common today, business-savvy painters who specialize in this artform can make a living doing their craft, since many businesses, organizations, and families still commission portraits.

stained-glass artist While many of us think of churches when we hear the words "stained glass," a boom in historic home renovation has created a resurgence in jobs for stained-glass artists. People who specialize in stained-glass artistry can make their living designing custom windows and other decorative fixtures for clients.

illustrator Those looking to make a living as an illustrator might find work at newspapers or magazines, or in advertising or children's book publishing. Whether you're drawing cartoons or illustrating a short story for a magazine, this career can offer flexibility and variety, since many illustrators work as freelancers.

printmaker A printmaker creates a template or "plate" for a piece of art, usually on some sort of material like a piece of wood or glass or even stones, and then prints the art from these plates. Printmaking is a specialty craft, and the possibilities for creating unique works of art are unlimited.

 you need to know about

The American Museum of Photography (www.photography-museum.com) is a virtual museum where you'll find tons of information about the history of photography, the development process, virtual photography exhibits, and much more.

For more on careers in art, check out the animator profile on page 231 and the museum curator profile on page 103.

Linda Chen

golf tournament director

the facts

▶ **what?** Event planners of sorts, golf tournament directors plan, organize, and manage golf tournaments. They oversee every aspect of a tournament—including planning a VIP guest list, finding and working with sponsors, handling all media and press requests, hiring caterers, and staffing the event.

▶ **where?** Golf tournament directors typically work at the golf resorts that host the event.

*Linda Chen,
Tournament Director,
Ginn Open*

▶ **how?** Linda has a background as a professional golfer, but this isn't a requirement. A love of the sport and a background in marketing, business, or event planning is.

▶ **$$$:** An average of $60,000 to $100,000 on up, depending on the size and level of the tournament

▶ **dress code?** Business to business casual, depending on the day

▶ **stress factor:** On a scale of 1 to 10, a 10

linda chen is the tournament director for the Ginn Open, a new women's golf tournament on the LPGA schedule in Orlando, Florida. The Ginn Open has the most award money of any LPGA tour at $2.5 million, and it is broadcast live on CBS and televised worldwide. It boasts two nights of concerts, a million dollars' worth of art from Chihuly glass displayed on the tournament grounds, and a food and wine event. You could say the event is *big*. So big, in fact, that tournament director Linda Chen literally spends an entire year planning for it.

"When you're an athlete, you train to build stamina so you can perform at that peak moment in the competition. I'm building stamina for this event, too."

"I kind of view it almost as if I'm the 'head conductor.' I work with my team of 'musicians'—everyone from security, marketing, and food and beverage to our reservations, accommodations, and sales department. I make sure that we're all in step with one another as we try to execute this huge event," Linda explains.

So what does being an event planner on such a megascale actually entail on a daily basis? Linda laid it out for us.

you asked . . .

"How did you know what you wanted to do with your life?" Jessie, age 15

linda answered . . .

"I didn't. Never in my life did I actually think, 'Hey, I really want to be a tournament director.' There's no way I would have even put that in my top ten things that I wanted to do. But I knew I was good at business development, and I have the ability to work with all sorts of people and inspire them, and that can really translate into any number of roles. Some people are very passionate about wanting to be a dentist or a vet and that's what they look toward doing. I just want to be in an environment where I'm always working toward the strengths that are my talents, and that can come in many different forms."

I usually wake up around six thirty a.m. and am in the office by eight thirty. A big part of my job is organizing things, both my time and my space. I've dissected this event into areas of responsibility, so I have certain piles on my desk that are about marketing or sales, sometimes there are administrative items, others are finance-related, and yet others might have to do with operations. I prioritize that stack every day based on urgency. It doesn't always work out that I can go through and touch everything in the order that it needs to be addressed, because I have an open-door policy. So what ends up happening is that I spend most of the day assisting different departments so we can move forward.

 the breakdown

IN MEETINGS: 3 hours a day

ON THE PHONE: 2 hours a day

ONLINE: 3 hours a day

SITTING: Most of the day

READING: 2 hours a day

WORKING SOLO: 4 hours a day

One of the great things about my job is that we work on a beautiful resort and there's a fitness facility on site. So for lunch, I jog down to the fitness room, I do my run and workout for an hour, come back, make lunch or a shake, hop in my shower, and I'm back at my desk all within an hour and twenty minutes.

The afternoon continues much like my morning, and then I use the hours between four thirty to eight p.m. to get caught up and stay on task with everything else. I go home for dinner and spend about another hour and a half in the evenings working to get everyone, myself included, up to speed in terms of tasks and responsibilities for the next day. I go to bed around midnight or one in the morning.

As the tournament date gets closer, Linda's job gets more and more intense. At the time I spoke with her, about two months before the big event, Linda was working seven days a week, and she was expecting things to get even busier. She noted that her background as a professional golfer actually helps her do her job.

"When you're an athlete, you train to build stamina so you can perform at that peak moment in the competition. I'm building stamina for

why wait?

▶ Get involved in the planning for a school event like homecoming or a big concert.

▶ Volunteer to work at a golf tournament near your hometown.

this event, too, not just in terms of energy, but sharpness. So all of the adrenaline is building so that you can run on all cylinders when it comes down to the event. The funny thing about an event like this is that on the surface it seems so peaceful and goes so smoothly, but it's all the behind-the-scenes work and planning that allows for that perception to come through," Linda explains. "It really can be crazy."

Working at such an intense pace and juggling so many things at the same time sounds pretty stressful, and Linda admitted that it can be. She says the biggest stress is all about expectations.

"There's quite a bit going on and you have to stay on top of it. At times it almost seems impossible, and it can be overwhelming to keep your hands and your eyes on everything, but it needs to be done," she says.

There are also the inevitable tensions that arise whenever many different people are working together, like legal disputes with contractors that have to be addressed, which is a difficult but necessary part of her job.

So, is the stress and breakneck pace worth it in the long run? It is for Linda. The perks are many. Because she's working with such a prestigious company, she gets to do things like interact with important executives, travel to great places, stay in wonderful hotels and resorts, and dine with heads of companies.

then to now

1994: Graduated from University of Texas, BA in kinesiology

1994–1996: Toured as a professional golfer

1996: Public relations manager, Futures Golf Tour

1996–1999: VP of marketing & business development, Futures Golf Tour

paying your dues

The most common entry-level position for work in sports tournaments is a one-year internship, where you'll do things like coordinate mailings, run business-related errands, answer phone calls, assemble binders or reports, or lay out and assemble marketing presentations.

On top of that, being a tournament director is the perfect fit for Linda because it taps into all of her expertise and experience in a way that is challenging and stimulating. She didn't seek out this career when she first graduated from college, but through a series of stepping-stones and happy accidents, she has ended up here.

I was curious, though—after working so hard all year to pull off a weekend-long event, what happens the morning after?

"When it's over, it's almost sad. You build up to all this, and you're on this adrenaline high and then you see this buzz and golf players from all over the world come in and you've got the media running around . . . that's the exciting part. And then everyone goes home and disappears and it's like, 'It's over.' I know the staff and I will be exhausted after the tournament. I've already planned on disappearing for two weeks after the event so I can recuperate," Linda says.

And next year's tournament?

"I'll probably start working on next year's tournament the day after I get back from vacation."

 ## what it takes

▸ Keeping your cool under serious pressure

▸ Excellent organizational skills

▸ The ability to inspire and motivate others

| 2000–2004: Manager, sports sponsorship and promotions, Walt Disney Company | 2003: Finished MBA at Stetson University, Florida | 2004–2005: Manager, Alliance Development, Walt Disney Company | 2005: Founded L2 Inc. with business partner |

▸ *Have an awesome attitude: Positive energy is addictive!*

▸ *Think about how to take care of the needs of people other than yourself. Your dreams, wishes, and desires will be fulfilled when you learn what it is like to be in other people's shoes.*

▸ *Think of your career as a puzzle. A few pieces of one area might fit perfectly together to form a cluster. So develop as many clusters as you can, keep your eye on the overall picture, and slowly pull the clusters together to form your career.*

in the field

Five More Careers Working in Event Planning

caterer Any planned event that includes food, whether it be delectable hors d'oeuvres or a five-course meal, involves the work of a caterer. Caterers help their clients develop a menu that suits the event and the venue, and they oversee getting and cooking the ingredients, hiring waitstaff, and ensuring a smooth event.

party planner Party planners plan events ranging from weddings and bar mitzvahs to anniversaries and sweet sixteens, working with their clients to find the perfect location, negotiate with caterers, organize music or other talent, and select a menu. They deal with the little (and big) details so the client can focus on the fun stuff.

invitation designer Custom invitations are the norm for many events. Invitation designers help their clients figure out what information needs to be on the invitation, identify any design preferences or logos clients want to incorporate in the invites, and then design and print the custom invites.

set and event designer Set and event designers create sets for events ranging from huge concerts to industry expos, dealing with things like large constructions, lights, and microphones. They handle all the logistics of set construction, as well as being on-site for the event itself in case there are any set-related emergencies.

corporate retreat planner Many companies plan corporate retreats, or getaways, for employees to strengthen their relationships with one another and reconnect to the mission of the company. Planners work at retreats, resorts, and other destinations, and they help companies plan a retreat experience that will meet all their needs.

lunch break

what *does* it take?

for each career, there are certain qualities and characteristics that go a long way toward making someone successful—you may have noticed some highlighted throughout this book in sidebars called "What It Takes." You'll also notice that some of these qualities show up time and time again, so much so that it became pretty obvious that there are universal keys to success, no matter what career path you find yourself going down. Here are the ten most commonly mentioned essential qualities identified by the women in this book. Do you have what it takes?

1. Persistence, drive, and patience

2. Solid interpersonal and communication skills

3. Being able to handle pressure well

4. Great networking skills

5. Willing to work hard and put in long hours

6. Ability to inspire and motivate others

7. Passion

8. Being a team player

9. Great organizational skills

10. Knowing how to trust your gut

Barbara Boxer

senator

the facts

Barbara Boxer, U.S. Senator, California

▶ **what?** U.S. senators serve in the Senate, which is one of the two chambers of the U.S. Congress. There are two senators for each state, and their job is to write and vote on bills, ultimately making decisions about what will be signed into law.

▶ **where?** Senators spend much of their time working and living in Washington, D.C., although they work out of home-state offices as well.

▶ **how?** Senators need to be at least twenty-five years old, have lived in the United States for a minimum of nine years, and be a resident of the state they are hoping to represent. Most senators have a background and experience in law and/or local or federal government, and they must run to be elected every six years.

▶ **$$$:** An annual salary of $165,000

▶ **dress code?** Business professional

▶ **stress factor:** On a scale of 1 to 10, between a 5 and a 10, depending on what's happening in the Senate

when it comes to having a successful political career, Senator Barbara Boxer of California is an expert. After a brief stint as a stockbroker when she first graduated from college, Barbara made the switch to politics and hasn't looked back. She's been working in national government for more than twenty years, first as a member of Congress from 1983 to 1993, and as a senator ever since. When she was elected for her third senate term in 2004, more people voted for her than any other senate candidate in the history of the United States!

"My job is more of an honor than glamorous."

As you can imagine, Barbara is an extremely busy woman, as she divides her time between her offices in Washington, D.C., and northern California, and she focuses much of her time and energy working toward improving the quality of public education and health care, as well as championing environmental and crime-fighting efforts. And that just scratches the surface. Barbara took the time to answer these questions about her job and life:

ME: What were your career dreams when you were younger?

BARBARA: When I was a little girl, I wanted to be a ballerina. When I was in high school, I decided I wanted to be a stockbroker.

ME: What kinds of tasks might you do on any given day?

BARBARA: In Washington, D.C., a typical day might consist of meetings with constituents* to find out their issues of concern, meetings with staff to plan legislative and communications strategy, committee hearings to fulfill my responsibilities as a committee member, press conferences to communicate issues of concern and action plans to address those issues, and Senate floor statements to discuss pending legislation and other issues. In California, a typical day might consist of meeting with constituents and groups, meeting with state

* **THE LINGO:** A **constituent** is someone who lives in an area represented by someone who's been elected. In this case, it's a citizen of California.

staff, visiting various cities and counties to see firsthand the needs of the people of California, connecting with elected officials in the state, holding press conferences to bring the issues to the hometown press, and giving speeches on topics ranging from foreign relations to flood control to education. Also, I often present certificates of merit to those Californians doing outstanding work in the fields of education and environment.

ME: How many hours do you work per week? And what are your hours, as in, what time of day or night?

BARBARA: I have no set hours—some days start at eight a.m. and end at one in the morning; some start at nine a.m. and end at seven p.m. It all depends on the schedule of the Senate.

ME: What's the first thing you do when you get to work in the morning?

BARBARA: It depends on the day. Sometimes I have breakfast meetings with constituents, other days I go straight to a committee hearing—there is no predictable schedule for me on any given day, except for our Tuesday mornings, when we have our Senate Democratic Leadership meetings.

ME: What is the last thing you do before you go home? And how much work, if any, do you take home?

you asked . . .

"How many times have you fought to keep your head above water?"
Mykaila, age 15

barbara answered . . .

"I have been in elected office since 1976. There have been more times than I could possibly recall where I felt a heavy load on my shoulders. But each time, I had a skilled staff, a supportive family, and an optimistic belief in the future, and therefore I was able to come out of those dark moments with even more experience and dedication to my work."

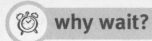
▸ Run for student government at your school and see what it's like to be part of a campaign.

▸ Volunteer in a local political campaign. There is always plenty of work to be done, like stuffing envelopes, making phone calls, and handing out flyers.

▸ Get a politician to come visit your school—part of their job is community outreach. When they get there, don't hesitate to ask questions!

BARBARA: There is no one thing I do each night before I go home— sometimes votes run very late into the evening. But almost every night, I have a large package of material from my staff to go through for the next day. I review drafts of letters to constituents, informational memos on legislative issues, talking points, testimony and statements for committee hearings, as well as press clips from as many as fifteen newspapers and transcripts of radio and television interviews.

ME: Your job appears so glamorous and exciting from the outside . . . what's the reality?

BARBARA: I think you can already tell from the description of my work that on an everyday basis, there is not much glamour in the Senate. My job is more of an honor than glamorous.

ME: What is the travel like? Do you split your home life between two cities?

then to now

1962:	1962–1965:	1972–1974:	1974:	1976–1982:
Graduated from Brooklyn College	Worked as a stockbroker	Served as Associate editor, *Pacific Sun* newspaper	Became a congressional aide	Elected as member, Board of Supervisors, Marin County, CA

BARBARA: Travel is a major part of my job, because I have family on both coasts and my work is on both coasts.

ME: What's the best part of your job?

BARBARA: The best part of my job is helping people.

ME: The most challenging aspect?

BARBARA: The most challenging aspect is bringing an issue across the finish line—it takes skill, determination, and enormous focus to get that done.

ME: Any advice for a teen girl hoping to succeed as a politician one day?

BARBARA: The best advice I can give any young person is to find an issue that you care about deep in your heart. If the issue is children, then map out a way to build coalitions to help our children If the issue is the environment or help for our seniors, the same applies. Once you build coalitions, show leadership by bringing everyone in and not being afraid to say what you think. Your skills will be noted, and eventually you will become a natural candidate for public office—starting at the local level. Another recommendation is to volunteer in a campaign for someone you believe in. Work hard, be part of a team, and again, your leadership skills will be noticed.

what it takes

▸ Excellent speaking and writing skills

▸ The ability to motivate and inspire others

▸ Being passionate about your ideas and vision

▸ A willingness to literally pound the pavement

1983: Elected as a member of the House of Representatives, California

1993: Elected U.S. Senator representing California

1997: Authored a Patient's Bill of Rights

2004: Elected for third term with 6.9 million votes—the highest total votes for any Senate candidate in American history

in the field

Five More Careers in Government and Political Science

lobbyist Lobbyists use their political savvy and powers of persuasion to try to convince voters—be they politicians or the general public—to make a decision that benefits their cause. They might work for private corporations or on behalf of nonprofit agencies.

press secretary Powerful politicians like Senator Boxer have the equivalent of their own private public relations department. At the head of this is the press secretary, whose job is to handle all media issues surrounding the politician's work, including holding press conferences and issuing statements on behalf of the politician.

campaign manager For major political races, campaign managers work tirelessly behind the scenes, handling all the details involved in running a bid for election. They might work for up to two years prior to an election, and they do things like manage thousands of volunteers, hire political consultants, and plan big fund-raisers.

speechwriter Government officials at high levels deliver a lot of speeches, and speechwriters work behind the scenes to write them, tailoring the speeches to the specific audience and using persuasive writing skills to convey the content in the way the official intended.

political pollster Political pollsters run frequent polls to get a pulse on where the public stands when it comes to a political candidate or issue. Then they analyze that information and work with campaign managers to address the concerns raised.

you need to know about

Young Politicians of America (www.ypa.org) is aimed at getting students ages fourteen to twenty-two interested in politics. YPA is not associated with a political "party"—its goal is to raise awareness of political discourse among teens and get teens involved in their own communities.

Susan Schulz

magazine editor

▶ **what?** An editor in chief manages the content for a magazine and is ultimately responsible for the people who come up with ideas, assign and write the articles, and design and lay out the magazine. Making sure the advertisers are happy with the placement of their ads is also part of the job.

▶ **where?** There are thousands of magazines across the country, although the hub for the industry is definitely New York.

*Susan Schulz,
Editor in Chief,
CosmoGIRL!*

▶ **how?** Most editors in chief started out like Susan did, as an intern, and then work their way up, position by position.

▶ **$$$:** From $55,000 to more than $125,000, depending on the size of the magazine

▶ **dress code?** Business casual is the norm.

▶ **stress factor:** On a scale of 1 to 10, between an 8 and a 9 (Susan says, "It's always stressful, but it's usually an exhilarating stress.")

i've always pictured magazine editors working in interesting old buildings in Manhattan, dressed in the lastest fashions, surrounded by lots of young, hip colleagues oozing energy, drive, and creativity. Well, I wasn't disappointed when I went to New York City to meet with the editor in chief of *CosmoGIRL!*, Susan Schulz.

Susan has a coveted job, so I wanted to find out how she did it. How did she get there? What does it feel like to work there? And most important, is it really as cool as it seems?

"I always wanted to be a magazine editor," Susan admitted. "When I was a teenager I read *Seventeen* magazine and ate it up, just died when it came in the mail. So I went into college as a journalism major, but switched to become an English major with a journalism minor. That switch just broadened my horizons. I totally loved reading, so it was a great major for me.

"I wasn't expecting to graduate and start out working for Vogue. *I just wanted to go and be somebody's assistant. I was like, 'Please, somebody, let me answer your phones."*

"When I graduated from college, everybody was freaking about what they were going to do and if they were going to get a job. But I didn't stress out about it. I was sort of like, 'Well, I'm going to graduate and I'm going to look for a job in magazines.' I just kind of had a belief. I decided to talk to anybody who could help me get in. I wasn't expecting to graduate and start out working for *Vogue*. I just wanted to go and be somebody's assistant. I was like, 'Please, somebody, let me answer your phones. I just want to be there, I want to learn, I want to help you.' That was my approach, and I think that's really what got me in.

"I started out at *Redbook* and then went to *Good Housekeeping*. But when I went to YM, that's when I started to realize that what I loved wasn't so much just writing articles and things, it was the idea of helping teens. When I got to YM, I realized I loved that age group so much and that's when I thought, 'I've found my passion.'

"When it came to moving up the ladder, I always took the approach that I'll get there when I get there and I'm going to work as hard as I can and do as good a job as I can. I've worked hard my whole life, I've gotten noticed for it, and it's worked for me. So I kept doing what I did, and luckily, I was in certain right places at certain right times. Plus, I always really liked what I was doing, and I think in a way that helped me," explains Susan.

While there is a certain amount of being in the right place at the right time in anyone's career success, there is also a lot of hard work, dues paying, and persistence, especially when it comes to the world of magazines. Susan worked her way up from the bottom as she moved around from magazine to magazine, and she landed at *CosmoGIRL!* when it was first launched, where she was the deputy editor, overseeing and nurturing the junior editors on staff. When the editor in chief left the magazine two years later, Susan moved up one step closer, becoming the number two at the magazine.

you asked . . .

"*In order to achieve your success, what did you have to give up along the way, and was it truly worth it?*" Mallory, age 15

susan answered . . .

"*Definitely, it was worth it. In my second job as an associate editor, I probably worked until ten o'clock at night for two years, and then I became a senior editor and probably worked until nine o'clock every night. When I first started here at* CosmoGIRL! *as deputy editor, I was working until ten o'clock a lot. So, I sacrificed a lot of 'going out with my friends.' But I think you have to want it enough that it really is your main priority, and that's what it is for me. I didn't mind those late nights so much, because if you like what you do, you're happy doing it and you're not thinking about what you're missing out on. It sounds so cliché, but the hard work does not go unnoticed.*"

IN MEETINGS: 5 hours a day	**STANDING:** Never . . . unless running from meeting to meeting
ON THE PHONE: 1–3 hours a day	
ONLINE: On and off throughout the day	**PUBLIC SPEAKING:** Occasionally
	READING: Constant, ongoing
SITTING: Almost the entire day	**WORKING SOLO:** 4 hours a day

"At the time, I thought, 'Oh my God, can I be the executive editor? I don't know.' And the new editor in chief said, 'Of course you can. There's like two more tasks that you haven't already been doing that you'll need to do,'" Susan relates.

Susan loved being the executive editor, but then things changed again. When Atoosa Rubenstein, then editor in chief of *CosmoGIRL!*, moved over to run *Seventeen*, she recommended that Susan pitch herself to management to be the new editor in chief.

"My response was, 'I don't think I can do that. Editor in chief . . . that's so huge.' But I couldn't say no, because Atoosa really believed in me. So I wrote up a proposal, and when I was doing it I realized that not only *could* I do this . . . but I *wanted* to do this. So I got the editor in chief job, and it was so surreal. I don't think my adrenaline came back down for literally a few months."

Moving to the present day, I asked Susan to tell us what goes on behind the scenes of one of the most popular teen magazines on the market.

then to now

Graduated from Loyola College in Baltimore	Started magazine career as editorial assistant at *Redbook* magazine	Became assistant editor at *Good Housekeeping*	**1997:** Made her move into teen mags as associate articles editor at *YM* magazine

I get up pretty early in the morning to read because as the EIC, I'm still just a cog in the wheel that is this entire magazine. You know, there's the art department and the editors and the production department and the research department . . . and if I don't turn first, then none of the other cogs turn. I do a lot of reading between seven thirty and nine thirty a.m., so that when we start work at nine thirty I can pass out a bunch of stuff that can then be fielded out to the different departments.

At nine thirty I meet with my managing editor, who deals with the schedules and budgets. So she'll come in and say, 'Oh, there's an issue with so and so,' like maybe there's a staff issue, or she'll say, 'Okay, the advertising department got an ad page and we have to figure out where we're going to put it.' For example, if we have a two-page story and we want to stick an ad in between it, we need to make sure it's going to look good. Maybe I need to ask the art department to do a redesign on that story so we can put the ad in between those two pages.

After that meeting, I'll often have a meeting with my deputy editor or my executive editor to talk about story ideas and the progress of certain stories.

Every day at eleven thirty I meet with my art director and my creative director and I look at the magazine layouts. Once they're approved, the copy or manuscript can be put into the layouts and cut to fit, because usually when you write a manuscript you write it much longer than will actually be on the page. At some point, the layout and the copy have to be married together by the production department, and then the editor goes back and cuts down the copy, and then I end up seeing it again and then one more time.

Then it's lunchtime, and I usually have a lunch that I'll go to, like today. Dove held a photo contest for their self-esteem campaign, so I judged the contest and they had a big luncheon for the winner today. Or

1999: Promoted to senior articles editor

2000: Joined *CosmoGIRL!* as deputy editor

2003: Appointed editor in chief of *CosmoGIRL!*

2005: Won a "Do Something" Award from the Alliance for Eating Disorders Awareness

the other day for lunch I met with a relationship therapist who might be an expert on one of our future stories.

In the afternoon, I usually have more meetings. Sometimes at four o'clock we'll have a lineup meeting, which is basically where we plan the next issue and figure out what stories are going to be in what sections of the magazine. The whole staff will be in those meetings. Other times we'll have a staff meeting where we'll go over a previous issue and talk about what we liked and what we could do differently in the future.

I try to have all my meetings over by five because with one meeting after another, I can get pretty fried. But usually at five o'clock or so, my design director may come back in and show me a few more layouts they've been working on, or the managing editor might come back in and say, 'This is what happened today,' or 'What's your decision on that?'" and that kind of thing.

Then sometimes I have events at night. Not that often, but sometimes it will be a charity event that I'll go to with my publisher. So those are the events where I'll have to wear a ball gown and I'll get my hair and makeup done. I always find those events are sort of fun, but it's also sort of weird. It's like getting ready for the prom and then not getting to go with your friends because you're working.

Just hearing about Susan's busy day made my head spin. I also knew that she was running late for a meeting, since her assistant buzzed in a few times during our conversation. Before we wrapped things up, I asked Susan to share some of the highs and lows of being an editor in chief of a magazine.

 why wait?

▸ See if there is a teen writing organization in your community where you can learn how to sharpen your creative skills.

▸ Many local newspapers have a teen page that is produced by teens, for teens—that's a great place to get some real-world experience.

paying your dues

The best way to break into magazine publishing is to do an internship while you're in college. You'll be doing lots of grunt work, but you'll also be in the mix at a very exciting atmosphere. Interns who prove their passion are often rewarded with assistant jobs upon graduating from college.

"The politics of the job is the hardest part for me, because it's like playing a chess game where you have to think three steps ahead. Like, 'If I do this, then this, this, and this are going to happen.' So if you can think that far ahead, and that's not the result you want, you've got to go back to square one. And sometimes the best decision that you can make for one part of the business is literally the opposite of what would make somebody else happy."

She adds, "On the flip side, the thing that makes me happiest is knowing that the magazine is selling really well. That's a really good day because I know it makes the company and everybody happy. Or when we get a really good celebrity for the cover . . . just the anticipation of a good sale is also great. Today is a good day, because I announced three promotions, and I love when I can reward hard work. I rarely have a bad day, because even when something bad happens, I know that this magazine helps so many girls, and that really feels good."

what it takes

▶ A willingness to work long hours

▶ The ability to handle tight deadlines

▶ Being able to work well with others

▶ Having great writing skills

▶ *Don't sell yourself short. Yes, there is competition out there and there are many other people going for the same position, but that doesn't mean that you're not going to be the one selected. Focus on your strengths, what you can do, and sell yourself as the best person for the position.*

▶ *Aim to be as helpful as you can be—think of the job as "here's what I can do for you" as opposed to "here's what I want to get from this job." If you focus on what you can offer a company, it puts you in the right frame of mind that no job is too small, and if you devote just as much energy and thought to a small task, you will perform well and get noticed.*

in the field

Five More Careers in Magazine Publishing

fact checker A magazine's reputation is only as strong as the material printed on its pages, so fact checkers go through articles and any other written material for the mag and make sure that every single word is correct, like making sure names are spelled correctly and ensuring that statistics and resources quoted in an article are true.

art director Art directors oversee how the text and images of a magazine are presented, laying out the pages and making sure the design is clear, cool, and true to the magazine's brand.

advertising sales manager The price you pay for your subscription to *CosmoGIRL!* doesn't cover the cost of creating, printing, and distributing it. Advertisers pay big bucks to have ads for their products in magazines, and every magazine has a sales team that finds new companies to advertise and keeps their current advertisers happy.

copy editor When the written content for a magazine article is turned in, a copy editor goes through the material and cleans it up, making sure there are no grammatical errors, rearranging things to make the text flow better, or sometimes cutting pieces to make it fit into the layout.

production manager Production managers at a magazine are responsible for the production aspect of printing a magazine—overseeing paper stock, colors, typesetting—and they make sure the finished product looks as great as the publisher intended, not to mention completed on time and within the budget.

 you need to know about

Teen Voices is a magazine written by, for, and about teen and young adult women. You can submit your poetry, fiction, and other writing to be considered for publication, or if you live in the Boston area, apply to be a part of their teen editorial board. Visit them online at www.teenvoices.com.

For more on careers in journalism, check out the journalist profile on page 222.

Lupe Valdez

sheriff

the facts

▶ **what?** The sheriff is the head law enforcement officer in a county. Sheriffs typically oversee all the police departments and jails within a county.

▶ **where?** There are more than 3,500 sheriffs offices across the United States—nearly every city and county has one.

▶ **how?** In most states and counties, the sheriff is an elected position, and sheriffs typically have extensive experience working at different levels of law enforcement, as well as an educational background in criminal justice.

Lupe Valdez, Sheriff, Dallas County, TX

▶ **$$$:** An average salary of $85,000 a year

▶ **dress code?** A sheriff's uniform, usually made up of pants, a button-down shirt, a hat, shoes, and badges

▶ **stress factor:** On a scale of 1 to 10, between an 8 and a 10

for someone who is in charge of one of the largest jails in the country, Sheriff Lupe Valdez of Dallas County has broken through a lot of barriers. Not only is Sheriff Valdez the first woman ever to be elected sheriff of Dallas County, but she's also the first Hispanic sheriff in the county. Lupe has an impressive career background in law enforcement, most recently working as a special agent with the Department of Homeland Security before being elected as sheriff in 2005.

I had a chance to talk with Lupe about what it's like to be in her shoes, and believe me, they're big ones to fill. Here is our conversation.

"What is the old saying? 'A woman has to work twice as hard and gets half as much credit.'"

ME: I've never met a sheriff before. Can you explain to me what you do?

LUPE: Dallas County is the ninth largest county in the United States. We have the seventh largest jail in the United States, and I have almost two thousand employees, so it's a pretty big organization. I don't think there's any other female who's got this much authority in law enforcement, so it's pretty much a frontier for women. I have at least thirty-five sections in the department reporting to me, from the jail to patrol to criminal investigation to courtesy patrol. We also have our own cooking facility, which takes a lot of management. Basically, I run a little city of eight thousand prisoners every night and at least five to six hundred officers on duty at all times, as well as another two hundred to three hundred patrol officers. There's no such thing as leaving it without any attention, so people are always here, working holidays and doing all sorts of things—criminal investigations, victims' assistance, transporting two hundred to three hundred prisoners a day.

you asked . . .

"What were your motives for getting involved in this career, and have they changed since you've started?" Sarah, age 18

lupe answered . . .

"I got into law enforcement by accident, and I've always taken the approach of, 'Okay, now that I'm here I'll do the best I can, and maybe I can get to the next level.' There's nothing wrong with having goals of being four or five levels ahead, but that wasn't me. I gave up a good job with the federal government in order to run for sheriff. I had come to the conclusion that being somewhere where I could mentor, where I could make a difference, and where I could influence for the better was important enough that even if I lost, it would have been worth trying."

ME: Do you find that there are special challenges being a woman in this job?

LUPE: What is the old saying? "A woman has to work twice as hard and gets half as much credit." Because I broke so many barriers, I really have to prove myself. There hasn't been a Democrat in this office in thirty-five years, and there's never been a minority sheriff here. There are some people who want you to succeed and there are some who want you to fail. So I think the difficulty comes in keeping your head above water and doing the things that are right for the department and keeping those other things out of the way.

ME: That sounds very stressful—how do you deal with it?

LUPE: For a while I wasn't dealing with it very well, so when I noticed it was having an effect on me, I started trying to catch a movie here or there or get together with friends more. And every year or so I schedule a trip to a monastery where they practice silence, and I'll go for three or four days where I can meditate and just totally be with myself

paying your dues

Before you become a sheriff, you'll need to spend time working in law enforcement, most likely as a police officer, and then work your way up the ladder.

and catch up with what's going on with me and my body. But there is a lot of stress. Recently I've noticed that I've been having problems with it, so I actually built a little room in my home that I call my "sanctuary room," and I just go in there every two or three days and sit for five to ten minutes and let my spirit catch up with me.

ME: Can you tell us a little bit about how you actually spend your day?

LUPE: This office essentially hadn't been given any attention for about ten or twelve years before I got here, and a lot of things that were needed were not even here to run a normal department. So right now my job is a lot of restructuring. I end up having a lot of meetings. The main thing for me is that I'm holding people accountable. That didn't happen before. If you were in a position before, you were there because somebody liked you. It didn't matter if you could do it or not. And now, if you can't do the position, then you don't belong there. Unfortunately, in situations like that you have to spend a lot of time getting to know people to figure out who would fit best in that position. For my first year as sheriff, I was literally working seven days a week, sixteen or seventeen hours a day on weekdays and seven to eight hours on the weekends. But there was so much that had to be redone. There was also a lot of backstabbing and working against each other in the department before I was elected. And I've been trying to change that mind-set to, "We are a team, we're going to work together."

ME: When do you feel the most satisfaction in your job?

LUPE: I know I'm making some good changes that are going to last.

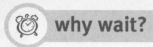
▶ This might seem obvious, but don't get in trouble with the law! If you're interested in being a police officer, you'll want to have a clean record when you apply to the police academy.

▶ Do volunteering in your community, where you'll have an opportunity to show your dedication to serve.

▶ Check with your local police or sheriff's department to see if they offer any special programs or classes for high school students.

ME: I know that you were elected into office. How well have you been received into the department?

LUPE: I didn't come up through the ranks. When I won the election, the newspaper headline said something like, "Five Strikes Against Her and She Still Won." Well, one of the strikes was that I did not come up through the department. My opponent's supporters were putting up charts of what was going to happen to the people in the department if my opponent didn't win, like people being fired and demoted. So of course when he lost, the people who had done this were scared about what I was going to do. When I started, I had a two-hour interview with all captains and above, and they literally came into my office shaking. I would say, "Why are you shaking?" and they would say, "I don't know what you're going to do to me." So I said to them, "I'm going to give you the opportunity to be the best officer that you have ever been."

then to now

Graduated from Southern Nazarene University, Oklahoma, with BS in business administration	Graduated from University of Texas with MA in criminology and criminal justice	1976–1986: Captain in the U.S. Army National Guard & U.S. Army Reserves	1978–1980: Correctional officer with the Department of Justice, Federal Bureau of Prisons

ME: Are there any misconceptions about the field of law enforcement?

LUPE: A lot of shows glamorize things that don't exist. No department has the money to spend on testing everybody's DNA. It's never going to be like it is on TV. Women leaders in law enforcement have to be way above the norm and have to work a lot harder and prove themselves much more than their male counterparts. Hopefully, ten years from now that won't be the case, but it is right now. When I came in there wasn't a single female on the whole executive staff except for a secretary. Out of fifteen on the executive staff, there was one minority. So that is changing. I'm trying to make the department look like the face of the community. You know, the community is not all white males, and we need to change things so that people can start identifying. I don't think we'll ever get to the point where the community totally trusts law enforcement, but we can get to the point where they can feel that they're being treated fairly.

 what it takes

▸ Dedication to the job

▸ Being able to handle office politics

▸ A fair and disciplined nature

ME: What would you have said if someone told you when you were a teen that you'd become the sheriff of Dallas County in 2005?

LUPE: I would have said you come from cuckoo land or outer space. I grew up extremely poor. My family were migrant workers. And there was a time in Dallas when Hispanic people were not allowed through the front door of restaurants. So the idea of ever being a sheriff was

1980–1983: Special Agent, GSA, Office of Inspector General	1983–1987: Special Agent, U.S. Department of Agriculture	1987–2003: Special Agent, U.S. Customs	2003–2004: Senior Special Agent, Department of Homeland Security	2005: Elected sheriff of Dallas County

just so far out from where I was at. I happened to get into law enforcement by accident, but I always remembered that I wanted to make a difference, and I think this job provides the most opportunity for me to do that.

INTERESTED IN WORKING IN LAW ENFORCEMENT? HERE'S LUPE'S ADVICE

Go for it! We need more women working in law enforcement. We need more people who are not concerned about their egos. When you go on official duty, you no longer represent yourself. It's not about you—it's about the whole department. And I think that women have a tendency to think that way—we're nurturing, so we think about the whole instead of just about "me."

in the field
Five More Careers in Law Enforcement

parole agent When offenders have been released from jail, they are often on parole and must check in with a parole agent at regular intervals. Parole agents might arrange for drug testing of the parolees or interview them about their living arrangements and job search, as well as offer support and direction to ex-offenders.

detective Detectives are in the business of investigating and solving crimes, from petty thefts to murders. They research the crime scene, search for clues, interview witnesses, and interrogate suspects, usually working around the clock until the crime is solved.

bounty hunter Bail bondsmen hire bounty hunters to find fugitives who skip out on bail, so they can get their bail money back. They then give a percentage of the bail to the bounty hunter as payment. In most states, bounty hunters can carry guns and go on people's property without a warrant in order to do their job.

police officer Police officers are the members of the law enforcement community most visible to us. Their primary job is to protect people and enforce the law, and they might be doing deskwork in the squad or driving around on patrol with their partner.

dispatch officer Whether they're looking for information or have an emergency and need a police officer immediately, people calling the police department reach the dispatch officer. They're based in the squad room and they keep tabs on where all the officers out on patrol are and what calls they're responding to.

 you need to know about

The National Center for Women & Policing (www.womenandpolicing.org) is an organization dedicated to increasing the number of women in law enforcement. On the website you'll find great information about how to become a police officer, articles and downloadable publications about the status of women in law enforcement, job links, and much more.

For more on careers in law enforcement, check out the district attorney profile on page 33.

Anne Corbett

urban planner

the facts

Anne Corbett, Executive Director, Cultural Development Corporation

▶ **what?** Urban planning, also known as city planning, deals with how cities are developed and shaped. Urban planners figure out what buildings and businesses should go where, and how the public transportation of a city should work to have the best impact on the community.

▶ **where?** Every city and regional government has a planning division that deals with things like transportation, real estate development, and historic preservation. Urban planners might also work for special interest groups or nonprofit organizations.

▶ **how?** Urban planners typically get their undergraduate degree in urban or city planning, but to advance in the field, they'll need a master's degree.

▶ **$$$:** $41,000 to $70,000 for urban planners with a master's

▶ **dress code?** Casual to business casual

▶ **stress factor:** On a scale of 1 to 10, an 8

there is actually a job shaping the cities of tomorrow. In researching urban planning, I discovered Anne Corbett, the executive director of the Cultural Development Corporation (CDC), a small nonprofit in Washington, D.C., that aims to make sure that artists and art organizations in the city have affordable spaces that support their art—from theaters and art galleries to housing for artists. Here's our conversation.

ME: Urban planning sounds like such an interesting concept, but I'm not sure I get what you actually do. How do you spend your days?

ANNE: On any given day I might be sitting down to meet with a real estate developer or landowner who has a particular project they're looking to build. It might be a big office building where the developer also wants to have art space on the ground floor, or because of the city rules they are required to have some sort of art space included. So my organization would help them think about that art space and come up with something that works well, given the other things that will be in the building and what else is going on in the neighborhood. So I spend a lot of time getting to know people who have property, projects, and buildings that they're planning.

"A lot of times my work and leisure time are the same thing."

At the same time, I might spend part of my day meeting with different people who work at arts organizations. Like this morning, I got a phone call from an organization of actors that is getting evicted from their space. They told us what their needs are, and we put the information in a database so that when we find people with buildings who have space, we can put the two together. That's really my specialty—having in my head a sense of things going on all over the city. When something is happening in the arts world as far as real estate goes, I'm the "go-to person" and can help broker those relationships.

Another thing I might be doing is sitting in a meeting with architects and talking about the design of a housing building, making sure that the apartments are big enough for the artists who live and work in them and that they've included the kinds of amenities that are important to artists—high ceilings, good windows with natural light, a freight elevator or heavy-duty electrical requirements. We help the architects figure out how to design it and then we come up with a plan for marketing those units to artists in our area, schedule open houses, and put ads in the paper.

ME: It sounds like you have a very full job. How do you squeeze it all into a workday?

ANNE: I used to come to work at nine or nine thirty a.m. and be here until seven or seven thirty p.m., and then go to events in the evening. A lot of my job is who I know, and I have to keep building relationships with as many people as possible, so I spend time going to business receptions and arts events like gallery openings or theater events. Other nights I might be going to a community meeting where a project is being presented to the community so they can give their input. I used to work more than ten hours a day, maybe fifty to seventy hours a week. And I love what I do, so usually I didn't have a problem with that. But now I have a child. He's sixteen months old and he's in day care, but he can only be in day care until six p.m., and

you asked . . .

"What is the most rewarding aspect of your career?" Rebecca, age 16

anne answered . . .

"A lot of times we're dealing with rundown buildings that have been vacant for a really long time, so seeing the before and after of a building that was maybe boarded up and covered with graffiti, and then seeing it totally refurbished and people doing arts activities and things that they love there—that transformation is really pretty magical."

the breakdown

IN MEETINGS: 4 hours a day

ON THE PHONE: 2 hours a day

ONLINE: 3 hours a day

SITTING: Most of the day

PUBLIC SPEAKING: 30 minutes a day

READING: 1 hour a day

WORKING SOLO: 2 hours a day

GUIDING STAFF AND REVIEWING THE WORK OF OTHERS: 3 hours a day

he has to be picked up regardless of what's going on at work, so either my husband or I have to get up and walk out of our office and do that. It's a very different balance for me. Now I spend more time at home on the computer, anywhere from half an hour to two or three hours at night after my son's gone to bed so I catch up. I can't go to all of the nighttime things that I used to—I really have to pick and choose. And that's good and bad. Most times I would rather be at home with my son than at a reception making small talk with building developers. But it makes it harder for me to do my job when I'm not able to put in all of that networking time.

ME: So between work and being a mom, how do you find the time to recharge?

ANNE: Well, I go to the gym, I take my son to the park, I go to the movies. I think my personality is really driven—I'm incredibly centered around my job and I'm ambitious. And a lot of times my work and

why wait?

▸ Volunteer or intern with an organization that interests you, especially as it relates to planning and running community events.

▸ Get involved with what's going on in your community by reading the paper and notices about community development or revitalization projects.

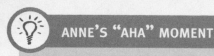

ANNE'S "AHA" MOMENT

When I graduated from college in 1992, there weren't a lot of jobs to be had, and I also didn't have a very good GPA coming out of school. So I ended up taking a job for [a corporation that owns fast food restaurants]. I was literally running restaurants, running the drive-through, and managing all of the people in it. After a couple of years I started helping them plan new restaurants. They would assign me a new restaurant that hadn't been built yet, and I would work with the contractors, start planning the marketing of the new store, hire all the people, and do everything to get the store open and ready. But I didn't think that the way the corporation was going about the whole process was very thoughtful—they never seemed to talk to the community or ask people what they wanted. So I started asking the people I worked for about trying to build in a community process, and they just didn't understand what I was getting at. I just kept hitting brick walls. So I literally had an "aha" moment where I realized that this was not how communities should be shaped. It shouldn't just be private companies trying to figure out how to make the most money— there's gotta be something more. So I started doing research and found the field of urban and community planning and decided I would get a graduate degree. I quit my job, went back to bartending and waiting tables, and went back to school and got a degree in community planning.

then to now

1992: Graduated from Wake Forest University, North Carolina, with BS in mathematical economics

1994: Quit Taco Bell to pursue urban planning

1996: Interned at an economic development consulting firm

1997: Received master's in community planning, University of Maryland

leisure time are the same thing—if I have to go to an art gallery opening because there are people there that I need to see, I can look at that as not just work, but as leisure time as well.

ME: What would you say is the most challenging part of your job?

ANNE: Because we're a nonprofit, we have to raise money for everything that we do. Sometimes people are paying us for our services, but not in the same way that most private companies work. Usually the projects we're doing can only partially pay for themselves, so we have to go to foundations, corporations, or individuals and ask them for the funds—make a case and tell them why what we're doing is really important. And when you're trying to run a project at the same time you're trying to raise money, it makes for a stressful situation. Sometimes you wish that you could just focus on doing a project and doing it right, and it would be nice if it could just pay for itself.

ME: But you really seem to love your job, despite the challenges and long hours. What makes it all worthwhile?

ANNE: When you negotiate a really great space or a project that provides great space for different people and the community is really happy, that makes it worthwhile. Say there's a new dance studio in a neighborhood. The people who run the dance studio are really happy because now they have a place to teach the classes and rehearse their dance stuff. The owner of the building is really happy because

what it takes

▶ A strong sense of community

▶ A creative vision

▶ Being a good negotiator and mediator

1997: Was inspired by hearing Kennedy Smith speak on downtown revitalization

1998: Began working at Cultural Development Corporation (CDC)

1998: Published the book *Arts in a Living Downtown*

2000: Promoted to executive director, CDC

his building has a dance studio in it and it turned out to be much better than he thought it might be. That's really, really rewarding when you see all of those different things come together and everybody feels like their neighborhood is much better than it was before.

INTERESTED IN URBAN PLANNING?
HERE'S ANNE'S CAREER ADVICE

▶ *Since you need a master's degree in city or urban planning, study whatever interests you in undergrad and try to do well in it.*

▶ *Get to know the city or community that you're in, and spend time paying attention to how a city runs—that might be seeing what your neighborhood association has going on or attending community meetings around big development projects.*

in the field

Five More Careers Where You Can Help Shape Your City

city manager You might not think of cities as "businesses," but they need to be managed as if they are. Think about it . . . cities have huge budgets, lots of staff, and a million details all needing attention at the same time. City managers report to the mayor and are in charge of managing the day-to-day "operations" of a city.

landscape architect Landscape architects plan what the landscape of public spaces—from courtyards and malls to playgrounds and zoos—will look like, figuring out how to incorporate trees and bushes, flowers, grass, fountains, benches, and walkways. Most are hands-on in putting their plan into action.

neighborhood weekly newspaper editor Most communities, big and small, have a weekly newspaper. These weeklies cover the local scene, including news, events, arts, and music, with a goal of bringing the community together. Editors at these weeklies assign stories and shape the tone and content of the paper.

director of tourism Most cities employ a director of tourism, who promotes businesses and events in the city with the goal of bringing in money to the community through tourism. Even small towns need tourism directors to promote attractions like the world's largest ball of paint in Alexandria, Indiana, or Lucy, the sixty-five-foot-high elephant statue on the Jersey shore.

community events coordinator Street fairs, Halloween parades, Christmas tree lighting ceremonies—these are the kinds of happenings that a community events coordinator might organize. No matter how big or small, community events coordinators are always looking for ways to bring people and businesses together to build community.

 you need to know about

The American Planning Association (www.planning.org) is the go-to source for all information on urban, suburban, regional, and rural planning. Through this organization you can find out about conferences, read publications about planning, research schools with planning degrees, and learn about student chapters of the APA.

For more on careers that change the landscape, check out the architect profile on page 198.

Michelle Carter

international development and relief worker

the facts

Michelle Carter, Assistant Country Director, CARE Mozambique

▸ **what?** An international development and relief worker works for a government agency or an NGO (nongovernmental organization) to provide emergency relief or development support to countries and regions in need.

▸ **where?** Development and relief workers can be found in all corners of the world.

▸ **how?** Getting into development and relief work is competitive—many relief workers have a master's or doctorate in international relations or other specialties that directly relate to the work they do, as well as a strong track record of volunteerism.

▸ **$$$:** $20,000 to $50,000 a year or more, depending on the agency. Most agencies also provide a stipend to cover housing and food costs of staff living abroad.

▸ **dress code?** Casual, but may be inspired by the country (like having to wear a skirt or veil in certain countries, not showing arms or legs in others)

▸ **stress factor:** On a scale of 1 to 10, a 9

fresh out of college, I worked for a relief and development organization called CARE. While working for CARE, I had a chance to travel to Africa, and I came back with an immense amount of respect for the relief workers who worked "in the field," sometimes in seriously difficult and even dangerous conditions.

I knew I wanted to profile a relief and development worker for *In Their Shoes*, so I decided to go back to my career roots. CARE put me in touch with Michelle Carter, the assistant country director for CARE Mozambique. Michelle was wonderful enough to write about what her life in the heart of Africa is like.

> *"Somehow, no matter how well I plan things, I end up with urgent issues at the end of the day that have to be handled immediately."*

MICHELLE'S WORK

I always knew I wanted to do something to help others, and that's probably why I studied psychology in college. Growing up, my father was in the military, so I had the privilege of living in Thailand and Europe, as well as visiting North Africa and Asia on family vacations. I loved traveling.

After college I took a year off and started thinking about being a diplomat, or finding a job where I could work on issues facing poorer countries. As I started researching these types of jobs, I realized that I needed a master's degree, so I applied and got into graduate school, where I focused on international economics and Sub-Saharan Africa. While in grad school, I figured out that it wasn't politics or international business that I was interested in—it was trying to find a way to make things work better for poor countries. I remembered traveling as a young girl and seeing the brown drinking water in Thailand or the incredible poverty in India and other places. I also loved the idea of working in a job where I would have the freedom to see the world and learn about Africa, a place where my ancestors came from many years ago, but I knew very little about it beyond the mostly negative portrayals in the media.

And now here I am. I'm doing exactly what I dreamed of. I work for a great international relief and development organization, CARE, and I'm living in Mozambique, which is a country in southeastern Africa.

I'm the assistant country director of CARE Mozambique, which basically means that I lead a team of coordinators and project managers in HIV/AIDS, agriculture, natural resources, and water programs in the country. I work with a team of specialists to design, plan, and implement the projects to help the people in need, as well as send reports on our work to the donors who fund our projects.

My hours are long. I'm usually up by five or five thirty a.m. to check e-mails on my laptop and see if there is anything I need to know about going on in the world or at CARE headquarters in the United States. There's a seven-hour time difference between where I live and headquarters, so getting up early gives me a chance to communicate with people there if I need to. Then I'll eat breakfast, shower, and drive to the office, which isn't too far from my house.

My job itself changes from day to day. If I'm in the office, a lot of my work is about the projects I'm involved in. Sometimes I'm having planning meetings with staff, writing and editing proposals and reports to describe CARE's work in the field. I make sure our projects are high quality and will have the positive, long-lasting impact that we're hoping for. Sometimes I'm meeting with donors to see if they're interested in funding some of our projects. I often have meetings with the local government or other NGOs to

you asked . . .

"How did you get to where you're at without getting distracted or drawn in by the peer pressure around you?" Kristin, age 16

michelle answered . . .

"Like all teenagers, I was very influenced by my friends. However, I was also lucky to have a strong family who instilled in me the basic values of not hurting myself or others. My father would always say to me when I went out, 'Remember who you are.' I think my family's faith and trust in me built up my confidence to remain focused on doing well and not get distracted by drugs, drinking, boys, or not doing well in school. I know that I'm one of the lucky ones to have a strong family and role models around me, but I think that even if someone has a tough home environment, we all need to be able to look at ourselves in the mirror and make sure that we're okay with who we are."

talk about CARE's programs, discuss policies, or to talk about how we can work together. Then there are days when I'm dealing with not-so-exciting but also important financial reports and budgets. The meetings and organizational part of my job isn't so glamorous, but it's an important part of what I do.

When I can, I try to grab lunch with folks from other organizations in the area to hear about their projects and work—it's a nice break from staring at the computer. I'm based in Maputo, which is a big city, so there are all kinds of restaurants—Italian, Thai, and so on. Mozambique has great food like matapa, *which is made up of cassava leaves and coconut milk, like a gravy over rice, or* chema, *which is pounded maize with a stew or greens.*

Somehow, no matter how well I plan things, I end up with urgent issues at the end of the day that have to be handled immediately. I try to leave work by six thirty p.m. or so. The hours are long, but the work really keeps me inspired, so I never really feel tired. I have a nice house in Mozambique with electricity and running water. I have most of the comforts of home . . . there's even an ice-cream store in Maputo. When I get home, I usually warm up some dinner and then relax with a book or watch TV to catch up on the latest events. Sometimes I get on the Internet to send e-mails or chat or call my family and friends. Other nights, there might be some cultural event going on in town—a dance, art exhibition, or something else that I go to.

My favorite part of my job is going out to the field to see our projects, which I try to do as often as possible. On those days, I get up really early (usually around five a.m.) and drive in a four-by-four or pickup truck long

the breakdown

IN MEETINGS: 3 hours a day

ON THE PHONE: 30 minutes a day

ONLINE: 4 hours a day

SITTING: Not very often

PUBLIC SPEAKING: Occasionally

READING: End up reading at night

WORKING SOLO: Rarely

why wait?

▸ Gain experience by volunteering in your community.

▸ Learn other languages, such as French, Portuguese, Spanish, or even better, Arabic, Russian, and Kiswahili!

what it takes

- ▶ A strong sense of integrity
- ▶ A willingness to live in less-than-comfortable environments
- ▶ A sense of adventure

distances over bumpy roads to get to where I'm going. I always wear a long skirt in respect of the culture, where rural women do not wear pants. When I'm in the field, my primary interest is getting a better sense of how the projects are helping the poor. For example, one of the projects we have is to help women's associations increase their peanut production so they can make more money. Then we teach them different ways to save monies for difficult times, like if there is a drought or a family member gets sick with malaria or HIV. So when I'm in the field, I take a look at how these programs are running and think about what can be improved.

Most of the time, the CARE staff in the field knows the community members really well, and they also speak the local language, so they translate for me. When I'm in the field, I also try to meet with local government officials and let them know what CARE is trying to do to help their communities and discuss any concerns there might be. It's always good to hear them thank CARE for the work we're doing to help people address their problems.

The last part of my day in the field involves the CARE staff. Usually we'll grab a sandwich and talk about what's going on. I'll let them know what I think can be improved, and I'll share my deep appreciation for the hard work they do in very challenging environments. I'll always leave time for the staff to share with me any concerns they might have, because they are our connection to the communities.

The work isn't easy. Poverty is very complex, and sometimes I get depressed because I know the world is unfair and that there are always going to be winners and losers. But then there are great moments too, like

then to now

1993:	1996:	1995–1996:	1996:	1997–1999:
Graduated from Smith College with a BA in psychology, minor in international relations	Graduated from Georgetown University with an MS in foreign science	Interned at USAID	Was a CARE Fellow, CARE Haiti	Assistant regional director, CARE Haiti

when I'm speaking with a woman who tells me that a project has changed her life—that she can provide more for her family and everyone's healthier, better educated, and empowered to make changes in their lives.

One of the best perks of my job is getting to live in another country, and I try to take advantage of all that it has to offer on the weekends. Some weekends, I travel around Mozambique or go next door to South Africa or Swaziland. Others I might go to the beach, enjoy conversations with Mozambicans in my best attempts at Portuguese, and learn a lot about the interesting culture in Mozambique, like art, dancing, and great African music. I'm very interested in their culture, and Mozambicans are also very curious about American culture. Because of music and movies, I spend a lot of time clarifying stereotypes about Americans, too! But this is all part of the big adventure that I'm on.

in the field

Five More Careers Working Overseas for a Relief and Development Organization

communications officer A big part of the work at relief organizations is getting information to the donors—the people who contribute money to the organization and its programs. Communications officers deal with the media and act as the face of the organization.

peace corps volunteer People interested in a career in international development sometimes start with the Peace Corps. Peace Corps volunteers help people in a developing country, doing anything from building schools and better plumbing systems to educating and counseling.

1999–2000:	2000–2001:	2002:	2002–2004:	2004–
Project manager/sub-office team leader, CARE Rwanda	Civil society technical coordinator, CARE Rwanda	Promoted to assistant country director for program, CARE Rwanda	Deputy regional director for East & Central Africa, CARE Atlanta	PRESENT: Assistant country director for program, CARE Mozambique

relief doctor If you watch ER, then you've seen Carter or Luka travel to Darfur, Sudan, to practice medicine. Relief doctors often work with organizations such as Doctors Without Borders (Médecins Sans Frontières) and use their expertise to aid people in regions where access to health care is limited.

logistics manager When working in relief situations in other countries, there are often a lot of logistical details—transportation, a shortage of gasoline, bad roads, security, and safety issues within the community. Logistics managers figure out how to work safely and efficiently within a village, city, or country.

missionary Associated with an organized religion, missionaries commit their lives to sharing their faith in the hope of converting others. While they don't have to work overseas, many missionaries live in developing countries and center their work on humanitarian efforts while spreading news of their religion.

 you need to know about

If you want to get involved in international issues, visit the website www.oneworld.net, a global network aimed at building a more just, global society through its partnership community. Here you'll be able to explore media from cultures around the world and connect with other motivated people and organizations looking to make a difference.

it may seem out of place to talk about volunteering in a book about careers, but volunteering and getting involved in social action is actually very connected to the working world. Most companies support the work of nonprofit organizations—encouraging employees to volunteer by giving them time off for volunteer activities, sponsoring employee teams for fund-raising events, and even making financial donations to charities their employees volunteer for.

Being a volunteer for a cause you feel passionate about can be extremely rewarding. And while knowing you're having a positive impact may be all you're looking to get out of it, there are actually many other side benefits of donating your time and energy:

▶ Just because you aren't getting paid for it doesn't mean it isn't real experience. The skills you can gain through volunteering, especially in a formal or regular capacity, are just as valuable to you and your future employers as any you'd gain through a paying job.

▶ Not everyone has the dedication to volunteer for an organization or to promote a cause on their own time, so doing it is a great way to show potential employers that you're motivated and willing to make a commitment. For some employers, this volunteerism can be more impressive than traditional experience on a résumé.

▶ Volunteering gives you a chance to practice all kinds of practical life skills—written and verbal skills, networking skills, organizational skills, and many more.

▶ Because there are opportunities in just about any arena, volunteering is an excellent way to try out different careers, even as a student. Who knows . . . you might get exposed to and fall in love with a career that completely changes your course!

▶ When you're volunteering with an organization whose work you feel passionate about, chances are you'll meet other people who share in your interests. You might even find a mentor or make great connections with people you can network with down the road.

Keep your eyes open for volunteer opportunities in your community—you don't have to make a huge commitment to get involved. It could be something as simple as handing out water bottles to finishers at a local road race or spending one afternoon a week at a local nursing home. There are many organizations with volunteer-based programs who would be happy to work with you to figure out an opportunity that would meet both of your needs.

Miriam Kramer

yoga instructor

the facts

▶ **what?** Yoga instructors help people practice yoga either through classes or one-on-one instruction.

▶ **where?** They usually work at yoga studios, in gyms that offer yoga classes, vacation resorts that offer spa and yoga services, or in their own private practice.

▶ **how?** Yoga instructors generally apprentice with a mentor to learn different skills and methods, as well as practice yoga for years themselves. There is no formal yoga certification requirement, but taking workshops or classes in different disciplines is important.

*Miriam Kramer,
Yoga and Movement
Instructor*

▶ **$$$:** $40 to $80 dollars an hour

▶ **dress code?** Cool, comfy, and casual yoga wear . . . lots of loose cotton

▶ **stress factor:** On a scale of 1 to 10, a 3

have you ever practiced yoga? I do it from time to time, and I really enjoy it. There's something about yoga that just makes you feel good—body, mind, and soul. Yet I know that for real "yogis" it's about so much more—breathing, tuning in . . . connecting. As a result, there's definitely something unique about yoga instructors. They have a certain energy and calmness that is really motivating and inspiring.

I got in touch with Miriam Kramer, a yoga and movement instructor in Los Angeles. I wanted to find out what being a yoga instructor was really like, beyond my perspective as a student. First things first: I asked Miriam how she got involved in becoming a teacher and to explain yoga and the lifestyle that goes along with it.

"In a career field where you're being a healer or a giver, the hardest part is making sure to recharge yourself so that you can be a giving person."

"I went to UCLA under their dance program, and I just fell in love with dance. I thought that every day was so joyful and was just about playing with the body. It was always something new. But I injured my foot when I was eighteen years old, so one of my teachers recommended I take Pilates to stay fit while my foot healed. When I graduated from college, I decided to go to New York and study with the master Pilates teacher Romana, got certified, and ended up teaching Pilates full-time and dancing professionally. A few years later, just for fun, I started going to the Iyengar Yoga Institute in Los Angeles, and once I took one class I knew it was my calling. I instantly fell in love with the process of yoga, and I haven't left since. I realized that the teaching of yoga was going to carry me throughout my life . . . it is a whole philosophy of living, and I could relate it to everything I did.

"In terms of what yoga is, the word 'yoga' means 'union.' And it's not just the union of the body and the mind, but it's the union of the individual self with the universal self, as well as the union of the body, the mind, the emotions, and the intellect. So people go to yoga

you asked . . .

"Has a loved one ever said something that made you feel like giving up?" Rebecca, age 12

miriam answered . . .

"I think the only person who's ever told me I can't do something is really myself. I've been my harshest criticizer, my own worst enemy, and I think that's the biggest challenge in this type of career. But what yoga really teaches you is to be true to yourself and the essence of you. So anytime anyone, myself included, says something that makes me feel like giving up, I remind myself of what I'm most passionate about. If you don't love having your job really be a part of your whole life, then it's probably not the right fit for you. You have to keep digging for that place."

classes to learn how to 'practice' yoga on their own and in their life. Our yoga teachers talk about how when we're going outside, we'll see what the weather is like. So for example, if it's cold, we'll wear pants and a big sweater. In yoga, we do that for our body—we ask 'what is the weather of our body and our mind and our emotions today?' From there we tailor the practice to what's going on inside of us.

"To be a yoga instructor, you have to be very flexible, body and mind, have a high amount of energy, and you can't be rigid in your ideas of what you're going to be doing on a daily basis, because you never really know who's going to be in front of you to teach. You also have to be willing to take time to build up your practice. It's not the kind of thing where you get certified and then suddenly somebody knocks on your door and offers you a fifty-thousand-dollar-a-year job. You have to be willing to start slow and ease yourself into it," Miriam explains.

The job scenario for yoga instructors is certainly different from many other more traditional careers. Most yoga instructors aren't full-time employees at a yoga studio unless it's their own studio— more typical is the path that Miriam has taken. She works at a variety of jobs to create what would be the equivalent of one full-time job. She teaches several yoga classes a week, does private Pilates instruction for about ten clients a week, and runs the creative movement program at a private elementary school, where she teaches improvisational dance and movement to pre-K through sixth grade. On top of all that, Miriam practices yoga every day for one to two hours. As you can imagine, all of these different pieces keep her fairly busy. I asked Miriam to tell us about the realities of the lifestyle.

"The lifestyle can be somewhat restricting because you're at the whim of other people's schedules, but at the same time there's a lot of flexibility, too. Since most people work eight to five, most yoga classes are either early in the morning or late at night. So oftentimes you may be teaching two classes a day—one at night and one in the morning—and then you'll have your day free to do your practice or any other endeavor that may interest you. Your 'job stability' is also very dependent on your performance, and if you get injured and it's serious enough that you can't teach, you can't work," she says.

the breakdown

ON THE PHONE: 10 minutes

ONLINE: 10 minutes

SITTING: 10 minutes

SOME FORM OF MOVING:
3–6 hours a day

WORKING SOLO: Only in own
yoga practice

I wanted to get a better sense of what a day in Miriam's life might look like, so she broke it down for us.

then to now

Graduated from UCLA with BA in dance performance and choreography	Received certification in Pilates from the Pilates Studio of New York	2000: Completed three-year teaching training at the BKS Iyengar Yoga Institute of Los Angeles

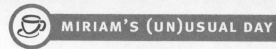

I wake up around five thirty a.m. and feed the cats, and then I do my yoga practice for about an hour and a half. Next I eat breakfast. And by the way, I always eat three meals a day. People who are dancers and movement and yoga teachers eat a lot. I get dressed and get ready to go—leggings and a T-shirt or some other kind of exercise clothing. Then, depending on when I'm teaching, I'll leave for work. Let's say I have a class at eight a.m. I'll leave by 7:40 and I'll start teaching at eight, and I'll teach for about an hour and a half. Then I'll have a short break and then maybe I'll teach a couple of private classes.

Next I take a lunch break. Usually I'll have some soup and toast and cheese and bread. My afternoon is generally pretty open, and then I'll teach another class in the evening, often a six o'clock to seven thirty p.m. class. Then I come home and have dinner and relax. Oftentimes before I go to sleep I'll do another breathing yoga practice, and then I'll go to sleep at around ten p.m. By the end of the day, my body is usually very, very tired. I try to be relaxing in bed by eight or nine p.m.

Hearing about her day made my body tired. It's exhausting enough doing one yoga class a day. Miriam is doing several, plus dancing and Pilates, not to mention her own yoga practice in the morning and evening. I asked her if she found the pace tiring.

"In a career field where you're being a healer or a giver, the hardest part is making sure to recharge yourself so that you can be a giving person. Because you're putting out energy all the time, you need to make sure that you go to class to recharge yourself and continue to teach yourself. I get body work sessions on myself—at least twice a month I'll get a massage or something like that, so I can really feed myself and get recharged," she explains.

2000: Started as Pilates teacher/apprentice at Drago's Gymnasium

2005: Became yoga teacher at Iyengar Yoga Institute of Los Angeles

⏰ why wait?

▶ If you don't already, start practicing yoga now—it's never too early!

▶ Attend yoga workshops that are open to the public to learn about various yoga techniques.

But I could tell that the payoffs of the career are worth it for Miriam. Her love for her work came through as we spoke, and it was obvious that she has found a career that allows her to have a perfect "union" between work and life. I wrapped up our interview by asking her what she loved most about her job.

Miriam answered, "I love when I'm looking out at my students and I feel a genuine joy coming from them toward me. It's an unspoken message we're sharing that this isn't just about movement or healing their aching back—it's about this greater process of discovery that we're all in together. I may have a day where I'm teaching and it's not my best class—maybe I wasn't watching my students as closely as I wanted to or giving them the right correction—but I realize that they look at it as a lifetime process that they're interested in experiencing themselves. Those are my favorite moments."

what it takes

▶ A love of yoga and a belief in the philosophy behind it

▶ Being good at inspiring others

▶ A calm personality

▶ Being very disciplined

INTERESTED IN BEING A YOGA OR MOVEMENT INSTRUCTOR? HERE'S MIRIAM'S ADVICE

▶ *You have to "do." Yoga is a life of action and it's really about integrating your whole life around a yoga lifestyle and listening to your inner self.*

▶ *There's so much more to this life than just making a certain amount of money—there can be so much fulfillment in doing a career that maybe isn't a big moneymaker.*

▶ *The joy of this type of work is acknowledgment that you do not have all the answers and there is always room for personal and spiritual growth. Don't allow others to dissuade you if you believe being a movement instructor is your true path. Stay focused on your desire, and the life practice of this art form will be your teacher and companion.*

in the field

Five More Careers in Fitness

personal trainer Personal trainers usually work at fitness centers or are self-employed, and they work one-on-one with clients to help them reach their fitness goals. They create training programs and often actually go through the fitness regime with their clients, acting not only as a fitness expert, but also as a supporter and motivator.

nutritionist Nutritionists specialize in creating nutritional plans for their clients, whether it's with a goal of losing weight, recovering from an illness, or simply eating a more balanced, healthy diet. They might cook for their clients, teach them how to food shop, or provide them with healthy recipes and monitor their diet.

wellness coach A career that has become more popular in recent years is a wellness coach. These coaches view their clients more holistically than personal trainers, and they provide guidance for healthy living not only with regard to fitness and nutrition, but also emotional, mental, and spiritual well-being.

gym manager Gym managers not only run the business side of a gym, but they also work to bring in more clients. They make sure the atmosphere of the gym is a positive one, develop ideas for fresh, new classes, and offer promotions and place advertisements to boost membership.

pilates instructor Pilates involves what's called "contrology," defined as the "complete coordination of the mind, body, and spirit." Pilates instructors are trained in this technique and use a variety of exercises involving repetition and coordination of the body so people can be physically, mentally, and spiritually balanced.

 ## you need to know about

Yoga Journal is both a print magazine and an online journal you can find at www.yogajournal.com. Check it out for tons of articles about yoga, information on yoga poses, a directory of classes around the country, and resources for training.

For more fitness-related careers, check out the professional athlete profile on page 159.

Ullika Pankratz

visual merchandiser

the facts

▶ **what?** Visual merchandisers design product displays for stores and boutiques, figuring out where products should be sold within a store and designing displays that showcase the merchandise in ways that will maximize sales.

▶ **where?** Many, like Ullika, are freelance and work exclusively with one or two big clients, while others work for department stores, chains, and small boutiques.

Ullika Pankratz, Visual Merchandiser and Display Designer, IKEA

▶ **how?** Most visual merchandisers have a four-year degree in visual design or merchandise, as well as experience working in retail.

▶ **$$$:** $25,000 to $50,000 or more, depending on experience

▶ **dress code?** Casual to business casual, depending on whether they're building displays or going to meetings

▶ **stress factor:** On a scale of 1 to 10, a 4

when i think of ikea, I think of affordable furniture, cool designs, an enormous building, and the most delicious Swedish meatballs around. When Ullika Pankratz thinks about IKEA, she thinks about how to design a product display within one of their stores around the world.

Ullika is a visual merchandiser and display designer, and for the past twelve years she has been working with IKEA, traveling around the world to design and set up mini "shops" within the stores. Ullika's travel schedule is intense: six weeks at a store anywhere in the world, two weeks home, and then back out to the next store for another six weeks, and so on. I caught up with Ullika while she was on a break between gigs at her home in Portland, Oregon.

> *"You have to like taking a drill in your hands, you have to like to hammer, to paint, get dirty, get on your knees, get a ladder . . . you have to be a very active person."*

ME: What does being a visual merchandiser entail?

ULLIKA: I do the interior setups and inside decor for IKEA, from space planning to visual merchandising to graphic setting and things like that.

ME: And so when you say you do the "inside decor," what exactly does that mean?

ULLIKA: I do anything from setting up the racking that is needed for the goods to be laid on, to doing podiums, decorations, displaying the products. Let's say we want to remodel a shop inside of IKEA. I'll do the whole floor planning with displaying and figuring out what we're going to do with each product. I specifically work in displaying the original merchandise, the little shops within IKEA, like the cook shop or the home organization department.

ME: Is that what your background is in?

ullika answered . . .

"I usually try to tell myself that maybe I'm just at a moment of my life where things are not quite going the way I want them to go. But I try to stay positive and focused on the future rather than the moment. I'll tell myself, 'Look, this is a difficult situation and this is hard, but there are good things to come and there is more to come. I just need to focus on that rather than what's happening right now.'"

ULLIKA: I'm originally from Germany, and they have an apprenticeship program there. So I did that for three years and got a degree in visual merchandising and shop window design.

ME: How long have you been working for IKEA?

ULLIKA: I did a store opening in 1994 and stayed there for nine years. In 2002 I became a freelancer for IKEA and now I just do international work for them.

ME: So if you're working with an IKEA in another country, how does it work?

ULLIKA: When we're doing a new store, usually I'll do the planning six months ahead of the opening, and I'll go to Holland to do that. And then once it's time to get a store ready, I'll fly to whatever country it's in. If it's a store that's already built, and the interior and shell is there, then I have an assignment of creating one of the shops. The racking is usually already up, so I start looking at the plans that I have and then do the merchandising. I usually have a group of salespeople who help me put all the goods on the shelves, trying to figure out what is the perfect spot for which kinds of products. There are a lot of special IKEA ways of doing things. Then when you're done with the merchandising, you get into the visual merchandising, which is usually organizing stuff on a shelf. You figure out how you want to display a specific candleholder or a specific quilt cover . . . that kind of thing.

ME: How long will it take you if it's a new store you're opening up?

ULLIKA: Six weeks.

ME: Six weeks that you would be in that country? Wow. What is it like to travel so much for your job?

ULLIKA: The reality is that you never actually quite know where you are, and you spend a lot of your free time flying, living out of hotels, and being in places that you don't really know. So you have to be really, really flexible when you do this kind of work. It can be very lonely at times. And it's not like you get someplace and somebody is right there to explain to you where to find your groceries. You have to do a lot of that stuff by yourself. So you have to be very self-motivated. We do have pretty good working hours and we don't do a lot of overtime, because things are very organized. But when I'm in another country, we get off work and I have a hotel room to myself that IKEA pays for, and that's it. So I try to organize myself—do I want to sightsee or do I just want to hang out in the hotel? I think the hardest part is that because I'm on the road thirty-eight weeks of the year, when I'm at home, I don't have time to have a "regular life," as in Tuesday nights I go to yoga, Wednesday nights I see my girlfriends. I don't have that at all.

ME: That's really intense. So where are you off to next?

ULLIKA: Australia.

 then to now

1992: Received a certificate of shop window design and visual merchandising from Hamburg Trade School, Germany

1993–1994: Worked at Nordstrom doing visual display and holiday setup

1993–1994: Worked at the Gap doing sales and visuals

ME: Cool . . .

ULLIKA: Yeah, this is the part that sounds really fabulous. And it is fabulous. I do love my job. It's the best thing that I've done.

ME: Do you get to travel business class?

ULLIKA: No. IKEA is about low cost and low budget, and the company expects its employees to not waste money. So we never have any kind of first-class or business-class travel.

ME: What kind of personality do you think is a good match for this type of work?

ULLIKA: You have to be open-minded and friendly, you have to like being around people, and you have to like working with your hands. It's hands-on work. You have to like taking a drill in your hands, you have to like to hammer, to paint, get dirty, get on your knees, get a ladder . . . you have to be a very active person.

the breakdown

IN MEETINGS: 30 minutes a day

SITTING: 1–2 hours a day

STANDING: 6 hours a day

WORKING SOLO: 2–3 hours a day

why wait?

▶ Try to get a job in retail while you're still in school, and get involved in how displays at the store are put together.

▶ Sign up for set design for your school theater productions to get experience working with tools and your hands.

| 1994: Started working at IKEA | 2000–2001: Participated in IKEA's Leadership and Management Training | 2000: Worked at IKEA in Budapest, Hungary, as visual merchandiser | 2002: Became freelance visual specialist |

paying your dues

As a beginning visual designer, you'll spend the first two to three years doing things like assisting and picking up after people you work with, doing the daily maintenance of displays, and prepping and building displays.

ME: What are the other challenges of your job, besides the travel?

ULLIKA: It can be challenging to always be working with different kinds of people. You never know who you're going to team up with, and you never know what kind of personality they have. Sometimes it can be very tough, especially because, although we work in English, for most of us English is our second language. So it's a challenge when you have to explain things to people.

ME: And what's the best part about your job?

what it takes

▸ Being comfortable with getting dirty and doing physical work

▸ Having a good sense of color and design

▸ Persistence . . . it's a tough field to break into

ULLIKA: It's never boring. I learn so much every time I go someplace, and because IKEA brings out new products every year, there are new ideas, new concepts every year, so that keeps the job really fresh all the time. And then, of course, being in all the countries and learning so much about other cultures is just fabulous and amazing. I feel really fortunate to have that.

ME: If you're having a really great day at work, what makes it so?

ULLIKA: If I listen to people's ideas and we can come together and brainstorm as a team and by the end of the day, we've done a whole display and it looks beautiful . . . that's wonderful.

▶ *Believe in yourself and believe in what you can do with your hands and your creativity. Don't let other people tell you that you're not good at something.*

▶ *It's a bit tough to get into visual merchandising, but when you're in, you're in, and that's the nice part about it. The best places to try to break in are department stores, the Gap—even galleries or small shops.*

▶ *Take a summer job in something that you like to do or that sounds interesting to you. Do it for a few weeks or a few months and check it out before making a decision about if it's really something you want to do for life.*

in the field

Five More Careers in Design

interior designer Interior designers pay attention not just to aesthetics, but also to designing spaces that are based specifically on how they will be used by the client. They must be licensed by the state and know how different design materials react or hold up in various situations.

home product developer Kind of like the fashion designers of the interior decorating industry, product developers might work for home furnishing stores like Crate & Barrel or Pottery Barn, and develop new products and furniture lines to be carried there.

kitchen and bath designer Kitchen and bath designers specialize in designing the two rooms that are used the most in any house, and they create kitchens and bathrooms that are not only attractive, but functional as well.

textile designer Textile designers usually have a background in art and design, and they use their creativity to develop new designs for textiles to be used in the home, such as sofa covers, pillows, curtains, and bedding, while also paying attention to things like durability and how the fabric will be used.

furniture maker Blending their love of creativity and design with the practical aspects of construction using wood, fasteners, fabrics, and other materials, furniture makers might create furniture for designers like Ethan Allen or hand-make unique pieces of furniture for individual customers.

you need to know about

The National Association of Visual Merchandisers (www.visualmerch.com) is an organization supporting the work of visual merchandisers in the world of retail. Visit their website to sign up for a free newsletter with info and articles on visual merchandising, see what kinds of jobs are out there, and get involved in the discussion forums.

Ellen Goldsmith-Vein

talent agent

the facts

*Ellen Goldsmith-Vein,
CEO & Founder,
The Gotham Group*

▶ **what?** Talent agents represent performers like actors, writers, animators, musicians, and comedians. Their job is to not only find work for their clients, but also to negotiate their clients' deals, guide their careers, and represent their involvement in a project or gig.

▶ **where?** Talent agents for big-name talent tend to work at the large firms in New York or L.A., while others work out of smaller boutique agencies or, like Ellen, start their own!

▶ **how?** Agents don't need a particular educational background, although a BA doesn't hurt. Breaking into the industry is very competitive— most people intern first and then start out in the mailroom at an agency, working their way up to a receptionist or assistant before representing clients themselves.

▶ **$$$:** $20,000 a year for agents just starting out, but there's no cap on earning potential, as agents earn a percentage of their clients' income

▶ **dress code?** In most agency environments, the dress is very businesslike . . . suits and other business attire

▶ **stress factor:** On a scale of 1 to 10, Ellen says it's a 40!

when i say that Ellen Goldsmith-Vein has built her own Hollywood empire, I'm not exaggerating. Ellen is the founder and CEO of the Gotham Group, a representation firm in the heart of Beverly Hills that focuses on the animation and family entertainment business. The producer of *Shrek?* Ellen's client. The director of Adam Sandler's *Eight Crazy Nights?* Ellen's client. The executive producers of *Lizzie McGuire?* Yeah . . . those would be Ellen's clients too.

I visited Ellen in her loftlike offices on Sunset Boulevard, and the energy in the air was intense—it was obvious there was lots going on and plenty of smart, attentive people working their butts off in every office and cubicle. Ellen had just gotten back from a business lunch, so I hung out on the plush couch in her office while she caught up with her assistant (who sat in Ellen's office next to her desk) and simultaneously returned a phone call, had a conversation with a colleague down the hall, and made notes on a stack of papers on her desk.

"I feel like I have a responsibility to my clients, but I still am able to have a critical eye when it comes to their work and ideas."

As an agent and manager in the animation and family entertainment biz, Ellen represents directors, artists, animators, writers, producers, animation studios . . . even publishing companies. She and her team act on behalf of the firm's clients, negotiating deals with studios and production companies, setting up pitch meetings, finding work for their clients, and being an advocate for anything related to their clients' careers. It's a big job, but somebody's got to do it. I had a chance to pick Ellen's brain and get all the details about what her daily life is really like.

ME: What were your career aspirations when you were a teen?

ELLEN: When I was a teenager, I think I had sufficient delusions of grandeur. I wanted to be the first woman justice on the Supreme Court. You know, that's the kind of "middle-of-the-road" thinker I was. Obviously that was not meant to be, because look where I am now—I'm in the cartoon business. When I went to college, I was initially pursuing a political science route in the hopes that that's what I would end up doing. And that was the dream until I took a creative writing class in college and somebody said, "You're a great writer" and I kept getting A's on anything that I had to write. So then I decided I wanted to be a novelist. And so I went into banking, which is exactly what you do when you are a novelist who wanted to be a justice of the Supreme Court. *(Laughs)* After five years of doing that, I decided that I was going to come back to Los Angeles, and I went to work for the William Morris Agency. I thought that would be a way to get back into the creative process. And from there I ended up representing writers as opposed to actually being a writer.

ME: Did it all sort of click for you when you realized that this was what you wanted to do?

ELLEN: Well, I had really been an agent when I was in the banking world. It was just a different commodity—money as opposed to talent. And I was pretty good at it, so it seemed natural. I was more of

the breakdown

IN MEETINGS: 1/3 of the day

ON THE PHONE: 1/3 of the day

E-MAILING OR IMING: 1/3 of the day

SITTING: All day

READING: Whenever I can

MULTITASKING: All day long!

a caretaker. I feel like I have a responsibility to my clients, but I still am able to have a critical eye when it comes to their work and ideas.

ME: There are all of these Hollywood takes on what an agent does—can you set us straight? What does an agent actually do?

ELLEN: Essentially, agenting, at its very core, is representation. And by that I mean it's going out into your client's world, whether it's publishing or film or television or music, and acting on their behalf. So you have to decide what projects and material make sense for your clients, and what other elements you can bring into a project that make sense for your client, and you have to make a determination about who the best people are for your clients to be in business with. It's sort of like being the angel on their shoulder if it happens the right way and if it's a good relationship.

ME: So how do you literally spend your day?

ELLEN: My day may be different from a lot of other people's days here, because a lot of the managers here do "coverage," which means they go out and talk to the studios and the production companies and figure out what's going on in the world and what's open in terms of writing and directing assignments. For me, it's not only checking in with clients, but it's talking to their other representatives and

then to now

1986:	1984–1989:	1989–1990:	1990–1992:	1992–1994:
Graduated UCLA with a BS in sociology	Mortgage banker at Merrill Lynch	Assistant to an agent, William Morris Agency	Development executive, Nelvana Entertainment	Manager/ partner at Atlas Management

keeping everyone informed, because in the entertainment industry, information means everything. It's also finding out what the status of client activity is. We usually "go out" with one piece of material a week, whether we have a book that we're out in the marketplace with, or a comic book, or an article, or we've got a pitch. So there's managing that process—talking to movie studios and producers, assigning territories. It just goes on and on and on. That's why my job is a 40 on the stress level!

ME: What are the hours like?

ELLEN: It's pretty much 24/7.

ME: If you're working those kind of hours, how do you juggle it with being a mom?

ELLEN: I have to get up at the crack of dawn. I basically spend time with my kids in the morning and then when I get home. For example, tonight I have a dinner, so I'm going to leave early, go home, spend a few hours with my kids, and then I'm going to go to meet my clients for dinner.

ME: What's the first thing that you do when you get to work in the morning?

 why wait?

▸ Keep tabs on what's happening behind the scenes in Hollywood by reading the trade and celebrity magazines.

▸ Read books and see movies with a critical eye to develop your own sensibility.

1993: Founded the Gotham Group

1999–2003: Partner/ head of Animation and Family Entertainment, Artists Management Group (AMG)

PRESENT: CEO, The Gotham Group

paying your dues

Believe it or not, many agents start out working in the *mailroom* (the official entry-level job at an agency), where they'll spend a year or two learning the ropes and soaking in the atmosphere before being bumped up to an assistant.

ELLEN: First I check my e-mail from home at six in the morning, because I have clients in London and all over the place, and I need to make sure that I know what they're doing. Then I read the trades* online and the newspapers and then I start making phone calls from home. Once I get in the car, I'm on the phone the entire way here. So usually it's a case of the tail wagging the dog. I may get on the phone with somebody, which precipitates needing to make another phone call, and so on.

ME: What does a great day at work look like?

ELLEN: I feel like I'm really lucky, because we are surrounded by so many incredibly talented people that every day for us is a great day. I remember I was so desperate when I first got into the animation business, all I wanted to do was represent Henry Selick, who directed Tim Burton's *The Nightmare Before Christmas*, that's all I wanted to do. I couldn't get him to return my phone calls. I just worshiped him. And about five or six years after I started this company I started having conversations with Henry and then we actually signed him, which was a big milestone because I think he's such a genius. So every day I just think to myself, *Man, I can't believe I'm lucky enough to be in business with the people we represent.* So whether it's Henry or it's an author or a publisher or Dark Horse Comics, or we just signed another Academy Award–winning director . . . how could every day not be a good day?

---

* **THE LINGO: Trades** is another word for trade magazines or publications that relate to a specific industry. In Hollywood, the trades typically refer to the *Hollywood Reporter* and *Variety*.

ME: What do you think are the most important traits of people who are successful in this business?

ELLEN: You have to realize that you're committing to making people's careers move along beyond where they are when they first come to you. So you have to take that obligation seriously. I always tell people that if you get into this business to make a lot of money, you never will. It's about having enough of a commitment to your clients that you can continue to move their projects forward. The other thing is having patience. There are times where I'm not up to the task—I don't have the patience. And when I'm not up to the task I have to take a beat or I have to ask other people for their help. It's really important when you're in the representation business to work collaboratively. The ultimate downfall of any agency is working in little fiefdoms as opposed to as one unit.

ME: Do you think there are any misconceptions about what it's like to be an agent?

ELLEN: Yes . . . I don't think people realize how much incredibly hard work it is. I can't tell you how many people have come in here who just don't get that it's as intense as it is, and the incredible pressure that

what it takes

▶ Amazing networking and schmoozing skills

▶ A drive to succeed

▶ Business savvy

▶ Being great with people

you're under when people's lives hang in the balance based on what you do or don't do, whose call you return or what you say or don't say. That's why I think the training programs at the agencies are important, because it gives you a great overview. It's really vital.

ME: Do you expect to stay in this career for the rest of your life?

ELLEN: I can't imagine doing anything else. At least until my kids stop liking cartoons and I'm no longer a hit at all their friends' parties.

in the field

makeup artist When celebrities are performing, making a guest appearance, or attending a red carpet event, makeup artists work their magic, giving them a finished, flawless look. Makeup artists may work long or irregular hours on television or film shoots.

talent manager There are some similarities between managers and agents, but while agents' primary role is negotiating deals for their clients, managers play more of an advisory role in terms of what projects make the most sense for their clients to work on.

personal assistant Celebrities have busy, busy lives. Personal assistants are the celebrities' right-hand people, organizing their schedules, running errands, answering phones. Many are on call 24/7 and have to drop everything to attend to their boss.

publicist Publicists shape a celebrity's image for the public. For example, if there's big news about Angelina, her publicist will figure out the best way to get the word out, including identifying the magazine or television show that might get the exclusive interview.

talent scout We've all heard stories about a celebrity being "discovered." Talent scouts find new talent by going to concerts, comedy clubs, improv shows, local theater . . . and sometimes just by keeping their eyes open as they walk down the street.

you need to know about

The industry trade magazines *Hollywood Reporter* (www.hollywoodreporter.com) and *Variety* (www.variety.com) publish daily and weekly editions, and while subscriptions are pricey, many libraries carry the weeklies, and you can view some headlines and articles for free online.

For more on careers in Hollywood, check out the publicist profile on page 89 and the movie studio executive profile on page 60.

lunch break

the freelance life

have you ever met someone who works as a "freelancer"? Being freelance essentially means that you're self-employed, and although you may take on jobs for one or more companies, you're not actually employed by them. For example, a freelance photographer might be hired by a magazine to do occasional editorial shoots, but she isn't actually on their payroll—the magazine just hires her when they need her.

If you're considering a career as a freelancer, make sure you're a motivated self-starter, since it's a lot of hard work to build up a sustainable freelance career. Like any career, being a freelancer has its upsides and downsides. Here are some things to consider if you think you might want to go this route:

upsides	*downsides*
You can work on the projects you really want to work on, and say no to the projects that don't interest you.	There is little to no job stability for a freelancer, and sometimes it can be months or longer between paying gigs.
The pay for freelancers might be better for certain jobs than if you were being paid as a full-time employee.	Freelancers have to pay for their own medical insurance and don't get any other paid benefits.
You can wear anything all day long, even your pajamas.	Working from home can be isolating.
You can set your own hours and work as much or as little as you like.	You often have no control over when jobs come up, so you might have no work for months and then get slammed with three jobs all at once.

Claudia Poccia

business executive

the facts

Claudia Poccia,
President, mark *(Avon)*

▶ **what?** Business executives work at high levels at a corporation, running either divisions within a company or an entire business.

▶ **where?** Every for-profit company in every city has business executives running it.

▶ **how?** A BA or BS in business, marketing, or finance is a great start, but most people get an MBA to accelerate their quest to be a high-level business executive.

▶ **$$$:** From $75,000 up to a million plus, depending on the level and size of the company. At very high-level positions, bonuses and other financial incentives are usually an additional benefit.

▶ **dress code?** Business dress

▶ **stress factor:** On a scale of 1 to 10, a 7

today you'll find more women in top positions of companies than ever before. Even so, the number of women running Fortune 500 companies (the five hundred companies with the highest revenue in the country) is still too small—in 2005 there were women at the top of ten.

Avon Products is one of those ten companies, and with CEO Andrea Jung at the helm, the company is thriving. Avon, based in New York City, has been on *Fortune* magazine's "most admired companies" list for more than ten years, and the National Association for Female Executives ranked it as the number one company for executive women to work in.

I was lucky enough to find time on Claudia Poccia's overbooked calendar for an interview. Claudia is the president of Avon's teen brand, *mark*, where she pretty much oversees every aspect of the business.

"My job is to set the vision for our brand and our company, and then develop and guide the team in terms of accomplishing their piece of the plan to get us to where we're going. That means making sure that all of the pieces of the business come together. In the case of *mark*, we're a brand that stands for young, mix-it-up,

> *"The challenge is to try to keep up without feeling overwhelmed. . . . I think it's important to be able to figure out what's 'need to know' and what's 'nice to know.'"*

customizable makeup for girls who are ahead of the curve and yet not self-absorbed. So my job is to think about our business plan. How do we want to reach our target? What products should we be bringing to the market? What should our packaging look like? What should the voice of our brand be? Should we be on the Internet? Should we be in magazines? Both?

"The first thing we do is bring together the people from research and development and tell them what types of products we want to develop. While they're developing the products, the packaging people are working on the packaging, you know, like the actual tube that the lipstick goes in. Then there's the marketing piece—how do we get our product out there, what's our channel of distribution, how do we want to communicate what we are and what we offer? Then there's the education piece—how do we teach the consumers and the people who sell the product? There's the operational piece—did we produce enough product, and did it come in at the right cost so that it can be a profitable business for us?

"Those are all of the pieces that go into what I do, and I'm responsible for setting those objectives and making sure everyone's managing to do it. On top of all that, I'm running a business, so it's dealing with finance matters and operational stuff, like how much product we're going to need and where it will be manufactured and can you really deliver the product at the right cost so we have enough money to promote it and still be profitable. In a nutshell, that's my job . . . to keep it all pulled together and on track," Claudia explained.

Okay, I know what you're thinking: *big* job. Keep in mind, though, that as the president of *mark*, Claudia isn't doing all these things by herself. She's like the captain of a ship, and the different department

you asked . . .

"Was it all worth it?" Courtney, age 15

claudia answered . . .

"Absolutely, and on so many levels. I've had to do some things along the way that were anything but glamorous. Early in my career I was working on a major fragrance launch, and we had all of the fashion windows at Saks Fifth Avenue for the launch. We had these wonderful tulips in the window, but it was unseasonably cold and they wouldn't open. So there we were at six in the morning with blow dryers trying to get the flowers to open without fogging up the windows. At moments like that, you say to yourself, 'Is this really what I want to do with my life?' But it was definitely worth it, because I also have moments where the work I do really makes a difference. And at the end of the day, I always go back to the fact that I truly and sincerely love the beauty business."

the breakdown

IN MEETINGS: At least 6 hours a day

ON THE PHONE: 30–45 minutes a day

ONLINE: 1–2 hours a day (usually during my commute)

PUBLIC SPEAKING: Occasionally for conferences

READING: Usually during commute

COACHING AND MENTORING YOUNG TALENT: All day long

heads and staff are her crew. She knows where the ship is going and charts the course while her crew makes sure the ship has fuel, the cargo is full, and they aren't about to ground the boat.

Still, Claudia has her hands full. So full, in fact, that she has her assistant actually schedule half-hour "meetings with herself" through-out her day so she can find time to return phone calls, follow up with e-mails, page through trade magazines, and stay on top of her game.

"I think it really requires some discipline to keep those appoint-ments with yourself. It could be something as simple as flipping through a few pages of *Women's Wear Daily* or giving yourself an opportunity to decompress and focus. Then you can get back out there with your team," Claudia says.

So, we know what kind of big-picture things Claudia is doing as president of *mark*, but how does she actually spend her day? Two words: meeting central. I asked Claudia to give us the rundown.

CLAUDIA'S (UN)USUAL DAY

Today is actually a great example of a typical day. This morning Debbie Coffey, who is the head of PR for our brand, and I had a breakfast meeting at eight fifteen a.m. with a reporter from a trade publication. We talked a little bit about our business and some of the issues and challenges that are happening in the retail community as well as within the industry. It was a good networking opportunity for our businesses and a good chance to talk about future collaborations.

why wait?

▸ Get a job working retail in beauty, fashion, or cosmetics.

▸ Join (or start) a chapter of Future Business Leaders of America (FBLA) at your high school.

After the meeting, we came back and sat in an advertising review meeting and listened to our media department make recommendations about what our print schedule should be for our new product innovation this fall.

Subsequent to that, we had a lunch meeting with a magazine that pitched us some ideas that tie in with some cause-related efforts we have on mark to help young women quit smoking. That was a different kind of meeting. It wasn't about placing advertising dollars—it was about partnering together to reach our audience with a message about helping young women change their behavior with respect to smoking.

I usually have a lunch meeting like the one I had today, but if I don't, I'll grab something at my desk, because when I get the rare opportunity to be in my office, I relish it. It's also very nice to take fifteen minutes and go for a walk outside. There's nothing like strolling on Fifth Avenue and popping into some stores to check out what the kids are looking at, what they're trying on, which cosmetic counters they're at, what stores they're in—it's like informal market research.

After lunch today, we're having our conversation with you, and after this I go into a creative meeting, where we'll look at our fall brochure or "magalog," which is like our retail store. We're looking at the key items that we're promoting, making sure that the photography is on-point, that the models are wearing the right things, that the makeup is correct, that the hair is right, that it's styled correctly, and that the copy resonates with our consumer.

When that concludes, I have a staff meeting with all of my senior staff members who run all of these areas I spoke to. We have a touch-base every other week so that we can make sure everyone knows what's going on in everybody's areas.

then to now

1980–1981:	1980–1984:	1984–1986:	1987–1992:
Worked as a flight attendant	Director of in-flight training, Air Florida, Inc.	Account executive, designer fragrance, Cosmair, Inc.	Various positions at Giorgio Beverly Hills, Inc.

Claudia works long hours Monday through Friday, usually seven a.m. to seven p.m., including commuting time, where she's reading, e-mailing via her BlackBerry, and doing phone work, as well as a few hours over the weekend so she can get a head start on the week.

"The challenge is to try to keep up without feeling overwhelmed, where you feel as though 'Gosh, I'm not going to be able to cut it because I didn't get these five hundred things done and come up with the next great big idea.' How do you keep it all in perspective and focus on what really matters and not get wrapped up in this constant onslaught of e-mail and IM and phone calls and all of the things that you need to do? I think it's important to be able to figure out what's 'need to know' and what's 'nice to know,'" she says.

I asked Claudia what she loves best about her job, and I could tell by her answer that she loves just about everything, which is probably why she's so good at what she does. Claudia has a quality that business leaders need in order to be successful: *passion.*

Claudia comments, "Every single day I get to do something I love. No, we're not surgeons or finding a cure for a horrible disease, but what we are doing is, in our own way, giving women self-confidence and making them feel a little bit better about themselves than they did before they interacted with us. Of course there are the more mundane pieces of the job, like making sure you're on your profit plan or putting together the analytics on something

 what it takes

▶ **Passion about what you do**

▶ **The confidence to take the lead**

▶ **The ability to inspire and motivate others**

▶ **Strong business skills**

1992–1994: Director of field marketing, Avon

1994: Began working with Estée Lauder USA

2000: Became VP sales & education, Stila

2003: Promoted to SVP, general manager, Stila

2005: Named president of *mark,* Avon's teen brand

before a big presentation. Those real nuts and bolts are the things that can sometimes be a little less glorified. But there's something so gratifying about that moment where you can connect with someone on a very real level and know that when you leave them they're in a better spot than when you first came together. That's what keeps me going."

CLAUDIA'S CAREER ADVICE

▸ *There are going to be parts of your job that you love and that you don't. But if when you wake up in the morning you can feel great about going to work, you have a spring in your step and you know that in some small way you'll make a difference, then you're in a good place.*

in the field

Five More Careers You Can Have with a Background in Business

trader "Online trading" gets a lot of press, but most traders work for international banks where they trade, or manage the buying and selling of, different assets such as bonds, stocks, futures, or options, worth millions of dollars. Traders try to predict the financial markets and figure out when to buy or sell to make the most profit.

financial analyst Financial analysts typically work in-house for corporations, analyzing financial transactions involving their business. Financial analysts might do things like work up budgets to determine if a project is worth taking on, develop financial plans for programs within the company, or analyze the finances of a competitor.

mutual fund analyst Mutual fund analysts are like researchers. Their job is to research and analyze different potential investment opportunities for mutual funds or pension funds, and make recommendations on which funds are good investments and which are risky.

mergers and acquisitions manager People who work in mergers and acquisitions, or M&A, typically structure deals for two companies who are merging or when one is acquiring the other. People in M&A might provide advice, figure out the finances, or set up deals for their client.

venture capitalist Venture capital firms are companies that invest in what are usually considered to be high-risk opportunities, like start-up companies or young, struggling businesses. Though these investments are typically much riskier than more traditional types of investing, the financial payoff can be high.

 ## you need to know about

Future Business Leaders of America (www.fbla-pbl.org), otherwise known as Phi Beta Lambda, is a national nonprofit organization whose aim is to help middle school, high school, and college students prepare for business careers. You'll find a ton of resources at this website, including an online kit to help you start a chapter at your own school.

For more careers as an executive, check out the nonprofit director profile on page 168.

Tamara Hayman

engineer

the facts

▶ **what?** Engineers use math and science to design and develop anything from small machines and computers to space shuttles. Systems engineers, like Tamara, develop the requirements for a system, like a computer program, and make sure it gets built the way it needs to, from start to finish.

▶ **where?** Depending on their field, engineers might work for private corporations, local governments, pharmaceutical companies, or big government contractors.

Tamara Hayman,
Systems Engineer,
Lockheed Martin

▶ **how?** A bachelor's degree is all an engineer needs to work in this industry, but getting a graduate degree will open up doors to more advanced opportunities and promotions.

▶ **$$$:** $55,000 to $90,000 a year, depending on field and degree

▶ **dress code?** Business casual to casual

▶ **stress factor:** On a scale of 1 to 10, between a 7 and an 8

tamara is a young star in her field. At the age of twenty-four, she juggles a demanding job as a systems engineer at Lockheed Martin in Bethesda, Maryland, a company that develops everything from space stations to defense systems for the military; graduate school; and taking part in a supercompetitive three-year program for young engineers called the Engineering Leadership Development Program. Only five engineers get into this program at Tamara's site each year, and in addition to training in all the different engineering disciplines, she participates in national conferences and mentors younger engineers as they pursue their own graduate degrees.

I recently had the chance to talk with Tamara about her job and her life.

ME: How did you get started in engineering?

TAMARA: I've always been involved in internship programs or leadership development programs. If someone told me about an opportunity, I'd apply. I kind of fell into engineering because everyone said that this is where the money is. Now that I'm here I can say, "Okay, I can do this." I remember one mentor who said to me, "Stop trying to figure out exactly what you want to do and just take advantage of every opportunity that comes your way, because one day someone will pull you into a position that you never thought you wanted to do or even knew existed, and that's when you'll realize that's the place you want to be."

> "I'm a nosy person, so this job is perfect for me because it allows me to know what everyone is doing."

ME: What does a systems engineer do?

TAMARA: A systems engineer writes the requirements for a system. So, say a computer needs to have an on and off power button. It must have a keyboard and the keyboard must interface with the CPU system. The user should be able to press *T* and *T* shows up on the

you asked . . .

"How have you stayed motivated?" Brie, age 14

tamara answered . . .

"I'm one of those people who wants to be the best at whatever I do. I love it when people know my name and know who I am, and I have a drive to keep learning more so I can be the best in my job and my field. And in a place where you have six hundred employees, in order to stay on top you have to work really hard. So that's my motivation. I know that if I work hard now, I'll get recognition later."

monitor. Those are all the kinds of things we tell the designer of the hardware so that the final system can do all of those things. The designer can make it look any way that they want to, but it must still meet the system requirements that I set up.

Part of what I love about this job is that I get to be involved in every stage of the process. So, while my job is to write the requirements, when we go into design, I'm making sure that the person designing the system is designing it according to the way that I wrote the requirements. Then when we move into development, I'm making sure that the person is developing the system in the way that I wrote the requirements. The same thing goes for the testing phase—I'm making sure that they're testing it to meet my specifications. I'm a nosy person, so this job is perfect for me because it allows me to know what everyone is doing throughout the whole life cycle of the system we're developing.

 ## TAMARA'S (UN)USUAL DAY

7:30 a.m.: I get up, get ready for work, and head out. It takes me about thirty-five minutes to get to work. When I get here, I get something to drink and get settled in. The first thing I'll do as soon as I get to work is look at e-mails to see what meetings I have and see what my day looks like. I'll go through e-mails and respond to those I can. I write myself a

"to do" list for all the things that I plan to accomplish that day. I don't necessarily accomplish everything, but at least I have a plan.

10:00 a.m.: *A lot of mornings I have meetings at ten or eleven, so I'll grab my little engineering notebook and scribe all the information I get from each meeting, any important discoveries that came out of that meeting, or things I want to follow up on. If I don't have a meeting, it will pretty much be me starting to accomplish some of my tasks for the day.*

12:30–1:30 p.m.: *I take an hour for lunch, and my other engineering friends and I will sit in the cafeteria and just talk about how our day's going so far or what was on TV the night before or the difference between men and women in relationships . . . that kind of thing.*

1:30–6:00 p.m.: *In the afternoon I tackle more of the tasks on my "to do" list. Sometimes the things I'm working on are related to the Engineering Leadership Development Program (ELDP) that I participate in at work. The ELDP is a competitive program for young engineers that gives them the chance to work in different engineering disciplines at the company. I'm the deputy manager of that program here, so I handle all the day-to-day operations of the program at this branch of Lockheed Martin. So the rest of my day will be juggling the work of an engineer—attending design reviews or writing requirements for new systems—and the work of managing the Leadership Development Program and being a mentor to entry-level engineers.*

 the breakdown

IN MEETINGS: Sometimes all day, some days not at all

ON THE PHONE: 4 hours a week

ONLINE: On and off throughout the day

SITTING: Most of the day

PUBLIC SPEAKING: Occasionally for presentations

READING: On and off throughout the day

6:00 or 7:00 p.m.: *Leave work.*

ME: What's your work space like?

TAMARA: Most engineers sit in cubicles. I sit in a three-person cubicle, but there are only two of us, so the other person and I share the third desk. My desk is always cluttered because of the two different jobs I'm juggling, so I try to stay organized and keep the paperwork for each job separate, but it never works out that way. Because I

why wait?

- Take math and science courses in high school—they'll be a prerequisite to most engineering programs in college.

- Look for apprenticeship and mentoring programs specifically designed for girls interested in engineering.

- Join an "Advocates for Women in Science, Engineering, and Mathematics" (AWSEM) club in your school or start one! Find out more at www.saturdayacademy.org.

work on government systems and we have a whole bunch of requirements, each system has its own requirements documents. I have all of these thick notebooks laying on my desk. I also keep notes from any training course I've had since I started—I've been here for three years, so you can just imagine how many notebooks I have. I like to say that I'm organized, but my desk is just a cluttered mess. I can find everything, though, even though somebody else might not be able to.

what it takes

- Paying attention to detail

- Having good math and analytical skills

- A desire to want to figure out how things work

- Being able to work in a team

ME: What's the toughest part of your job?

TAMARA: Because we're developing systems that are used on actual navy ships, you really have to pay a lot of attention to detail and keep the end goal in mind all the time, because whatever you do in your job today is going to affect someone's life later. So just because I'm tired or

then to now

| 1997: Interned at law firm through Law Links | 1998: Interned at University of Maryland through Youthworks | 1999: Graduated high school in Baltimore | 2001–2003: Worked as part-time cashier at university bookstore | 2003: Graduated University of Maryland, BS in computer science |

I really don't want to go through all the details or research a system like I should, I have to remember that my taking the easy way out now could affect the way the system runs later. It could ultimately backfire and even affect someone's life. So you really have to pay a lot of attention to detail.

ME: How do you deal with that pressure?

TAMARA: Lunch is my refresher every day. My friends and I go to lunch and we don't talk about work . . . we just talk about "stuff." I'm also a serious soap opera junkie, so even though I can't watch them, I'll go to CBS.com and read what happened yesterday on *The Young and the Restless* if I feel like I need a quick break or distraction.

ME: What's the best part of your job?

TAMARA: With everything that I work on, we have meetings and peer reviews, which means my coworkers from the different engineering areas come in and review the requirements that I wrote. I'm writing from a systems perspective, but an electrical engineer might approach the project in a different way, and the same goes for a mechanical engineer and a software engineer. So having the other engineers come into a meeting to review my work and find no defects in my requirements is the best thing ever, because it means that I really am doing my job well.

 paying your dues

> Wannabe engineers usually start out as associate engineers, a position they have for about two years. Associate engineers have an engineer mentor and learn the ropes by doing the job with supervision.

2001–2003: Interned at Lockheed Martin through INROADS	2003: Hired at Lockheed Martin as software engineer	2005: Began working as a systems engineer at Lockheed Martin	2006: Graduated Johns Hopkins University, MS in technical management

INTERESTED IN A CAREER IN ENGINEERING? HERE'S TAMARA'S ADVICE

▶ *Pay attention to detail, be nosy, and want to know how things work.*

▶ *Be a people person. We're not all geeks or bookworms—we have to be able to interact with people.*

▶ *Remember that engineering is not just about math and science— it's about making your ideas a reality.*

in the field

Five More Engineering Careers

mechanical engineer There is an engineer behind every machine— dishwashers to jet engines. Mechanical engineers know all about how machines work, and they might have jobs developing and test- ing new products for companies or maintaining equipment for major manufacturing plants.

civil engineer Civil engineers design and maintain the infrastruc- tures that we encounter in our everyday lives—things like highways, bridges, airports . . . even skyscrapers. They consider how these infra- structures will be used, what their impact will be on the environ- ment, how much energy they'll use, and how safe they will be.

agricultural engineer There are actually engineers who spend their workday figuring out the most efficient ways to handle, process, and distribute the food that ends up in our kitchen. Agricultural engi- neers develop new and better ways for preserving or packaging food or even create new and improved technologies for cooking food.

aerospace engineer Flip through the employee directory at NASA and you'll find it's full of aerospace engineers. They're the ones who design and test new space shuttles, military jets, missiles, and commercial airplanes. They usually work for organizations like the Federal Aviation Administration (FAA), NASA, or private companies.

industrial engineer Industrial engineers figure out the best way to keep everything moving smoothly in the production and distribution of a product or service. They may work on anything from a radio station broadcast to a bank service—and integrate people power, budgets, schedules, and the mechanics of how to actually get the process done.

 you need to know about

The website Engineer Girl (www.engineergirl.org) is part of the National Academy of Engineering's Celebration of Women in Engineering project. Its goals are to expose women and girls to engineering careers, and this awesome website includes tons of info on how to get ready for college, inspirational books to read, fun facts about engineering, quizzes, and essay contests.

Maria Carrillo

teacher

the facts

Maria Carrillo, Teacher

▶ **what?** Teachers educate students, from preschoolers through adults.

▶ **where?** There are teachers everywhere there are schools and students. They might work in private or public schools, or teach outside of the classroom, too.

▶ **how?** At the very least, teachers need a bachelor's degree in education or the subject they want to teach, although teachers with a graduate degree may earn more money. To teach in a public school, teachers need to pass a licensing test in their state and may need graduate-level education, too.

▶ **$$$:** An average salary of $45,000, depending on school and level of experience

▶ **dress code?** Casual

▶ **stress factor:** On a scale of 1 to 10, a 6 ("With an occasional 9," says Maria.)

i stumbled on bilingual high school science teacher Maria Carrillo while researching this book. Maria is a recipient of the prestigious Milken Family Foundation National Educator Award in 2005, and she embodies the qualities that make a great teacher.

A native of Mexico, Maria has made it her personal mission to help Latino students overcome their language obstacles and thrive in the American school system, virtually creating a bilingual curriculum that addresses their needs and gives them their best shot at succeeding academically. Maria's work alone has reduced her high school's student dropout rate.

I had a chance to interview Maria and find out from her what being a teacher is really like, what she loves about it, what she finds most challenging, and why she's going back to school again.

> *"The first years that I was teaching were hard for me because I really wanted to make all my students succeed. But then I realized that you can't get them all."*

ME: When did you know you wanted to be a teacher?

MARIA: It was after I graduated from college. I got my bachelor's degree in biology and I was living in Mexico. I couldn't get a good job doing fieldwork as a biologist because there were mostly men in those jobs. So I started teaching in a school for adults and then in public schools as a substitute. After I moved to this country, I worked as an instructional assistant for the Beaverton School District for a couple of years, and then started working with the ESL students, the ones learning English. I saw how difficult it was for them to succeed in school, and that's when I realized I needed to get my teaching certificate. So I did. I actually quit my instructional assistant job and got my master's degree. About a year after I got my master's, I started working for Beaverton again, this time as a teacher.

ME: So now that you're teaching, do you feel fulfilled? Are you able to achieve what you were hoping to when you first got into the field?

MARIA: Yes, but I still don't think it's enough. There are so many things that we still need to do to improve the services we provide for minority students. They are so left behind. I've actually started working on my doctoral degree because I want to find a way to do more. I really want to be able to make a big difference at the administrative level.

ME: Teens interact with teachers every day, but they see the job from their own perspective. Can you tell us what kinds of things you do on a given day that students might not be aware of?

MARIA: Well, they might not realize how much research goes into being a teacher. I teach special classes for ESL students, or students for whom English is their second language, and I have to find the right material or I need to simplify and modify the materials that I use in the mainstream classes, paying attention to the vocabulary, making sure that there's not a lot of slang or words that can confuse my students. They also probably don't realize the amount of extra work that teachers have to do. I teach science in Spanish, and that's been hard because there are not enough instructional materials and I have to translate everything and try to find teaching material online. Then there's grading papers, contacting parents, dealing with things like making copies . . . stuff that's boring. Plus a lot of meetings and things that they don't think about, like all of the politics in school.

ME: Is dealing with "politics" a big part of teaching?

MARIA: For me it is, maybe because I work with minority students. When I first started teaching here, some people didn't believe that I could actually teach science in Spanish. A lot of teachers thought that the students needed to learn English before they started taking science classes. It was hard because I knew that some people didn't really accept what I was doing, and it didn't put me in a great position. It's still an issue today, especially with increasing class sizes and things like that. I'm always fighting for smaller classes even though I never get them, because if we want to reach minorities, we need to have small classes to do a better job. It's been difficult.

ME: What are some of the things that make it worthwhile?

MARIA: When my students actually understand what I'm trying to do, when you see that they get it. Like right now I'm working on genetics. We are learning about how genes work—how they combine and the different ways in which you inherit traits from your parents.

why wait?

- ▸ Look into being an assistant or aide to a teacher at your school.
- ▸ Volunteer at a preschool or summer school as an assistant teacher.
- ▸ Be a volunteer tutor in a subject you're an expert in.

what it takes

▶ Being a good public speaker

▶ Staying calm even when frustrated

▶ Being an expert in the subject(s) you want to teach

▶ Dedication to your students

I had a good day today because I know that they really understood what I was trying to get across, and they were really enjoying what they were learning.

ME: Are there any other parts of your work that you find especially rewarding?

MARIA: The fact that I see more and more of my minority students graduating every year and actually get to see some of them moving on to college—that is really good.

ME: When you get the rewards that you're telling me about, does that make up for the challenges that you experience?

MARIA: Yeah, it does. Because most of my students are Hispanic, the fact that I have the privilege to help them is really something. But there are parts of the job that I don't really like—sometimes it's hard to see students who have such big problems, knowing that I can't really help them.

ME: How do you handle that on a personal level?

MARIA: The first years that I was teaching were hard for me because I wanted to make all of my students succeed. But then I realized that you can't get them all, you know, you're never going to be able to. So realizing that if I made a difference in one or two of their lives, I think

then to now

Graduated from Universidad Autonoma de Nuevo León, Mexico, with a BA in biology

1984: Worked in the ecology department at the Nuevo León Government

Taught at Nuevo León Public Schools

that's good enough. Because they identify with me, I also really get to know my students, whether I like it or not. And that can be rough because you get to know all their problems. But it's also good because that means they trust you.

ME: I bet that long after they graduate, your former students look back on high school and say, "That Ms. Carrillo . . . she really made a difference in my life."

MARIA: Yeah. *(Laughs)* I push all their buttons.

ME: That's good . . . that means you're a good teacher! What are your hours like? What time do you get up? Do you ever work at home?

MARIA: My work schedule is seven to three, but I have to confess that I never get to work at seven, and often I come home early. A lot of times I bring my work home because I prefer to work here. Lately it's been getting better—I don't work that much at home anymore. But at the beginning I was working maybe twelve hours a day, because I had so many things to do. I had to design the curriculum, I had to translate everything—I had a lot of work to do. But I think that teaching gets easier as you get more experience.

ME: So, the first couple of years teaching can be difficult?

MARIA: Yes, those are killer years. I think that's the reason a lot of teachers change careers—because you get burned out. But if you can stick to what you're doing and teach for five years, then you've made it over the hump.

| 1995: Became bilingual instructional assistant in Beaverton School District, Oregon | 1998: Received MA in Teaching from Pacific University | 1998: Became teacher in Beaverton School District | 2005: Started doctorate program at Portland State University |

ME: Is public speaking an important part of being a good teacher?

MARIA: I think it is. You have to be able to get your point across, be able to speak their language. I tell my students I am trilingual. I speak my language, I speak English, and I speak their language. I think it's very important that you're able to talk to them and understand what's important to them.

MARIA'S ADVICE FOR FUTURE TEACHERS

▶ *Treat all students with the same respect and recognize that everyone is different. Help your students realize their potential by holding them to high standards.*

▶ *Be sure that you want to be a teacher, because it's not an easy job. You're not going to become a millionaire, but you can make a good living and you get to help others.*

in the field
Five More Careers in Education

principal Principals are the heads of schools, and they oversee teachers and staff, and make decisions about and enforce the school rules. Since they're usually appointed by the school board, principals also deal with administrative duties like managing the school budget and making policies.

college professor There are some similarities between college professors and middle school or high school teachers, but in addition to preparing lectures and educating students, professors spend a good deal of time doing research and writing papers to help them become experts in their academic field.

university dean If professors are like teachers, then deans are like principals. They are generally former college professors who have moved from an area of expertise to overseeing a larger unit within the university, such as a group of departments or an aspect of student life.

special education teacher Special education teachers might work with students with physical, emotional, or psychological disabilities, or gifted and talented students. They provide specialized instruction requiring specific training and certification.

school nurse School nurses manage the overall health of the student body, from scheduling health-related educational programs to figuring out the best way to manage an outbreak of chicken pox. They might administer hearing tests one day, and make sure that a child with special needs is being taken care of on another day.

 you need to know about

The website TeachersCount (www.teacherscount.org) has resources for teachers and people interested in the teaching profession. Here you'll find a whole section dedicated to people who want to teach, including info on why it's such a great career and details about scholarship opportunities.

For more careers working with children, check out the educational psychologist profile on page 130 and the nanny profile on page 378.

Kay Lakey

physical therapist

the facts

Kay Lakey, Physical Therapist, Private Practice Owner

▶ **what?** Physical therapists work with people's physical structures, whether to help them recover from an injury or because they're experiencing chronic pain. They use a blend of exercises, stretches, massage, electrotherapy, and other tools to help rehabilitate their clients.

▶ **where?** You'll find physical therapists in hospitals, clinics, schools, or, like Kay, in their own private practice.

▶ **how?** Physical therapists need undergraduate work heavy in biology, anatomy, and other sciences, and they must attend an accredited graduate program for physical therapy and become licensed to practice.

▶ **$$$:** An average salary of $60,000

▶ **dress code?** Depends on the work venue . . . business casual for private practice or maybe scrubs if at a hospital

▶ **stress factor:** On a scale of 1 to 10, between a 5 and a 6

physical therapy is a very popular field among women—in 2002 more than 70 percent of physical therapists were female. I interviewed Kay Lakey, who runs her own physical therapy clinic, to find out what a physical therapist's work involves.

"Basically what we do is work with people's structure—their muscles, their bones, their tendons, their ligaments—and help them improve function. So if you were to get hurt doing a sport, a physical therapist would be the one who would help you transition back into your sport with no pain, or if you have a spinal cord injury or a head injury, they would help you get back into society without any assistance or with minimal assistance. So we're helping people get back to being functional in their life, and hopefully, pain free," she explained.

> *"That is the piece that is so cool about physical therapy and working with people—as soon as you're the teacher, the students actually teach you."*

As the owner of her own clinic and the only person on staff, Kay wears many different hats. To give us a better picture of what her day looks like, I asked Kay to break it down.

you asked . . .

"How did you know what you wanted to do with your life?" Jessie, age 15

kay answered . . .

"When I was a kid, I always wanted to be a doctor or an astronaut, so there was a part of me that always knew that I was going to do something that was not just getting married and having kids. I had no idea that I'd become a physical therapist, but when I took a college course for it and saw everything that was involved in the field, I thought, 'Oh, this is really cool.'"

KAY'S (UN)USUAL DAY

I start my day by opening the office. I don't have an assistant or anything—I'm a sole practitioner. So just like anybody, I come in and turn the coffee pot on, open everything up, unload laundry because I need to keep clean sheets on my massage table, those kinds of things. Throughout the day I'm answering phones and taking appointments, canceling appointments, dealing with faxes and e-mails from doctors, insurance companies, and patients.

I schedule my appointments from nine to six, usually seven a day. But that's just me. I've worked in hospitals before where I've had twenty-four patients scheduled a day, for fifteen-minute appointments. But I can't schedule as many now because I handle all of the administrative parts of running my business too.

the breakdown

IN MEETINGS: Not often

ON THE PHONE: 1–2 hours a day

ONLINE: Maximum of 1 hour

SITTING: 2–3 hours a day

STANDING: 7–8 hours a day

READING: 1 hour a day

When my clients come in, I do an evaluation of them. I'll watch them walk, watch them move, test their range of motion and joint function and strength. I'll have them fill out a form with specific questions about what their pain is and what their function is, what their goals are or what they want to accomplish. Then I'll do some work with them, like joint mobilization or ultrasound or craniosacral. We decide together what their program is going to be, and each time I see them, I reassess them. Based on what I see, the program might shift slightly. These appointments typically last fifty-five minutes or so. When we're done, I come into my office and make notes on their chart about what we did, what I observed, and so on.

then to now

Graduated from University of Montana with BS in health education and recreation	Received certificate from the Mayo Clinic School of Health Related Sciences, Rochester, MN	**1977–1981:** Worked as physical therapist at Elks Rehabilitation Hospital in Boise, ID

At lunch I'll run errands. I'll go to the bank, I'll go to Kinko's to make copies, I'll go to the post office. So the tasks of running a business get slipped in since I don't have anybody who's working for me. In between all of the appointments, I'm doing other work, like calling insurance companies, calling doctors' offices, or dictating my notes.

As a physical therapist, Kay puts together a plan of action to help her patients reach their goal, whether it's to free themselves of pain or to run a marathon someday. I wanted to get a better sense of what a physical therapist does in working one-on-one with patients. These are the kinds of things that Kay might do with a patient who's come to see her for an appointment, using some of the techniques she used while studying physical therapy at the Mayo Clinic:

▶ Have the patient walk around the room and see what part of the patient's body her eye is drawn to

▶ Gather information about what's happening in a patient's body through her hands

▶ Check range of motion in an area that they're working on

▶ If she picks up that there's a misalignment, then she'll use an osteopathic muscle energy technique.

▶ If it's the first time she's seen the patient, Kay will teach him or her how to do the energy technique for themselves at home.

While Kay's work clearly has a positive impact on her clients, it's not without its challenges, the biggest of which, according to Kay, is dealing with insurance companies and all the paperwork that goes along with it. On top of that, she finds herself challenged by working with clients who have been treated poorly by the medical system, mainly because no one has been able to diagnose what's wrong with them.

1985–1987: Worked at the Sports Physical Therapy and Back Clinic, Davis, CA

1988–1994: Worked at the Puget Sound Physical Therapy Registry, Redmond, WA

1993: Started own physical therapy practice

why wait?

▸ Look into volunteering with a sports medicine clinic for events like road races or walkathons.

▸ Take courses in biology and science in high school.

"Those people who have been severely curbed and not supported are the hardest. They get cut off by insurance companies, but they're still disabled and are struggling to figure out how to function with a level of pain that most of us couldn't handle. And there's a lot of anger and emotion around that. So it's harder to figure out what to do to help those people. I feel really bad for them because I'm a pretty compassionate and empathetic person," Kay explains.

what it takes

▸ An abundance of patience

▸ Being able to tune in and connect with people

▸ Physical stamina—you're on your feet a lot

Despite these challenges, Kay finds her work as a physical therapist extremely fulfilling. "One of the true gifts of what I do is watching and witnessing the journey of us as human beings and supporting a person's struggles. I'm learning all the time, and that is the piece that is so cool about physical therapy and working with people—as soon as you're the teacher, the students actually teach you. When I started my own business, my life began to get healed in ways you would not believe," she says.

KAY'S CAREER ADVICE

▸ *Have the courage to do what excites you and what fulfills you, even if it's not going to make you a lot of money.*

▸ *If you're going to take a profession for status, money, or power, you're not going to be happy in it. Keep asking yourself, "What makes me happy and what do I enjoy doing?"*

in the field

Five More Careers Working as a Therapist

occupational therapist These therapists work with people who have permanent disabilities or have been injured, to give them tools to become as self-reliant as possible. They teach their patients how to do everyday things, such as grocery shopping and using public transportation.

speech language pathologist Also known as speech therapists, they work with people who have difficulties speaking. Patients can include children who are slow in developing their verbal skills and victims of head injuries who have lost language skills.

recreational therapist Activities like playing music, making art, even cooking and hiking can relieve stress. Recreational therapists work with physical therapy patients and find ways to incorporate these sorts of activities into their work to speed up recovery and strengthen their clients' overall mental, physical, and emotional health.

massage therapist Massage therapists are trained in massage and anatomy, and they provide massages to relieve stress, promote recovery from an injury, reduce pain, and improve the overall well-being of their clients. They often work in spas or gyms.

kinesiologist Kinesiology is a relatively new science focused on healing pain and illness in people by tuning in to the body and figuring out what is at the root of the imbalance that is causing the pain. Kinesiologists look at the whole body as opposed to just the symptom, and they perform muscle testing on their patients as part of their therapy.

 you need to know about

> The American Physical Therapy Association (www.apta.org) is the national organization for physical therapy professionals. The website features a whole resource section for students interested in becoming physical therapists.

Sara Lynch

nanny

Sara Lynch,
Full-time Nanny

▶ **what?** A nanny is a professional child caregiver for a family. Nannies do things like dress and feed the children, drive them to and from school, prepare meals, and sometimes do light housekeeping.

▶ **where?** Nannies tend to work in private residences, hired either through professional nanny services or by individuals.

▶ **how?** Many nannies have extensive experience babysitting and working with children, and most have taken some sort of child-care training. Being CPR and first-aid certified is a benefit as well.

▶ **$$$:** Nannies earn anywhere from eight to twenty dollars an hour or more, depending on where they work and how many children they're providing care for. Some also receive room and board as part of their salary.

▶ **dress code?** Casual

▶ **stress factor:** On a scale of 1 to 10, a 1 according to Sara (but probably depends on the children you're watching!)

if you've ever babysat and you like children, you may have wondered what a career as a nanny might be like. Wonder no more! Full-time nanny Sara Lynch is here to shed a little light.

ME: How did you get into being a nanny?

SARA: I've always loved working with kids, ever since I was old enough to take care of little ones, and I babysat over the summers when I was in high school. Once I graduated from high school, I knew I wanted to work with children, so I worked in a day care. I loved the work, but by the end of the day I was wiped out and just didn't feel like I was getting paid enough. I had heard that being a nanny was a great job—that it pays really well and that a lot of people would prefer a nanny to putting their children in day care—so I decided to try to find a nanny position. But it's definitely something that not just anybody can do. You have to have high qualifications.

> *"There is a big difference between giving the child some dinner and a bath and putting them to bed and what I do."*

ME: What do you mean when you say it's not something anybody can do?

SARA: There is a big difference between giving the child some dinner and a bath and putting them to bed and what I do. Babysitting is

you asked . . .

"Have other people ever not taken your career dreams seriously, and if so, how did you handle it?" Julia, age 14

sara answered . . .

"When people make comments to me about what I want to do, it's just one of those things that shouldn't matter. Because they're my dreams and goals. It's really mind over matter—if you think you can't do it, you won't, and if you think you can, you will. It's just that simple."

usually a couple hours long, but most nanny jobs are all day, every day. Somebody who doesn't have a ton of patience is not going to be able to do it. You also have to come up with somewhat of a curriculum, ideas for activities and entertainment.

ME: Can you tell us what a typical day looks like?

SARA'S (UN)USUAL DAY

My hours are eight a.m. to five p.m., Monday through Friday. I commute eleven miles to work every morning, so I have to get up at six forty-five a.m. and then leave the house by seven thirty to be here on time. Campbell's two, and she's on a really good schedule, so our routine is kind of set. Here's what it looks like:

what it takes

▸ Oodles of patience

▸ Being extremely responsible, professional, and trustworthy

▸ Liking children of all ages

8:00–8:30 a.m.: Take over feeding Campbell and clean up the kitchen after breakfast. While I'm cleaning and getting things ready for the day, Campbell reads books or does her independent play.

8:30–11:00 a.m.: I get Campbell ready for the day and then we have "outside activity" time, where we get out and get moving. If it's during the summer, we'll go swimming; other times we'll go to the park or the zoo. We try to get out and walk as much as possible, which can be tough in the winter. It's challenging to find things to do so we aren't stuck in the house. My mind is like a kid's—I can't be in the house all day long.

11:00 a.m.–12:30 p.m.: We have lunchtime and get ready for naptime. I prepare lunch for both of us—we go by the food pyramid, so I make sure she eats something from each food group. Campbell's parents are good about keeping everything stocked, so I don't have to do much grocery shopping,

then to now

1997: Started babysitting while in middle school

2003: Graduated from Anacortes High School, Anacortes, Washington

2003: Became live-in nanny for a family

although every once in a while we'll go to the store and get something. Campbell and I eat together, and we start the nap process as soon as she's done. I change her diaper and get her ready and then we'll read books and sing songs. It takes her a while to fall asleep, but once she's down she usually sleeps for between two hours and fifteen minutes to three hours. After she goes to sleep, I clean up the kitchen and her toys, which are usually everywhere. Maybe I'll do her laundry, empty the trash, play with the kitties. And then once all that stuff is done, I relax. Sometimes I watch TV or read, especially books about toddlers and discipline. The quiet time is kind of considered my break, because I don't get traditional breaks during the day.

3:00–4:45 p.m.: *Campbell usually wakes up from her nap by three, so then she'll have a snack. She has a lot of energy when she wakes up—she wants to go. Sometimes we'll just head outside right away for a walk, and I'll give her a snack in her stroller. Other afternoons she might have a class, like Wednesdays she has her gymnastics class and Fridays she has a music class, but most of the time it's just whatever we feel like doing. On rainy days the afternoon would be our time for hands-on stuff like reading and bubbles, music and dancing, working on her vocabulary and her colors. It's kind of like her "class time."*

4:45 p.m.: *Good communication with the parents is really important when you're a nanny, so I write in Campbell's journal about the day—what she ate, how she ate, what her mood was like, what she did. And then I write a short paragraph in her voice, from her point of view.*

 ## why wait?

▸ Babysit! You can get lots of experience with kids of all ages by being the neighborhood babysitter.

▸ Seek out opportunities to volunteer with children—at summer camps, preschools, and tutoring centers.

▸ Get certified in CPR and first aid—many people looking to hire babysitters and nannies require these certifications.

2005: Started in current position as full-time nanny

2006: Began going to school for Certificate of Proficiency for Child Care Professionals

5:00 p.m.: *I go home, go to the gym, and relax. I'm real exhausted by the end of the day.*

10:00 p.m.: *I'm usually in bed by ten because I get up so early. It's not a job where you can function if you don't have a full night's sleep.*

ME: It sounds like you have a big responsibility in your job.

SARA: It's ridiculously big. Campbell is in my hands, and she's my responsibility if something happens.

ME: What is your relationship with Campbell's parents like? Is that an important component of your job?

SARA: I don't know how it worked out so well . . . it just did. They were offering the same hours I wanted and they had an infant when I was hired, and that's the age level I wanted to work with. It just seemed like everything kind of fell into place. Things started out really well, and now, after being here almost a year and a half, they're like my second family. And I think that's really important, because if you can't work together as a team, it's not good for anybody.

ME: What is it about being a nanny that you love?

SARA: Campbell. *(big smile)* Sometimes I feel like it's not a job and that I'm just playing with my best friend—my very "little" best friend. Campbell's parents, Tia and Doug, are so sweet. And it's definitely rewarding when Campbell does something that I teach her. That's one of my favorite things.

ME: And what are the toughest parts of your job?

SARA: Keeping up with Campbell's growth and progress. I can't say it's not hard, but there aren't too many negatives. I think every day has its challenges, but nothing really extreme. The biggest one is making sure that she's progressing well from day to day and that I'm adapting to where she is.

▸ Take it very seriously—the people hiring you are placing a huge amount of trust in you.

▸ Make sure that it's something you're really interested in, because a lot of people want a long-term commitment—at least a year or more. Children need someone consistent in their life, so be straightforward from the very beginning about how long you want the job to be.

in the field
Five More Careers Working with Children

preschool teacher If you like children and want to be paid to act silly and have fun, you might look into being a preschool teacher. These teachers work in private or public preschools and help run classes with ten to twenty children or so. They have to be very patient and enthusiastic and enjoy singing, planning arts and crafts, and reading stories.

children's bookstore owner Children's bookstore owners tend to love both children and literature. They specialize in carrying new, and sometimes used, books that appeal to children of all ages, and much of their work involves community outreach and planning events such as weekly readings and book clubs.

pediatrician Chances are you've interacted with one of these during your own childhood, or maybe you still go to one. Pediatricians are doctors who specialize in working with children—some work at hospitals, while others might start their own practice and see children from the time they are babies through adulthood.

day care owner As there are more working moms than ever today, day care is a big business. In many states, day care owners must get a license to run their center, and their job is to ensure that the environment is a safe and nurturing one for babies and children.

children's photographer Some photographers specialize in taking photos of babies and children because they want to marry their love of photography with their love of children. They might work at photo studios or have their own business, and they focus on creating an environment where children are comfortable.

you need to know about

The International Nanny Association, or INA (www.nanny.org), is a nonprofit organization with a goal of educating and supporting professional nannies and the people who hire them. You'll find articles about being a nanny, educational resources, and even a nanny mentor program online.

For more careers working with children, check out the educational psychologist profile on page 130 and the teacher profile on page 364.

Maura Tierney

actor

the facts

▸ **what?** Stars of stage and screen . . . The gal behind the counter in a Wendy's commercial . . . The extras walking around in the background of the new Bond film. They're all actors— getting paid to play a role in order to entertain or inform.

▸ **where?** Actors perform in television shows, movies, regional theater, Broadway, commercials, cartoons . . . even marketing gigs for corporations. While there are acting opportunities just about everywhere, the main hubs for this profession are New York City and L.A.

Maura Tierney, Actor

▸ **how?** Most actors hone their craft by studying dramatic arts in college or even grad school. For access to most auditions, actors need an agent, and to get an agent, they need some experience, a prepared monologue, and a head shot.

▸ **$$$:** While big-time actors such as Maura Tierney can earn more than a million dollars a year, the average salary for an actor is around (gulp) $5,000 a year. Because many actors don't have steady gigs, they often supplement their income with full-time or part-time jobs.

▸ **dress code?** Actors wear whatever their role or audition calls for, whether it be a suit, jeans, or a chicken costume.

▸ **stress factor:** On a scale of 1 to 10, a 7

maura tierney has, by any definition, enjoyed a very successful career as an actor. For the past eighteen years Maura has been seen on big and small screens everywhere, from starring with Jim Carrey in the movie *Liar, Liar* (1997) and with Ben Affleck in *Forces of Nature* (1999) to playing a lead in NBC's cult favorite sitcom *NewsRadio* in the 1990s. She's probably best known for her role as Dr. Abby Lockhart on the hit medical drama *ER*, which she's starred in for more than seven years.

I had a chance to catch up with Maura at her home in New York City to find out what life as a successful actor really looks like.

"Acting really is a collaborative art . . . no matter how prepared you are, you have to be ready to throw everything out the window once you start working."

ME: It seems like starring in a weekly TV series must be pretty demanding. What kind of hours do you work?

MAURA: It varies, because I'm in an ensemble cast show. A standard workday for us is twelve hours, and if you have a lot to do, you can have a week where you work a twelve- or thirteen-hour day every day. And then some episodes, I'm a little bit lighter. So it really varies according to the script.

ME: Could you walk us through a typical day on a *busy* week?

MAURA: Every day is different, but I seem to be on the set *a lot*. On a busy week, my call time is six a.m., which is an hour before the crew gets there. I have to get up around five fifteen, which is a drag if you're not a morning person. I've been doing it for eighteen years, and still my body has not switched around to enjoying the mornings, but that's okay. So I get up really early and get there about six, go through hair and makeup, and then the crew and the director and everybody else arrives and we go to work at seven. We shoot for six hours and then we break for lunch. Then we shoot four or five more hours in the afternoon.

ME: And are you on your feet a lot of that time?

MAURA: On my show, yeah, because we're always running around the hospital.

ME: Do you have work to do once you're home?

MAURA: I do have work to do. I live close to the studio, so I get home probably around seven fifteen. Luckily, I don't have too much trouble remembering and learning lines. At this point when I have to say medical things on the show like "pericardiocentesis pneumomediastinum," I've been saying them for a long time, so it's not so bad. In the beginning it was a lot more arduous learning my lines, but fortunately for me, it's not something I have to work so hard at. Unless it's more of an emotional scene, a personal scene for the character . . . that stuff I have to prepare for. But the medical jargon kind of goes in and out of my head at this point.

ME: Many people forget about that part of the job—memorizing lines. Are there any other behind-the-scenes challenges that people might not be aware of?

MAURA: Well, you never know what can happen on the set when you show up. You can sit at home and work on a scene and think, "This is the way I think it's going to go, and this is what I think my

you asked . . .

"How have you stayed grounded?" Alexandra, 16

maura answered . . .

"Well, I do love acting. I think that's part of it—I love the work. And I still have all my same friends that I met in college twenty years ago who I'm very close to, and I think that that's helpful because in this business you can sort of get turned around easily. Having remained friends with this group of people who I love so much has been very helpful."

why wait?

- ▸ Join the drama club at your school, or if there isn't one, start one yourself!

- ▸ Audition for school productions or local community theater and see how you like being on stage.

- ▸ Take acting classes, or if you're interested in musical theater, try dancing or singing lessons.

character is thinking and feeling," and then you get to the set and the director or the actor you're acting with has a completely different idea, and the whole thing is sort of turned on its ear. Acting really is a collaborative art, whether it's theater or TV or the movies or whatever. No matter how prepared you are, you have to be ready to throw everything out the window once you start working.

ME: You also mentioned that it's a lot of work to prepare emotionally . . . is that challenging?

MAURA: Again, that depends. Sometimes it is, sometimes it isn't. Sometimes the writing and the material is very moving to me and I respond to it almost immediately when I read it. I sort of know, "Okay, so that's in my body . . . I know that." Other times, the muse is not with you, and you have to work a little harder to try to find an authentic emotional place. I guess the gist of what I'm saying is that there's a fluidity. You can't be rigid about anything.

ME: And what are the best parts of your job?

 then to now

| Attended New York University | Studied drama at Circle in the Square Theatre School, New York City | 1995–1999: Starred in NBC sitcom *NewsRadio* | 1997: Starred opposite Jim Carrey in *Liar, Liar* |

MAURA: My favorite part of this job? Well, I don't know . . . it's a wonderful job. If you get lucky like I did, it's a great job. I mean, it's difficult in terms of the fact that everybody's a critic of your work, but if you're okay with that inside yourself, then it's great. I love how many different people I meet. And because they're actors or actresses or writers, you know, sometimes they're kind of weird and usually very interesting. *(Laughs)* It's kind of like being in a circus.

ME: I haven't heard that one before.

MAURA: I love that aspect of it.

ME: And what about the recognition factor? Would you consider that a pro or a con? Or is it just part of the job?

MAURA: It is a pro. I mean, sometimes people are so sweet about it, and it's really nice when they come up and say, "I watch your show with my daughter every week." It's a great thing to hear. Sally Field and I did a big story line together on the show where Sally's character has a mental illness, and people have come up to me and talked about how real that was and how much it meant to them to see it portrayed realistically on TV. So that kind of stuff is really rewarding.

ME: Yeah, I can see that. . . . Just to know that you're really having an impact on people.

 ## paying your dues

Breaking into the industry can be tough, but many actors gain valuable experience, make connections, and find an entryway by doing small theater work, student films, and extra work.

| 1997: Profiled in *InStyle* magazine | 1999: Began her tenure on the drama *ER* as Abby Lockhart | 2001: Nominated for an Emmy Award for her role on *ER* | 2006: Starred with Eric McCormack in the Off Broadway play *Some Girls* |

what it takes

▸ Patience . . . your dream gig will take a while to land.

▸ Persistence and passion.

▸ A high tolerance for stress and pressure.

MAURA: Yeah. And today, someone said to me, "You know, from across the street you looked like that chick from *ER!*" And then I was ordering coffee and he said, "Jeez, you even *sound* like her." *(Laughs)*

ME: That's funny.

MAURA: It was really funny.

ME: Acting is one of those careers that a lot of girls are interested in pursuing. Is there any one thing you could pinpoint that they might be surprised to find out about the job?

MAURA: I'm always very encouraging to people who want to do this, but they should realize that it's hard work. You need to have a lot of stamina in terms of putting yourself out there. For many people it does involve a lot of rejection in the beginning. And you need to find a way not to take that personally, because it's not personal. I've been on both sides of casting—I've auditioned for a million things that I didn't get, and I've also been in the room auditioning other actors. A lot of times three great actors will come into the room and then a fourth one comes in and that's just the person who's going to play the role. And it has nothing to do with how talented or not talented anybody is. So it's important that you go into it knowing that if you don't get a job, it's not necessarily personal. I don't want to be negative about it, but sometimes you don't get a job you want and it's really, really hard, but you know, you have to keep going.

You have to love acting. I think a lot of people perceive it as glamorous, which it can be—you get to go to parties, dress up, be on TV, and have people recognize you. But those trappings should not be the reason why someone wants to get into this field, because again, it's hard work. If you're in it just for the celebrity, I think there's less of a chance of enjoying a long or satisfying career.

in the field

Five More Careers Working as a Performer

stand-up comedienne Being a stand-up comic has got to be one of the toughest jobs out there, but women who do it say they love performing in front of a crowd and getting laughs. And while most never land on *The Tonight Show*, there are plenty of opportunities for gigs in small comedy clubs or open mic nights.

stunt double Some actors do their own stunts while filming, but most of the time the more challenging stunts, like jumping off the roof of a tall building onto an air mattress, are performed by stunt doubles. Though doubles are highly trained in safety techniques, the work is not without risk, and it definitely never gets boring.

dancer Whatever your dance style—ballet, hip-hop, tap, ballroom—there are opportunities to dance and get paid for it. Some dancers are part of touring companies, while others might become teachers, open their own studios, become choreographers, or perform on variety shows and TV specials.

TV show host With the boom in reality shows, job ops for TV show hosts keep growing and growing. Think about it.... Where would we be without Ryan Seacrest guiding our journey on *American Idol?* TV hosts have to be comfortable in front of the camera, charismatic, and quick on their feet.

voice-over actor Turn down the volume the next time you watch *Family Guy.* Without the distinctive voices of Stewie or Peter, something will definitely be missing. Some voice-over actors bring animated characters to life, while others find work narrating documentaries or performing voice-overs in commercials.

 ## you need to know about

> *Back Stage* (www.backstage.com) is the main online resource for actors. Here you'll find career resources, advice for dealing with agents and casting directors, interviews with and articles about important people in the biz, and notices for auditions.

For more careers working in Hollywood, check out the movie studio executive profile on page 60 and the TV show creator profile on page 2.

Roxanne Coady

independent bookstore owner

the facts

▶ **what?** Independent bookstore owners typically run the day-to-day business operations of local bookstores, as well as interact with customers, organize community and author events, and keep the shelves stocked with books.

▶ **where?** Wherever there are people who love to buy books!

▶ **how?** There are no formal educational requirements for this career, although a love of books, business savvy, and perseverance are essential.

Roxanne Coady,
Owner, R.J. Julia

▶ **$$$:** An annual salary of $20,000 on up, depending on the size and success of the store

▶ **dress code:** Casual

▶ **stress factor:** On a scale of 1 to 10, an 8

independent bookstores have often been romanticized by Hollywood. Rent the oldies but goodies *You've Got Mail* with Tom Hanks and Meg Ryan (1998) or *Notting Hill* with Julia Roberts and Hugh Grant (1999) and you'll see what I mean. There is something very appealing about the idea of spending long days in a warm, cozy bookstore, sipping hot tea, surrounded by books.

The reality may look different, but for Roxanne Coady, owner of the well-known indie bookstore R.J. Julia in Madison, Connecticut, setting up her own cheerful reading nook was a way of creating a comfortable space that would have a positive impact in the community. She opened her store in 1990, when after nearly twenty successful years working in accounting, Roxanne realized it was time to make a major career shift.

"I thought, I'm forty years old and I have enough money and enough time to have a career that feels like it makes a difference in society. So I made the decision to leave my firm. I always knew my new career would have something to do with reading, so I thought about starting a publishing company or a bookstore. But I realized that I really didn't know anything about publishing—I wasn't an editor, I wasn't a writer. But what I always loved doing was picking out the right book for somebody. So I thought about opening a bookstore, and that's what I did," she explains.

"I may have challenges and sleepless nights worrying about cash flow and hiring and firing people, but still, my life is about books."

Owning an independent bookstore is, in many ways, like running any small business. There are general operations tasks to do, such as renting and maintaining retail space, handling the financial side of things (such as payroll and accounts with vendors), and managing a staff of employees. And like other jobs in retail, bookstore owners might spend a fair amount of time behind the cash register or on the floor arranging displays or helping customers. More specific to the world of books, independent bookstore owners also have to figure out ways to raise the store's profile in the community, as well as find creative ways to keep the store thriving even as competition increases every year.

Books are now sold just about everywhere—from online sites such as Amazon.com to the big chains such as Barnes & Noble and specialty stores such as Urban Outfitters. A career as an independent bookstore owner can be a precarious one, since the competition is fierce and the financial risks are high. Yet there are more than 2,400 such bookstores across the country facing these challenges every day, and keeping their community hub afloat. According to Roxanne, one of the biggest challenges of running an independent bookstore revolves around money.

"When you run something like a bookstore, there's not a clear line of whether it's for-profit or not-for-profit. You know, there's a kind of expectation that running an independent bookstore is about being a good member of the community. So we're stuck in the middle— there are people who expect it to be like the library, yet we need to make money in order to pay staff, pay rent, and run a business in a smart way.

you asked . . .

"Once you've achieved a certain level of success, does running your own business ever get easier?" Chloe, 17

roxanne answered . . .

"I worry every day. I've had to put another ton of money into the store this year. No . . . it's never out of the woods in a kind of sustainable way, but I just keep on doing it. And part of it is that I'm also on the board of a publicly held bank, which both keeps the other part of my brain occupied and helps me earn additional money. I do a bit of consulting for publishing companies, and I'm very active in the nonprofit world. It's a very full and satisfying life."

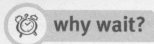
"What has intensified that challenge is that we sell a commodity—*books*. And this commodity has a fixed price, and we have formidable, well-capitalized competitors. It's harder to find a tougher business environment than that. So the real challenge is, how can we add value to what is basically a commodity? You know, a copy of *State of Denial* by Bob Woodward is still a copy of *State of Denial* by Bob Woodward, whether the buyer gets it at a discount online or pays full price at a bookstore. And so we have to find ways to add value—by the experience of coming into the store, or by the experience of talking to us on the phone, or by being sold a good book," Roxanne says.

But like many independent bookstore owners, Roxanne couldn't imagine doing anything else, despite the challenges. When I asked her what she loves about her career, Roxanne emphasized that it has enabled her to create her ideal work environment.

"It's worthwhile to run an organization where the employees are treated in a way that's respectful, and to create an environment where there's mutual goodwill. It's pretty satisfying to go to work every day when people are collaborative and kind to each other. Having a place that matters to the community and the customers—that's pretty satisfying too. And I like that my world is books. I may have challenges and sleepless nights worrying about cash flow and hiring and firing

then to now

Graduated from University of New Haven, Connecticut, with a BS in accounting and economics	Became partner and national tax director at BDO Seidman, New York, New York	1989: After a twenty-year career in accounting, quit job and moved to Connecticut

people, but still my life is about books. On really bad days, I might wish for a job pumping gas. But most days I feel like I'm doing exactly what I want to do. I just wish it were a little easier financially," she says.

As owner of her own business, Roxanne has also managed to create a flexible schedule that allows her to be where she needs to be, when she needs to be there. That's an important factor since she's involved in a number of other business and volunteer activities, from participating on a bank board to consulting for publishing companies.

She explains, "My workday totally varies. There are some weeks where I'm in the bookstore every day early to late, although sometimes even when I'm there every day, some of what I'm doing is not about the bookstore. But if I work sixty hours a week, probably thirty-five or forty of those hours are devoted to the bookstore, on average. When you're talking about the pros of owning your own business, you do have a lot of autonomy. Not *freedom*. You don't have *freedom* because you have employees and you have responsibilities. But you have a lot of *autonomy*. So I can decide how my day is going to go. That's a big deal to me.

Is it possible to have any downtime when running a business that needs so much hands-on involvement?

"If I'm exhausted, and I want to take a day off, I'm a little bit torn, because there's always something to do. And that's the tough part. There really aren't good boundaries, but I make it work."

 what it takes

▶ A willingness to devote time and energy to your vision.

▶ Love for books of all kinds.

▶ A desire to be a visible community member.

ROXANNE'S CAREER ADVICE

It's important for teenage girls not to react to the noise around them, and instead really think about what it is they want to do in their heart. Girls shouldn't let society dictate whether they should or shouldn't have kids, or whether they should or shouldn't get married, or whether they should or shouldn't make money. Talk to women who are happy and content in their lives and try very hard to think independently about what it is you want to do.

in the field

Five More Careers Working with Books

editorial director Editorial directors work for publishing companies and oversee the authors writing books for their imprint (publishing brand), as well as coordinating the different stages involved in successfully publishing and promoting books. They play a key strategic role in the editorial direction for an imprint.

book cover designer You can't judge a book by its cover, but the design of a book cover will most likely have an impact on sales. Book cover designers create covers that will be noticeable, will appeal to the book's target demographic, and will hopefully lead a potential reader to pick up and purchase the book.

literary agent Like a talent agent, literary agents are in the business of representation. They present their authors' work to editors at publishing houses in the hope of getting publishing deals for their clients. Literary agents work on commission and earn a percentage of their clients' publishing income.

sales account manager Sales account managers work for publishing companies, and their job is to ensure that their books make it from the publisher's warehouse to the shelves of independent bookstores, bookstore chains, and other retail outlets. They also help develop marketing and promotional plans for book launches.

acquisitions editor These editors have one primary responsibility, and that is acquiring new titles for their publishing company's imprint. Acquisitions editors nurture relationships with literary agents so they can be apprised of up-and-coming talent, as well as actively solicit new authors and projects to fill out their publishing slate.

 you need to know about

The American Booksellers Association is the national organization devoted to supporting independent booksellers. On their website (www.bookweb.org), you'll find interesting articles and research, resources, and a directory of independent bookstores nationwide.

For more careers working with books, check out the librarian profile on page 80.

women in the workforce

while a lot of progress has been made in the past century when it comes to women in the workplace, things are not equal—not yet, anyway.

Some careers have been traditionally female-dominated, like nursing, and others have been traditionally male-dominated, like engineering. That remains the case even today. Here are recent statistics about where women are working, courtesy of the U.S. Department of Labor, Bureau of Labor Statistics. As of 2003, women made up:

▸ 98 percent of preschool and kindergarten teachers

▸ 92 percent of registered nurses

▸ 82 percent of elementary and middle school teachers

▸ 36 percent of chemists

▸ 30 percent of physicians and surgeons

▸ 28 percent of lawyers

▸ 9 percent of civil engineers

▸ 3 percent of all aircraft pilots and flight engineers

Any shockers there? If not, this next statistic ought to do it. Are you ready? On average, a woman still earns 25 percent less than a man who's doing the *exact same job*. That's right . . . the *exact same job*. In fact, according to the Women's Caucus, the earnings gap (meaning the difference between what men and women earn) for full-time managers actually got *bigger* between 1995 and 2000.

Here are examples from the Bureau of Labor Statistics for 2003:

- Female physicians and surgeons earn 41 percent less than their male counterparts.

- Female college and university professors earn 21 percent less than their male counterparts.

- Female computer programmers and systems analysts earn 19 percent less than their male counterparts.

Disturbing numbers, to be sure, but it's not all bad news. Women have made serious headway in the past century, especially when you consider that in the year 1900, women made up only 18 percent of the labor force, while today we make up nearly 50 percent. And women are surpassing men when it comes to education—more women than men today go on to get bachelor's and master's degrees.

Karen Lederer, a professor at the University of Massachusetts, teaches a class called Career and Life Choices for Women, and she shared her thoughts on how these statistics actually trickle down to working women.

Karen suggested that at some point in their careers, most women are going to encounter a situation where their gender impacts their career in a negative way, like being given different responsibilities from a male counterpart or being passed over for a promotion.

As I talked with Karen about this reality for women in the workplace, she said something that really resonated with me. Karen said that it's important for young women to remember that if and when this sort of gender discrimination happens, *don't take it personally*. There is a tendency for women to wonder what we did wrong, or even worse, what's wrong with us.

My hope is that some of you reading this book are going to be the first women not to experience any gender discrimination in your career journeys. To get off to a solid start, join up with professional women's organizations—most industries have them—and connect with experienced women who've successfully navigated their own careers despite these inequalities and ask them how they did it.

career chooser

Check out this checklist of job traits to help you choose your ideal career!

get to attend hip work parties

* Actor
* Advertising Executive
* Architect
* Business Executive
* Golf Tournament Director
* Independent Bookstore Owner
* Magazine Editor
* Movie Studio Executive
* Museum Curator
* Photographer
* Professional Athlete
* Publicist
* Screenwriter
* Senator
* Stylist
* Talent Agent
* TV Network Executive
* TV Show Creator
* Urban Planner
* Video Game Programmer

have own office

* Advertising Executive
* Animator
* Business Executive
* Coast Guard Lieutenant
* District Attorney
* Educational Psychologist
* Golf Tournament Director
* Magazine Editor
* Marine Biologist
* Movie Studio Executive
* Museum Curator
* Nonprofit Director
* Publicist
* Real Estate Agent
* Recruiter
* Senator
* Sheriff
* Social Worker
* Talent Agent
* TV Network Executive
* TV Show Creator

get lots of free stuff

* Actor
* Advertising Executive

* *

* Business Executive
* Golf Tournament Director
* Magazine Editor
* Movie Studio Executive
* Professional Athlete
* Publicist
* Screenwriter
* Stylist
* Talent Agent
* TV Network Executive
* TV Show Creator

have stocked kitchen at work

* Actor
* Chef
* Firefighter
* Movie Studio Executive
* Nanny
* TV Network Executive
* TV Show Creator
* Video Game Programmer

never off duty

* Actionist
* Business Executive
* Coast Guard Lieutenant
* District Attorney
* Educational Psychologist
* Entrepreneur
* Environmentalist
* Forensic Scientist
* Golf Tournament Director
* Independent Bookstore Owner
* Journalist

* Magazine Editor
* Movie Studio Executive
* Nonprofit Director
* Photographer
* Publicist
* Real Estate Agent
* Recruiter
* Relief Worker
* Senator
* Sheriff
* Talent Agent
* TV Show Creator
* Veterinarian

up against inflexible deadlines

* Actor
* Animator
* Business Executive
* Golf Tournament Director
* Journalist
* Magazine Editor
* Movie Studio Executive
* Photographer
* Screenwriter
* Stylist
* TV Network Executive
* TV Show Creator
* Video Game Programmer
* Visual Merchandiser

can create flexible work schedule

* Accountant
* Actionist

* Actor
* Chef
* Commercial Airline Pilot
* Entrepreneur
* Environmentalist
* Firefighter
* Golf Tournament Director
* Independent Bookstore Owner
* Museum Curator
* Nurse-Midwife
* Photographer
* Physical Therapist
* Professional Athlete
* Real Estate Agent
* Screenwriter
* Stylist
* Talent Agent
* Urban Planner
* Video Game Programmer
* Yoga Instructor

can work from home

* Actionist
* Entrepreneur
* Environmentalist
* Photographer
* Professional Athlete
* Real Estate Agent
* Recruiter
* Screenwriter
* Stylist
* Talent Agent
* TV Network Executive

involves travel to interesting places

* Actor
* Advertising Executive
* Business Executive
* Coast Guard Lieutenant
* Commercial Airline Pilot
* Environmentalist
* Golf Tournament Director
* Journalist
* Magazine Editor
* Marine Biologist
* Museum Curator
* Photographer
* Professional Athlete
* Publicist
* Relief Worker
* Screenwriter
* Senator
* Stylist
* Talent Agent

frequent business lunches

* Actor
* Advertising Executive
* Business Executive
* District Attorney
* Golf Tournament Director
* Magazine Editor
* Movie Studio Executive
* Nonprofit Director
* Publicist
* Recruiter
* Screenwriter

* Senator
* Stylist
* Talent Agent
* TV Network Executive
* TV Show Creator
* Urban Planner

can be your own boss

* Actionist
* Architect
* Business Executive
* Chef
* Educational Psychologist
* Entrepreneur
* Independent Bookstore Owner
* Nanny
* Nonprofit Director
* Nurse-Midwife
* Photographer
* Physical Therapist
* Publicist
* Real Estate Agent
* Recruiter
* Screenwriter
* Stylist
* Talent Agent
* Veterinarian
* Visual Merchandiser
* Yoga Instructor

job might entail significant busywork

* Accountant
* Engineer

* Independent Bookstore Owner
* Librarian
* Nurse Midwife
* Physical Therapist
* Real Estate Agent
* Social Worker
* Teacher

might receive public recognition through work

* Actionist
* Actor
* Advertising Executive
* Animator
* Architect
* Business Executive
* Chef
* District Attorney
* Educational Psychologist
* Environmentalist
* Firefighter
* Golf Tournament Director
* Independent Bookstore Owner
* Journalist
* Magazine Editor
* Marine Biologist
* Movie Studio Executive
* Museum Curator
* Nonprofit Director
* Photographer
* Professional Athlete
* Publicist
* Screenwriter
* Senator

* Sheriff
* Talent Agent
* Teacher
* TV Network Executive
* TV Show Creator
* Urban Planner

collaborate with others as part of job

* Actionist
* Actor
* Advertising Executive
* Agent
* Architect
* Business Executive
* Chef
* Engineer
* Golf Tournament Director
* Magazine Editor
* Marine Biologist
* Movie Studio Executive
* Nonprofit Director
* Relief Worker
* Senator
* Sheriff
* TV Network Executive
* TV Show Creator
* Urban Planner
* Visual Merchandiser

work alone much of the time

* Actionist
* Animator
* Engineer
* Forensic Scientist
* Photographer
* Screenwriter
* Video Game Programmer

job involves interaction with the public

* Actionist
* Actor
* Chef
* Commercial Airline Pilot
* District Attorney
* Firefighter
* Golf Tournament Director
* Independent Bookstore Owner
* Journalist
* Librarian
* Museum Curator
* Photographer
* Real Estate Agent
* Relief Worker
* Senator
* Sheriff
* Social Worker
* Urban Planner